THE LAND BEYOND

T0308763

The Land Beyond

A Memoir

JACK D. IVES

UNIVERSITY OF ALASKA PRESS
Fairbanks

University of Alaska Press
P.O. Box 756240
Fairbanks, AK 99775-6240

Library of Congress Cataloging-in-Publication Data
Ives, Jack D.
The land beyond : a memoir / by Jack Ives.
   p. cm.
Includes bibliographical references and index.
ISBN 978-1-60223-077-4 (pbk. : alk. paper)
   1. McGill Sub-Arctic Research Laboratory—History. 2. Earth sciences—Research—
Newfoundland and Labrador—Labrador—History—20th century. 3. Earth sciences—
Research—Québec (Province)—Nord-du-Québec—History—20th century. 4. Ives, Jack D.
—Travel—Newfoundland and Labrador—Labrador. 5. Ives, Jack D.—Travel—Québec
(Province)—Nord-du-Québec. 6. Graduate students—Newfoundland and Labrador—
Labrador—Biography. 7. Wilderness areas—Newfoundland and Labrador—
Labrador—History—20th century. 8. Wilderness areas—Québec (Province)—
Nord-du-Québec—History—20th century. 9. Natural history—Newfoundland and
Labrador—Labrador. 10. Natural history—Québec (Province)—Nord-du-Québec. I.
Title.
   QE48.C23M35 2010
   557.19072'0718—dc22
                         2009035479

Cover: Lower Komaktorvik Lake, Torngat Mountains, after a snow storm on 24
August 1956. Photo by the author. "The land beyond" is one of several interpretations
of the word "Ungava," itself derived from Inuktitut.

Cover design by Dixon Jones, UAF Rasmuson Library Graphics

Contents

Place Names That Have Been Changed Since the 1950s

Original	Current
Fort Chimo	Kuujjuaq
Knob Lake	Schefferville
Indian House Lake	Lac de la Hutte Sauvage
George River	Rivière George
Whitegull Lake	Lac au Goélands
Pyramid Hills	Les Pyramides
Koroksoak River	Rivière Koroc
Great Whale River	Rivière de la Squaw
Dorval Airport	Pierre Elliot Trudeau International Airport (Montréal)
"Essay Lake"	Lac des Essais
"Shoreline Lake"	Lac Tasiguluk
Wedge point	Pointe Wedge
Sukaliuk Brook	Ruisseau Sukaliuk

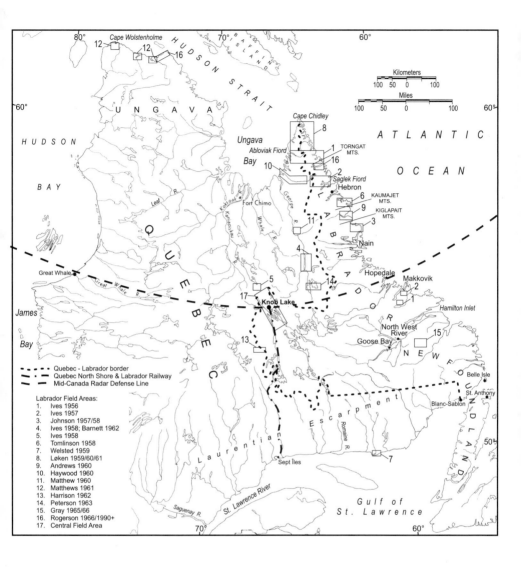

An outline of the Labrador-Ungava Peninsula showing locations of field research sites (place names in format of 1950s). Prepared by Thom Millest.

To Pauline
Stalwart field assistant and lifelong companion

Preface

This book has three closely related objectives. One is to provide a history of the establishment and the early period of operations of the McGill Sub-Arctic Research Laboratory (the Lab) in central Labrador-Ungava. The second is to relate the beginnings of the Lab's exploratory research in a seemingly endless wilderness at a time when there were no set ground rules and little firmly established underlying theory on which to base field plans. The third objective is of a more autobiographical nature. It describes how I was one of a small group of immigrant graduate students who were able to make use of the Lab facility and to develop field research programs and begin our own academic and research careers.

The narrative begins in the immediate post–World War II period at a time when almost three-quarters of the vast area that is the world's second-largest political entity was virtually unknown. The Canadian government was entering the initial phase of growing awareness of its northern regions in the light of events of the war itself and the onset of the Cold War. The International Geophysical Year (1957–1958) was harnessed to augment development although, regrettably, government interest appeared to subside during the 1970s and 1980s.

The period from about 1950 to 1970 provides a mirror for the early twenty-first century. Now there is another surge of national concern brought on by the widespread perception of climate warming, loss of sea-ice cover in the High Arctic, and potential for an open Northwest Passage. Today the issues are natural resource development, sovereignty (especially access to submarine resources and international navigation), environmental threat, and the rights of the Inuit and Innu to influence development of the landscape that they have depended upon for millennia. Once again, an international scientific event (the International Polar Year, 2007–2009) is used to advance claims of national sovereignty. The government's response has not yet been sufficiently robust or adequately focused either to realize the enormous opportunities or to appreciate fully the appropriate role of the aboriginal Canadians.

The results of scientific endeavor are usually widely available in the standard peer-reviewed literature, and today also on the Internet, but it is comparatively rare that the personal stories and interrelations between some of the principal players are told anecdotally. As the oldest surviving field director of the Lab (1957–1960), I have been prompted by a sense of responsibility to record the opportunities and challenges that faced new, field-oriented graduates, the majority of whom were inexperienced, at that earlier time when the northern reaches of Canada were little known.

The history of the Lab, as related here, illustrates the ambitious vision of Professor F. Kenneth Hare and my own good fortune to arrive in Canada at the critical time to participate in the development of that vision. It also emphasizes how much Canada depended on academic immigration to fulfill its responsibility to learn more about its northern territories.

The book is a recognition of the work of Ken Hare. His leadership not only led to the establishment of the Lab, but substantially influenced the careers of many of his colleagues and students. The book also pays tribute to Norman and Patricia Drummond, who rose to the challenge of putting the Lab in full working order and joined with Ken Hare to create an effective platform for fieldwork in the eastern Canadian Arctic and Subarctic. The series of short biographies, appended to the main text, demonstrates one aspect of the significant impact of the Lab's creation—how it attracted to its isolated and severe environment so many gifted young graduates in their formative years.

Jack D. Ives
15 July 2009
Ottawa, ON, Canada

Acknowledgments

Many friends and colleagues have read parts, or the whole, of early drafts of the manuscript. Without their generous support my task would have remained far more incomplete than it is. Peter Adams, John T. Andrews, Roger G. Barry, George Falconer, Olav Løken, Jim Lotz, Jean Macnab, and Geoff Sherlock had access to all or parts of earlier drafts, and many valuable comments and criticisms are acknowledged. Pat Drummond kindly read the first half of the manuscript and provided photographs from her and Norman's early years at the Lab. Diana Rowley read the entire text and, in addition to applying her formidable editorial skills and repeatedly taking me to task in her gentle yet firm manner, was a vital sounding board for my attempts to portray events and personalities associated with the immediate prewar and early postwar periods. Dr. Louis-Edmond Hamelin (professor emeritus, Université Laval) and Dr. Bill Mattox (lab field director, 1960–1963) undertook the delicate task of reading and offering advice on the section dealing with the loss of Brian Haywood and André Grenier on the Koroksoak River (Rivière Koroc) in 1960.

After reading Lawrence Coady's remarkable book, *The Lost Canoe: A Labrador Adventure*, I contacted him and our ensuing correspondence led to his generous offer to read the entire manuscript and to contribute many helpful suggestions. At a late stage in manuscript preparation, Keith Greenaway kindly elaborated for me the circumstances of the RCAF 408 Squadron's reconnaissance of winter ice conditions over Hudson Bay with Ken Hare, Tuzo Wilson, and others.

Pauline Ives critically read the entire manuscript and eliminated the worst of my indiscretions. Much more important was her constant companionship and support in what I have always regarded as a series of outstanding holiday adventures across Labrador-Ungava that others might say were arduous and frequently painful, or at least uncomfortable, slogs. For this, and for many other reasons, the book is dedicated to Pauline.

Many friends assisted at various times and in many different ways during my Labrador-Ungava years, especially the Moravians of the Labrador: Dr. Paul Beavan and staff of British Newfoundland Exploration (BRINEX), including our outstanding bush pilot, Paul Saunders, who was able to extract us from the Torngats in very rough weather in 1956; Dick Geren, Hugh and Jean Amor,

Buzz and Carol Neal, David and Barbara Selleck, Peter and Pat Young, and staff of the Iron Ore Company of Canada (IOCC); Dr. E. P. "Pep" and Eleanor Wheeler, J. Peter and Ellie Johnson, Noel Odell, Professor Gordon Manley, and my doctoral adviser, Professor J. Brian Bird, provided encouragement and inspiration. I am delighted to acknowledge substantial assistance throughout the actual preparation of the book for publication. David Murray, of Parks Canada, was a great help in providing cartographic assistance for Figure 14. Thom Millest, my regular "port in a cartographic storm," completed all the drafting and digitization for Figures 6, 14, and 52. Dave Andrews, photographer par excellence, worked over, cleaned up, and framed, where necessary, and rendered the very old photo collection shining and new. The editorial staff at University of Alaska Press endeared themselves to me by their sympathetic encouragement, precision, and professional excellence throughout: Elisabeth B. Dabney, managing editor; Sue Mitchell, production editor; and Melanie Gold, copy editor. I am also grateful for the close companionship, team spirit, sense of adventure, vigorous academic exchanges, and lifelong friendships and loyalties formed during my years at McGill. There are undoubtedly a number of minor misrepresentations, slips in precision, and other errors. At least most of these I must credit to lapses in memory over a fifty-year period; of course, they are entirely my responsibility.

Prologue

Romantic notions of Labrador-Ungava and the Torngat Mountains loomed large during my early upbringing in England. Sunday School stories of Sir Wilfred Grenfell and of the Moravian Mission were especially inspiring, in part, because my hometown was Grimsby. The dangers that beset the fishing fleet were embedded in my family life. As a schoolboy I made two deep-sea fishing trawler trips up the Norwegian coast to Svalbard and into the Barents Sea. The spirit of the north, or Arctic, was further enhanced through my undergraduate student leadership of three university expeditions to Vatnajökull, Iceland's largest ice cap.

This memoir really begins in May 1954. I had been camping alone north of what was then the very remote farm of Skaftafell and taking measurements on one of the Vatnajökull outlet glaciers. The arrival of my Nottingham and Cambridge university colleagues who would form that summer's expedition was still almost two months away. My close friend, Ragnar, the farmer, handed me a letter that had been delivered by a local farmer on horseback. Written on McGill University letterhead and signed by a Professor F. Kenneth Hare, it was addressed not to me but to Professor K.C. Edwards, my professor and head of the Geography Department at Nottingham University, UK. Hare explained to Edwards that a small research laboratory at Knob Lake in the center of Labrador-Ungava, which he had planned, would open the following September. He still needed to complete the roster of graduate students who would also serve as weather observers. He recollected that Edwards, on a visit to Montréal the previous summer, had mentioned a certain Nottingham student of his who was all fired up about the Arctic and had just completed his bachelor's degree in geography. Hare was writing the letter in the hope that Edwards would bring the "offer" to the student's attention. The letter had been forwarded to me intact, with a postcript in characteristic professorial fashion of the times: "Ives, you might care to look into this, KCE."

I had previously spent several weeks under canvas in the solitude of the beautiful mountains of Skaftafellsfjoll, with only a weekly walk back to the farm for mail and good farm food. Hare's letter was like a lightning strike. Here was the possibility for a winter in central Labrador and prospects for the following summer on the isolated north coast—the Torngat Mountains.

At the time, however, I did not suspect that letter would be a major turning point of my life.

I was in my first year as a graduate student with no immediate prospects for employment in any normal sense. I was engaged to Pauline. In those days, however, young men did not generally contemplate marriage until they had at least some financial security. What to do? I hastily dispatched four letters by horseback to the coastal beach landing strip to be picked up by the biweekly Flugfelag Islands DC-3: to Pauline—what did she think about marriage and living in Canada?; to Hare—yes, I would accept the position at Knob Lake, but was married accommodation available, as I was engaged to be married?; to my parents in Grimsby—what advice had they to offer? And a thank-you, of course, to Edwards.

I then continued with the frequent ascents of my favorite glacier, Morsárjökull, while anxiously awaiting the return post. Remarkably, three replies reached me together on the same horse that crossed the glacial rivers of the county of Öraefi. Pauline and I were decided on marriage and emigration to Canada. She would visit Canada House in London to obtain information about immigration, although her parents were very apprehensive. My parents were circumspect; they urged acceptance of "such a wonderful offer" but cautioned that it would be unwise to make conditions—Pauline could follow later! And Hare explained that there was no married accommodation at Knob Lake. In view of this, he offered me a McGill-Carnegie-Arctic Research Scholarship, tenable in Montréal, hoping that I (we) could arrive before the end of September. It transpired later that he had no authority to make such an offer, as the scholarship committee had disbanded for the summer. Unknown to me, he had entered my name as a lecturer in the Geography Department, as a precaution.[1] Nevertheless, Hare assured me that after the 1954–1955 academic year in Montréal, I would be able to go to the Knob Lake lab the following summer.

Despite all the uncertainty, the wedding date was set for 11 September, giving me a tight but exhilarating schedule, although Pauline was left with all the arranging—appointments for application for landed immigrant status, reservations for a sea passage to Québec City, a new passport for herself, in addition to the wedding preparations.

But how was I to handle my responsibilities as expedition leader in Iceland? The crew arrived a month later and we managed to push the fieldwork well ahead of schedule. Even then, there remained one further obstacle. This was my third summer based at Skaftafell. About once every ten years a gigantic glacier-flood, sometimes equal to the volume of the River Amazon in full summer spate, burst from beneath the nearby glacier, Skeiðarárjökull. The *jökulhlaup*, as the Icelanders called it, was expected to occur that very summer. The question was: precisely, when? Ragnar explained that an Englishman would only have one chance during his lifetime to see such an event, but he could get married whenever he chose; surely Pauline would understand? Not a happy prospect. Then Ragnar consulted his "jökulhlaup bible" (a long family record of such events dating back more than 150 years) and predicted 18 July for the climax of the flood, a remarkable "nonscientific" forecast. That would give me a chance to witness the glacier burst and a day to inspect the source of the jökulhlaup after the climax. There would be a day to spare so that I could mount a horse and gallop 25 mi (40 km) south to the beach landing strip, catch the DC-3 for Reykjavik, and be in time for the next of the fortnightly sailings of the passenger ship MV *Gullfoss*, bound for Scotland.

Ragnar's forecast proved correct. One of the spectacular photographs that I was able to take is reproduced to indicate my good fortune.[2] Although I have been back to Skaftafell more than twenty times since that momentous occasion, my visits have never coincided with another jökulhlaup. Ragnar's second prediction, that an Englishman would have only one opportunity in his lifetime to see a jökulhlaup, also seems to have been accurate. I will never give up trying, although time appears to be running out now that I have reached my seventy-eighth year (Ives 2007).

Jökulhlaup, Skaftafell, Iceland, 18 July 1954. Peak of the flood, the climax of glacier processes taken immediately before leaving Iceland.

In July 1954, the Nottingham University expedition was left in the hands of
Jim Exley, as leader in my stead; my undergraduate tutor, Dr. Cuchlaine King;
Malcolm Mellor; and three Cambridge students.[3] My share of the Iceland fieldwork was originally intended to form the basis of a master's degree to be submitted to Nottingham University. However, the surprise decision to emigrate
to Canada caused a significant reorientation and it became a McGill University
doctoral dissertation.

I did get to the church on time. After the wedding ceremony the vicar presented Pauline with her new passport that he had kept under lock and key awaiting the legal name change. We celebrated with family and friends and immediately changed from our wedding clothes. Our honeymoon was a voyage to
Québec City as first-class passengers on the liner SS *Atlantic*. We had persuaded
friends and family to consider a cash donation rather than a traditional wedding
gift, since our late application for a berth on a passenger liner meant that only
first-class accommodation was available. We eventually arrived in Montréal in
late September with $210 in cash and two cabin trunks of clothing and books.
The voyage was unprecedented luxury, although it woefully depleted our worldly
resources. I, at least, was immune to seasickness and was able to impress (or
horrify) our elderly first-class dining table companions by eating methodically
through the entire menu—a conspicuous change from my expeditionary diet of
pemmican, oats, chocolate, and ship's biscuits. The passage up the St. Lawrence
to Québec City, across tranquil water, with both shores gleaming under full
autumn color, was impressed on our minds' eyes forever.

We settled into Montréal very quickly, renting the upper floor of a small
house north of the Mountain and commuted daily from Monkland railway
station. Pauline was offered a clerical job with Canadian Industries Ltd.
(CIL), then a subsidiary of Imperial Chemical Industries (ICI), with whom
she had worked in London. I was allotted a student office on the top floor
of Bishop Mountain House, then home of the Montréal office of the Arctic
Institute of North America (AINA) and the hangout for the dozen or so
McGill-Carnegie-Arctic scholars from all disciplines. Here I met Dr. Svenn
Orvig, the AINA-Montréal office director, as well as Fritz Müller, Anne-
Marie Krüger, Mike Marsden, J. Peter Johnson, Frank Cook, Marjorie Findlay,
Andrew McPherson, Arthur Mansfield, David and Johanna Sergeant, Adam
Bursa, and Don Oliver, all young arctic enthusiasts who were to play impor-
tant roles in our lives as new Canadians.

The original uncertainty over married accommodation, or rather lack of it,
at Knob Lake turned out to have a fortunate resolution. There were several
immediate benefits. I had the full academic year in Montréal to become ori-
ented to the Canadian Arctic and Subarctic; graduate courses and advice were
offered by professors Ken Hare, Brian Bird, Hakan Kranck, Max Dunbar, Svenn

Orvig, and Bogdan Zaborski. Occasional visits to Bishop Mountain House by out-of-town senior members of AINA, including Dr. A. Lincoln Washburn, Mr. Tom Manning, and Dr. John Reed, facilitated contacts that were of great importance later in my career.

What do European, arctic-oriented students do when the Montréal winter sets in? They join together to rent an inexpensive unwinterized cottage in the Laurentians, for weekend skiing, for Christmas, for general conviviality, and for the true Canadian experience. Our "house mother" was the redoubtable and ebullient Barbara Battle. Bar had been widowed the previous year when her husband, Ben, tragically disappeared in a glacial melt-stream on Baffin Island. Bar had struggled with her loss while she taught at a Montréal high school, and by befriending newly arrived European and British (we still considered Europe quite foreign in those days) arctic scholars. Her one-room apartment near McGill and the rural cottage beyond Ste. Adèle were lively social and academic gathering points. Fritz Müller, a Swiss glaciologist, alpinist, and first-class skier, set up ski lessons for all comers. Within two years Bar became Frau Müller-Battle.

The cottage decorum, where we spent most weekends, was remarkable. Some of us learned the hard way what the fireplace damper was for, and what happens when the temperature drops far below 0°F (as it was then). After a hard day's skiing (usually cross-country, as we couldn't afford lift tickets), dinner and evening animated discussion, often about various theories of glacial erosion, we prepared for sleep. Banking up the huge open wood fire, we would turn down the space heater, and dive into our sleeping bags on the large living room floor before the indoor temperature plummeted. There were exceptions. Anne-Marie Krüger from Hamburg believed that an unmarried young lady should not sleep in mixed company. She selected one of the frigid bedrooms, until a memorable February morning when she awoke early to find her nose frozen and her bedside thermometer reading −17°F (−27°C).

We gradually adjusted to the Montréal winter. Pauline and I discovered all we could about Knob Lake and the wilderness of central Nouveau Québec-Labrador, almost 1,000 mi (1,609 km) to our northeast. So we prepared ourselves for life in Canada.

The McGill Sub-Arctic Research Laboratory (the Lab) opened in September 1954, as Professor Hare had predicted, and the weather station was in full operation by 1 October. Norman Drummond, who had made a pioneering canoe traverse with Harry Lash up the Romaine River and onto the inland plateau[4] as part of his master's-degree study, had been appointed field director. He and his wife, Pat, took up residence at the Lab, along with three graduate students: George Michie (geography, University of Toronto); Jean-Claude Langlois (geography, Université de Montréal), and Les Viereck (botany, Dartmouth College, NH, USA).

Pat and Norman Drummond in front of the Lab during the first winter, 1954–1955 (photograph courtesy of Pat Drummond).

The accommodation at the Lab was luxurious compared with the small mountain tents I had previously called home in Iceland. For the entire subarctic winter, however, it was somewhat confining. Norm and Pat had a well-equipped kitchen, a comfortable living room, a large bedroom, and a store room. The "boys" each had a small bed-study room, the Weather Room office was their living room, and they cooked on a single hot plate in a tiny anteroom packed with scientific instruments.

Norman and Pat Drummond with baby Janet, August 1957. The great green monster (the Lab jeep) is behind (photograph courtesy Pat Drummond).

The Lab was located 2 mi (3 km) from the main IOCC offices, the bunkhouses, the canteen, and the rapidly developing townsite of what was then called Knob Lake, a company town.[5] There were very few married couples in the early days. The Lab looked onto the airstrip and a small Department of Transport (DOT) radio shack (with a crew of three) that also served as the airport terminal. The only contact by land with the "outside"—the civilized south—was a ten-hour journey on the Québec North Shore and Labrador (QNSL) railway to Sept-Îles that was scheduled once a week. The only other connections were the telephone line and the weather station teletype, usually restricted to weather data transmission. The irregular commercial airplane flights to Montréal were too expensive for Lab staff, but available in the event of possible emergencies.

The financial base of the Lab was a DOT contract with McGill University for the operation of a first-order weather-observing station. It provided salaries for three weather observers (the graduate students), a partial salary for the station chief (the other part of Norm's salary was from his appointment as assistant professor of geography), and general operating costs.

A first-order station is responsible for weather observations at hourly intervals. Intermediate observations were added whenever there was a change in weather conditions that was significant for aircraft. Twenty-one shifts of eight hours each week were required to fulfill the contractual commitments. Norman, as field director with many other responsibilities, took three of these, the boys took six each. Other fixed duties were weekly measurement of lake ice thickness (which became a major operation when thickness exceeded

Christmas dinner, 1955. From left: Morton Fraser, Rowland Twidale, Art Morris, Pat, Norman, David Fox, two not identified (photograph courtesy Pat Drummond).

Christmas dinner, 1956. From left: Graham Humphreys, Ivan Hamilton, Art Morris, Ken Jones, Edward Derbyshire, and Pat and Norman Drummond (photograph courtesy Pat Drummond).

3 ft [0.91 m] as winter progressed), an extensive snow survey, operating various sets of scientific equipment (for example, a seismograph and magnetometer for Dominion Observatories, aurora borealis observations for Dartmouth College), special weather forecasts as requested by the IOCC, and general upkeep of the buildings, including the frequent and arduous task of snow removal. Blowing snow was a regular feature of the Knob Lake winter that caused large drifts to develop on the lee side of the buildings.

Norman, as assistant professor, offered two graduate courses two evenings each week. They were set up in Norman and Pat's living room and usually followed by coffee and cookies provided by Pat, a first-class hostess.

But back to Montréal. Easy access to the McGill libraries enabled me to read several McGill master's theses (geography and geology) and a doctoral dissertation. I was prompted to consider that three years of fieldwork in southeastern Iceland might be sufficient for a McGill doctoral dissertation. I may have been presumptuous. Nevertheless, after Professor Brian Bird had scanned my extensive field notes and specially prepared outline, he rather forcefully agreed with me. Professor Hare had assumed he would direct my doctoral dissertation on a study of the glacial geomorphology of the Labrador-Ungava Plateau and had suggested that I could write up my Iceland work on the side (as originally planned before I left England) for presentation to Nottingham University as a master's thesis. This was one of the few occasions when I provoked his anger. He refused to be my dissertation director. Brian Bird took over responsibility for supervising my doctoral dissertation.

I tried to appease Professor Hare by pointing out that, with a doctorate on southeast Iceland out of the way, I would be free to publish much more speedily on the glacial geomorphology of Labrador-Ungava, which was surely the main objective of my scholarship. He did not retract! Many years later he publicly confirmed that I had far exceeded his original expectations. He even introduced me, on occasion, as one of his favorite doctoral students.

Hare confirmed my planned 1955 summer at Knob Lake. I was to serve as acting field director so that Norm and Pat could take a two-month vacation. Consequently, in early May, with his wife, Helen, and Pauline to see me off, Professor Hare drove to Dorval (Pierre Elliot Trudeau) Airport to put me on a Hollinger-Ungava DC-4 flight to Knob Lake. After my departure (our first separation since the wedding), Helen casually asked Pauline why she was not going with me—did she prefer to stay in Montréal? On learning her answer, an indignant Helen reprimanded her husband for being so unthinking. Arrangements were made for Pauline to follow me north a month later on a similar Hollinger-Ungava flight, also courtesy of the IOCC. Nevertheless, no consideration was given to the problem of married accommodation at the Lab.

My First Summer at the Lab, 1955

The Hollinger-Ungava flight left Dorval behind just before noon on 4 May and headed northeastward into low cloud over the Laurentians. It was a long, monotonous, and uneventful flight, with only occasional glimpses of the ground. Through gaps in the clouds I could see a seemingly endless succession of rolling tree-clad hills separated by innumerable ice-coated lakes of all sizes. For me this was really a venture into the unknown, with not a sign of human habitation throughout the flight. As we approached Knob Lake the view opened out as the partial cloud cover progressively cleared. Coming in to land, I could see low parallel ridges with bare white windswept crests, scraggly conifers on their lower slopes, and frozen lakes between. Soon we were bumping along a gravel landing strip and came to rest opposite a forlorn shack. All in all it was a somewhat uninspiring landscape, especially for me, as I had been seduced by the North Norway fiords, Svalbard, and Iceland's mountains and ice caps.

The first signs of spring were already evident: wet snow, muddy puddles, and small openings of iron-ore-red ground where the snow had melted completely. Regardless, the welcome was encouraging and I descended from the aircraft to warm greetings from Norman and Pat Drummond. There followed tentative handshakes with three bearded characters who were to be my comrades for the next four months: Les, very tall and lean, with bright, sparkling, and friendly eyes; George, also tall but heavily built and rugged; and Jean-Claude, a slight, diffident Canadien with an attractive Québécois accent.

The red-trimmed white buildings of the McGill Sub-Arctic Research Lab stood out prominently above the mud and melting snow at the side of the airstrip, a hundred or so paces away. My personal luggage was quickly in the hands of the McGill crew, who walked me across to the Lab. There followed room assignment, tucking away of luggage, and a much-appreciated coffee with a large plate of Pat's freshly made brownies.

I was to be with Norm and Pat for four weeks to learn the intricacies of taking weather observations, the operation of the weather station and Lab, as well as my administrative responsibilities as acting field director and station chief. This was an especially valuable period, because the shortage of academic time in Montréal meant I had had to forego the usual three-week weather observer training course at DOT-Dorval.

The weeks with Norm and Pat proved a highly memorable experience for me. I liked them immensely. Learning the job of running a first-order weather station was fascinating. Norm was a meticulous instructor. This was especially apparent when the time came for the exacting check and certification of all the weather data logged during the preceding month—a large, multifaceted balance sheet that just had to balance before being dispatched to DOT-Dorval within the prescribed forty-eight hours. Our collegiality was further enhanced by Norm's assumption that I would possibly succeed him when his term of appointment was completed two years hence.

My relationship with "the boys," however, was clearly uncertain. Almost immediately on arrival I had sensed that something was very wrong. I quickly warmed to Les as a kindred spirit. The previous summer, with three colleagues, he had made the first traverse of the summit of Mt. McKinley (Denali). One of the team perished in a tragic accident just below the summit on the way down. The third member was badly injured and had to be left in the single tent that had been salvaged, while Les and Morton Wood walked out for assistance. As former captain of the Dartmouth College Outing Club, a stern, rugged, yet quietly humorous man of the wilderness, Les was an instant friend. Furthermore, he had taken a short winter leave to marry Teri, a zoology major and student president of Smith College, New England. They were planning for Teri to come to Knob Lake for the summer, and Les was delighted with my news that Pauline also would be with us in June. Understandably, Les and I found ourselves firmly in step.

It quickly became apparent, however, that I was very much out of step with George and Jean-Claude. The first serious problem concerned our wives. The difficulties went much deeper than that, however, and I soon learned the meaning of what was, to me, a new expression—the phenomenon of "being bushed." The long winter had taken its toll. Within a few days of my arrival, George took me aside and quietly informed me that I was expected to join with the boys in their opposition to Norman and Pat. I was startled to learn of the deep resentment that had gradually built up during the winter. It was much more than the disparity in living accommodations. Despite Pat's warmth and friendly personality, George and Jean-Claude had convinced themselves that the Lab was no place for women. It was a man's theater. Furthermore, George cautioned me that, being an Englishman, I should be careful not to belittle real Canadians. There followed a threat: if I did not fall into line, they would make things impossible for me, as they were well aware that I had received no meteorological training at Dorval and was therefore dependent on their goodwill for the fulfillment of my station duties.

At this time George and Jean-Claude did not know of the forthcoming intrusion by Teri and Pauline. I shared my concerns with Les and we quickly agreed on a plan of action. We informed George and Jean-Claude of the situation they would soon have to face when Teri and Pauline arrived. We assured them, however, that we fully understood that accommodation would be a problem, so we planned to establish a permanent camp for the summer, away from the Lab. The confrontation was both tense and unfortunate. George and Jean-Claude accepted the inevitable with very bad grace and told us they expected that our wives should never set foot in the Lab.

Les and I had decided on a diplomatic approach rather than confrontation. We established a camp on John Lake about 2 mi (3 km) through the spruce forest to the east of the Lab. Under the tutorship of an obvious Alaska backwoods expert, I enjoyed helping set up a very comfortable wilderness camp. And we were able to enjoy tranquil evenings with our wives, watching the evening sky reflected in a beautiful stretch of water, away from the very noisy weather office with its constantly chattering teletype and frequent incursions of flight crews seeking the latest weather forecasts. For me, the entire summer was a vital learning experience that stood me in good stead for my three years of managing the Lab from 1957 to 1960.

The month of May brought a mixture of snow, rain, occasional sunshine, and progressive melt, so that the entire area between the Lab and the mines became a sea of red mud. With the prospect of Pauline's resignation from employment with CIL, financial ruin once more stared us in the face. However, the Imperial Bank of Commerce had just set up a suboffice at Knob Lake. (Some five thousand miners were employed by the IOCC.) Jack Eakin, the bank manager, was more than pleased to employ a well-educated teller, so Pauline had a salaried position for two months, with August reserved for fieldwork.

Norman and Pat left for their two-month summer vacation. Les and I completed construction of our elaborate camp by John Lake. Pauline arrived by air at the end of May, and Teri on the train a day later, together with the anxiously awaited new canoe. So Les and I were ready to move out to the wilderness. This did not encroach upon our weather duties, although in-house difficulties remained.

The first inconvenience from living by John Lake hit Pauline. She was required to be at a counter, wearing a skirt and hose, in the small shack that served as a bank. The 2-mile (3 km) walk through the bush every day made her a tempting target for the swarms of black flies and mosquitoes. More amusing, possibly shocking for Pauline at the time, was her initial introduction to banking duties. After explaining the details of a teller's responsibilities, the bank manager took out a revolver, gave Pauline a short course in aiming and firing, and told her to keep it loaded and handy in her desk drawer at all times. With five thousand workmen and virtually no women in town, she wondered what the gun was for—self-defense, or to secure the cash?

Chapter One

History of Labrador-Ungava: An Introduction

T he great peninsula of eastern Canada that lies between Hudson Bay and the Atlantic Ocean had held various names throughout the thousand years or so since its discovery by Europeans. The Greenland Vikings referred to Helluland (more probably southeastern Baffin Island, although it could have included the Torngat Mountains of northern Labrador) and Markland (certainly the south-central Labrador coast). Labrador Peninsula is a very old name, although the word *Labrador*[6] is of uncertain origin and is possibly Portuguese. Hudson Bay and Hudson Strait derive from some of the earliest explorations seeking a route to the Far East through the Northwest Passage. They are a memorial to Henry Hudson, whose life was lost in 1611 in pursuit of that heroic quest. Ungava (meaning "the land beyond"), between present-day Ungava Bay and Hudson Bay, is an Inuit derivative used by the Hudson's Bay Company for the northwestern extension of the great peninsula. In combination it provides the name *Labrador-Ungava* (Hare 1950; Ives 1959a).

In 1869 the Hudson's Bay Company transferred its authority over the world's largest tract of land under the control of a private company to the Dominion of Canada. Following the enlargements of the original provinces, and the creation of new ones between 1867 and 1912, the Province of Québec attached the name Nouveau-Québec to its newly acquired northern territories. It also laid claim to most of the Labrador-Ungava peninsula, arguing that an old name, *Coast of Labrador*, should be interpreted to mean a narrow coastal strip facing the Atlantic Ocean. Newfoundland contested this definition, and the issue was resolved in its favor by the Judicial Committee of the Privy Council, Westminster (London), in 1927. The land settlement was based on the concept of the "height-of-land" for most of the boundary between the Province of Québec (Dominion of Canada) and the Dominion

of Newfoundland. The southern boundary was defined as a straight line running due west from a point some 120 mi (193 km) inland of Blanc-Sablon on
the Gulf of St. Lawrence. From there westward it coincided with latitude 52° N
as far as the Romaine River, then again adhering to the height-of-land into the
interior to the vicinity of Knob Lake. The Westminster ruling notwithstanding,
the actual height-of-land was virtually unknown in 1927, and this led to many
later disputes. On Québec provincial maps published as late as 1958 there
was an explanation that the border with Newfoundland was not shown "*pour
cause.*" It clearly indicated lack of acceptance by Québec of the 1927 decision,
even following Newfoundland's amalgamation with Canada in 1949.[7]

Even after the World War II years, the vast interior was regarded in many
quarters as a worthless wilderness of myriad lakes, swamps, stunted conifer
forests, tundra, and swarms of mosquitoes. This was a reflection of its much
earlier designation as "The Land God Gave to Cain," deriving from Jacques
Cartier's original sixteenth-century dismissal of the region that lay to the
north of his westward thrust. In the 1890s Dr. A. P. Low, the Canadian federal
government geologist, detected iron ore in the central and most inaccessible
region. The stage was set for a major reevaluation as the commercial market for
iron ore escalated in the late 1940s.

The history of the McGill Sub-Arctic Research Laboratory begins in 1954
after completion of the 320-mile (515 km) railway line between Sept-Îles, on
the Gulf of St. Lawrence North Shore, and Knob Lake (to become Schefferville
in 1958). The extensive reserves of high-grade ore provided the foundation
for one of the world's major extractive industrial developments of the mid–
twentieth century. This was closely followed by harnessing the hydroelectric
potential of Grand Falls on the Hamilton River (to become Churchill Falls on
the Churchill River). The colossal scale of these activities transformed much of
the wilderness. In light of this, Professor F. Kenneth Hare grasped the opportunity to establish a McGill University presence at its center. Some notion of the
contemporary geography is needed to provide a proper setting to the scale and
boldness of Hare's enterprise.

Labrador-Ungava or Nouveau Québec-Labrador, while situated in relatively low latitudes (approximately 50° N to 62° N), had been largely ignored
by Europeans throughout the previous three and a half centuries. Most of the
thrust of exploration was for discovery of the Northwest Passage and the race
to the North Pole. Labrador-Ungava is vast: about 1,000 mi (1,609 km) from
east to west and 800 mi (1,287 km) from north to south. The shortest north-
south transect from Sept-Îles to Kuujjuaq (formerly Fort Chimo), Ungava Bay,
is about 500 mi (805 km), and the length of the Labrador coast from Belle Isle
to Cape Chidley is about 700 mi (1,126 km). Apart from Hamilton Inlet, which

penetrates the southern third of the Labrador coast, the waterways are navigable only by canoe and frequent portages are necessary. The interior is largely a morass of lakes, swamps, muskeg, trackless boreal forest, tundra, and rocky plateaus. The relief, except near the Labrador coast, is scenically uninspiring. Winters are long and very cold; temperatures regularly fall to −40°F (−40°C) and below.

These basic elements of physical geography impressed me. As a new immigrant and McGill graduate student in 1954, my previous field research experience had been restricted to a mountainous and ice-capped area of southeast Iceland about 25 mi square (40 km by 40 km). Labrador-Ungava appeared to me as a major piece of Earth's terrestrial estate, nearly the size of Western Europe: a single railway line, seemingly to nowhere; coastal access for a small part of the year to tiny Hudson's Bay Company trading posts, Moravian and Grenfell Mission outposts; and rare temporary indigenous camps. The Naskaupi and Montagnais peoples were believed to consist of a few groups living off the land in the interior,[8] although most of them were beginning to shift toward permanent settlements close to Knob Lake, Fort Chimo, Sept-Îles, Goose Bay, and the Labrador coast.

The great interior wilderness was just that. Topographic maps at scales of 1:500,000 and 1:250,000 often contained a warning to aircraft pilots: "highest point unknown." Some parts of the coastline, eastern Ungava Bay, for example, were indicated by dotted line only (this designated them as unsurveyed). In contrast, a section of the interior, prompted by iron ore exploration and developments at Knob Lake, was covered by a block of high-quality 1:50,000 map sheets.

In the early 1950s Professor Hare and Professor J.T. Wilson initiated two separate large-scale air-photo research projects,[9] involving systematic interpretation of the only available air photographs—trimetrogon. The photographs provided vertical coverage for a very small percentage of the total area with oblique coverage of the 30 or so miles (48 km) between the flight lines of the photographing aircraft.[10] Hare's team of graduate students had begun mapping the great peninsula's vegetation and general physiography. Using the same minimal photography, Wilson led a group to map the tectonic lineaments and the glacial geology, not only of Labrador-Ungava but the whole of northern Canada. However, Hare's *Photo-reconnaissance Survey of Labrador-Ungava* (Hare 1959), while providing an excellent generalized picture of the cover types (principally vegetation) and topography, was of limited use to those struggling on foot or with canoe to define a doctoral or master's degree study.[11]

Given the general geographical position of Labrador-Ungava, together with its trackless interior, it is hardly surprising that little was known about it until well into the twentieth century. The Atlantic coast had been traversed by the

Viking Greenlanders in the tenth and eleventh centuries, but it was 1960 before archeological proof was found that they had attempted permanent settlement at the northern tip of Newfoundland. The Grand Banks and Newfoundland's numerous harbors and coves had become known to Basque and Portuguese fishermen by the fifteenth century and to other European fishing fleets shortly thereafter. The government and merchants of Elizabethan England, intent on outflanking the Spanish Empire in the struggle to reach the Spice Islands and the East Indies, directed voyages of exploration northward into Hudson Bay or further north through Baffin Bay to Lancaster Sound. French adventurers penetrated the westward-leading and seemingly endless St. Lawrence estuary and river system eventually to the Great Lakes and beyond. These thrusts effectively bypassed Labrador.

It was the fisherfolk, the *livyers*—those who live here all year round—as distinguished from the summer schooner fishing population, who were the first of European descent to settle the southern third of the Labrador coast. The Hudson's Bay Company, in turn, set up a series of small trading posts along the coast, along Hudson Strait and Ungava Bay, and on the shores of Hudson Bay. They had been preceded on the Labrador coast by the Moravian Mission, which sought to bring the Gospel, medicine, and education to the coast Eskimo (Inuit). This resulted in the establishment of a series of small settlements beginning with Nain in 1771. Thereafter, mission posts were built at Hopedale, Makkovik, Okak, and Hebron and as far north as Ramah and Nachvak Fiord in the southern Torngat Mountains. As early as 1811 the Moravians Gottleib Kohlmeister and George Kmoch, with Inuit guides, had rounded Cape Chidley and penetrated deep into Ungava Bay, naming the George River for King George III and ascending the Koksoak River to the present site of Fort Chimo. However, the Moravians were not able to obtain a permanent presence in Ungava Bay and did not establish a mission at Cape Chidley (Killinek) until 1905. The Hudson's Bay Company added trading posts to Moravian settlements, thus causing competition, both spiritual and commercial. After 1949, the year Newfoundland became part of Canada, the Royal Canadian Mounted Police (RCMP) used the same small settlements for police posts. The Grenfell Mission, founded by Sir Wilfred Grenfell, was initially established to provide medical support for the desperately poor fishing population of the southern coast. Permanent hospitals were set up at St. Anthony, on the island, and North West River, on the mainland. The mission's ship, MV *Strathcona*, a floating hospital, carried assistance far up the coast. The Grenfell Mission became a vital presence toward the end of the nineteenth century and continues to provide essential services today.

The first crossings of the forbidding inland wilderness from Ungava Bay to North West River achieved by Europeans occurred in the nineteenth century.

The Hudson's Bay Company established a trading post at Fort Chimo in 1830. Using this as a base, Bay traders John McLean and Erland Erlandson, with Naskaupi and Inuit guides, undertook a series of impressive overland journeys between Ungava Bay and North West River in the second half of the 1830s and the early 1840s. They canoed the George, Whale, Naskaupi, and Koksoak rivers and were the first Europeans to visit Grand Falls on the Hamilton. These exploratory journeys led to the establishment of trading posts in the interior, such as Fort Nascopie and the two posts on the George River system, both on its estuary and at the southern end of Indian House Lake. Excepting the George River estuary post, these survived for only a few years because of extreme difficulty of communication, accompanied by the apparent indifference of the Naskaupi to trading.

In 1891 Bowdoin College, Maine, organized a scientific expedition to the southeast interior. Two student members made a grueling journey up the lower Hamilton River as far as Grand Falls and left the name of their college on the map as Bowdoin Canyon, the tortuous canyon below the falls.

In the late 1890s, A. P. Low traveled great distances throughout the interior and produced an outline map of the entire Labrador-Ungava peninsula that provided an overview of its geography in the broadest possible terms. Nevertheless, his map, dependent in part on hearsay information from his Naskaupi guides, contained significant flaws. The inaccurate representation of the "Nascapi" River, for instance, contributed to Hubbard's fatal decision in selecting a route to Lake Michikamau in 1903 (see below). In the 1920s Gino Watkins, the famous University of Cambridge student, led a winter venture into the southeastern Labrador interior to provide members with experience in extreme cold and isolation in preparation for the trans-Greenland expedition that cost him his life.

Another component of exploration was introduced early in the twentieth century: that of gentleman adventurer. Names such as William Cabot, Hesketh Hesketh-Prichard, G. M. Gathorne-Hardy, and especially Leonidas Hubbard and Dillon Wallace, became widely known through their books and travel accounts. They were essentially elitist travelers propelled by the "lure of the Labrador wild" (to borrow the title of Wallace's first book [1905]): fishing, hunting, and adventure exploration, frequently to augment journalistic ambition. Hubbard's death by starvation and hypothermia in 1903 prompted the remarkable journey of his young widow, Mina, in 1905. Her book, *A Woman's Way Through Unknown Labrador*, not only added significantly to the cartography of the North West River–George River sector but also created a legend (Hubbard 1908). For its time, the journey of a high-society lady in long skirt, with elegant headdress draped in mosquito netting, and carrying a hot-water bottle, supported by Native and half-breed companions, as they were known then, was not only high drama in itself but created a fascination that has outlived a century. A dozen books, including her diaries and republication of her original 1908 edition, have appeared in the last twenty years. Canoeists have attempted to repeat the "woman's way," or that of her ill-fated husband; and feminist writers have provided intriguing reinterpretations of her journey that, for such a woman to travel "alone" through the wilderness with male half-breeds and Natives, had shocked many of her contemporaries.

By about 1900 another form of travel into the Labrador-Ungava wilderness was introduced: that in the interests of scientific research. The U.S. Navy had launched an expedition to Eclipse Harbour in 1861 to undertake astronomical measurements. The Bowdoin College expedition of 1891 preceded university and Canadian government expeditions with northern Labrador as a primary focus. The research of Bell (1884), Daly (1902), and Coleman (1921) led to the earliest predictions about the history of the Ice Ages in Labrador-Ungava. In 1931, Alexander Forbes, a wealthy American under the flag of the American Geographical Society (AGS), took a schooner and two seaplanes to the Torngat Mountains (Forbes 1938). In that same year an Oxford University student expedition reached Akpatok Island in Ungava Bay.

Forbes added a geological and botanical component to his 1931 expedition, although the main challenge was experimental topographical mapping from oblique air photographs taken from his two seaplanes. Thus, after two subsequent journeys north, Forbes and the AGS published a series of four accurate topographical maps, scale 1:100,000, of the Torngat Mountains, together with some of the finest black-and-white low-level oblique air photographs of glacial landforms ever acquired (Forbes 1938). Independently E. P. (Pep) Wheeler II, a geologist based at Cornell University in Ithaca, NY, undertook extensive coastal and inland journeys from the mid-1920s until shortly before his death in 1974. He single-handedly made the best available topographical maps of a large section of the Labrador coast north of Nain (Wheeler 1935). He also traveled overland from Nain by dogsled and snowshoe to Indian House Lake in the spring of 1935. From the lake he proceeded westward to the Whale River and followed it all the way to Ungava Bay. He then entered the estuary of the Koroksoak River and traveled eastward through the southern Torngat Mountains to Saglek Fiord and thence down the coast to Nain (Wheeler 1938).[12]

The 1931 Forbes expedition deserves credit for that other component of wilderness adventure: mountaineering. Forbes chose as geologist Noel Odell, who a few years earlier had been the last person to see George Mallory and Andrew Irvine approaching the summit of Mt. Everest. Thus Odell had reached one of the highest altitudes ever attained by that date. He undoubtedly devoted more energy in the Torngat Mountains to climbing Mt. Razorback, Precipice Mountain, Mt. Tetragona, and many others, than to geology. However, Odell sparked a controversial discussion about the extent of Ice Age glacierization and overthrew the widely supported assumption of the time. Bell, Daly, and Coleman had concluded that there had been limited ice cover and that above about 2,000 ft (about 600 m) above sea level the Torngat Mountains had projected far above outlet glaciers that penetrated through the main east-west valleys from a large continental ice sheet to the west (Odell 1933).

Coleman and Bell had ascended several Torngat summits, but these ascents were not mountaineering endeavors. Odell's introduction of mountaineering to the Torngat and Kaumajet mountains, however, was not followed up until very recently. Pauline and I, in the 1950s, were certainly not mountaineering, although we climbed some two dozen of the higher summits within Odell's "territory"—mainly steep scrambles—to test his theory about the maximum thickness of ice during the Ice Ages.

The first major field research ventures to study the geography of Newfoundland-Labrador, ranging from bedrock geology, geomorphology, Ice Age history, biology, and palynology, to its human geography came in the late 1930s. Professor Väinö Tanner organized and led the Finland-Labrador Expedition of 1937 and the Tanner Labrador Expedition of 1939. He was accompanied by several Finnish scientists who went on to establish international reputations. They included Carl-Gösta Wenner, palynologist; Ilmari Hustich, forest ecologist; and Hakan Kranck, geologist. They returned to Finland as that small country was swept up in the Winter War with the Soviet Union, during which Tanner lost his only son, who served with the valiant Finnish ski troops. This contributed to the father's wartime illness and premature death. Nevertheless, these highly successful Finnish expeditions completed the first systematic studies of Labrador.[13] The two most notable publications are Tanner's nine-hundred-page *Outlines of the Geography, Life and Customs of Newfoundland-Labrador* (1944) and Wenner's *Pollen Diagrams from Labrador: A Contribution to the Quaternary Geology of Newfoundland-Labrador, with Comparisons between North America and Europe* (1947). Kranck become professor of geology at McGill after World War II and was an active and supportive member of my own doctoral committee. Ilmari Hustich developed a close relationship with Ken Hare as the latter sought to build McGill's reputation for arctic and subarctic research. Hustich later became prime minister of Finland.

In the immediate postwar years Dr. Jacques Rousseau, under the aegis of Les Jardins Botaniques de Montréal and subsequently the Museum of Nature in Ottawa, and in collaboration with Dr. Erling Porsild, made substantial contributions to the botany of the Canadian Arctic and Subarctic. In particular, in 1947 he made an impressive canoe excursion down the George River to Ungava Bay, and up the Koroksoak River, and walked well into the southern Torngat Mountains. Odell, Tanner, Hustich, Kranck, Rousseau, Porsild, and Richard Foster Flint (see below) all positively influenced my own efforts to establish a Labrador-Ungava research program in physical and Quaternary geography.

Tanner, by accepting and publicizing Noel Odell's conclusions about the extent and thickness of the Laurentide Ice Sheet, in turn influenced Professor Flint at Yale. With his three major textbooks on Quaternary geology (1947, 1957, and 1971) and numerous scientific papers, Flint became the doyen of post–World War II Quaternary geologists and established the all-powerful and dominant hypothesis of Ice Age history. Much of the academic focus of this book is the story of the struggle to first test and then overthrow this entrenched hypothetical construct.

Mountaineering, aside from the pioneering efforts of Noel Odell in 1931, came so late in the history of Labrador-Ungava that it postdates the events of the present narrative. Nevertheless, for the sake of completeness, a brief comment is included here. The formal identification of Mont D'Iberville/ Mt. Caubvik and determination that it was the highest summit on mainland Canada east of the Rocky Mountains (5,420 ft/1,652 m asl) touched off a strong response in the 1970s.[14] The first ascent was made in 1973 and since then Mont D'Iberville/Caubvik and the surrounding peaks have been the objective of numerous mountaineering and hiking ventures.

Several developments facilitated a great expansion of the geographic knowledge of Labrador-Ungava during and immediately after World War II. The first was the wartime establishment of a major air base at Goose Bay. The second was widespread mineral exploration. Its focus on the Labrador Trough, extending from south of Knob Lake to the west coast of Ungava Bay, could have been anticipated as it was based, in large part, on the 1890s explorations of A. P. Low. But following the merging of Newfoundland with Canada in 1949, a large consortium, to become known as BRINCO (British Newfoundland Corporation), and its subsidiary mineral exploration enterprise, BRINEX (British Newfoundland Exploration), set off an intensive search for minerals and hydroelectricity potential across the length and breadth of Newfoundland's share of the peninsula.

These activities resulted in a rapid increase in geographical knowledge. However, it was of a specialized character focused on commercial development and, especially in the case of mineral exploration, it was not in the public domain. Hare recognized the need for a great extension of knowledge of this huge area and applied his initiative to establish McGill University as the geographical icon of Labrador-Ungava. Thus, despite the flurry of postwar mineral and hydro-power exploration and development, and regardless of the tenuous exploration routes traversed by the canoes of the Hudson's Bay Company and various missionaries and adventure travelers, it can be claimed that Hare entered an arena with about 90 percent of his chosen territory virtually unknown.

Founding of the McGill Sub-Arctic Research Laboratory, 1954

Geography, as an academic discipline, was established at McGill University only after World War II. Professor George Kimble founded the department in 1946, and Hare was persuaded to join him immediately following his wartime demobilization in England. While Hare gives much credit to Kimble for his early ideas and initiatives, it was Hare's vision and pioneer spirit, and especially his seemingly limitless opportunism, that established McGill as Canada's leading academic institution in arctic and subarctic teaching and research. He was abetted by Professor Max Dunbar's marine biological teaching and research that included extensive expeditions with the MV *Calanus* in arctic waters, and by Professor J. Brian Bird, the Geography Department's senior geomorphologist and subsequent chair. He and his wife, Beryl, undertook a series of bold summer research journeys into central Keewatin and Southampton Island.

Hare was preeminently a renaissance man, a much-sought-after public speaker and university lecturer, a man of unbounded ambition. Good looking and highly articulate, he had an outstanding presence and possessed a near-photographic memory. He tended toward excessive overwork. His enthusiasm for classical music was well known to all Geography Department graduate students. A new Canadian immigrant, Hare knew how to cajole friends and influence powerful people, as attested by his autobiography, which regrettably has never been published and from which much in the following paragraphs is derived.[15]

Hare claims that Kimble had foreseen that Canada and Canadian universities needed to find out and teach more about the Arctic and Subarctic. It was not only Labrador-Ungava that was a vast empty space in the late 1940s and early 1950s, but also the whole of Canada located farther than 150 mi (241 km) from its border with the United States.

Few Canadians today realize how little was known about the North before the 1950s. The federal government did not establish a separate department to administer its northern territories until 1954. At the second reading of a bill to do so, on 8 December 1953, then Prime Minister Louis St. Laurent commented in the House of Commons:

It has been said that Great Britain acquired her Empire in a state of absence of mind. Apparently we have administrated these vast territories of the North in an almost continuing absence of mind.

As an example, it seems unbelievable today that in 1948 Hudson Bay was thought to remain ice-free, except around its margins, throughout the winter. Hare's ability to identify with and influence individuals and institutions led to partial correction of this serious lack of knowledge. Hare and Tuzo Wilson together were able to benefit from the rapidly expanding interests of the Canadian Defence Research Board and the Canadian military that enabled them to explore the winter characteristics of Hudson Bay. To quote directly from Hare's autobiography:

> If 1948 was typical, then the Arctic Pilot and the United States Ice Atlas were absurdly wrong, as were the people who lived around its shores . . . [Hudson's Bay Company staff, Royal Canadian Mounted Police, missionaries, Inuit hunters[16]]. From this I learned that there was a huge need for a detailed, science-based reconnaissance survey in the north. The existing maps were often blank and where they were not they might well be wrong. Traditional [Canadian] survey methods,[17] largely inherited from the British Ordnance Survey, would never fill the gaps.

The reconnaissance from the air with Wilson (Churchill, Manitoba, Rankin Inlet, Southampton Island, Frobisher, Goose Bay, Great Whale) set the stage for the two large air-photo interpretation projects mentioned above. At the same time, with support from a seemingly surprising source, the Carnegie Corporation of New York, Hare and Kimble established the Stanstead Summer School on Arctic Geography. Symbolically located on the Canadian/U.S. border between the Eastern Townships of Québec and the state of Vermont, it attracted as teachers such well-known arctic and alpine experts as Vilhjalmur Stefansson, Sir Hubert Wilkins, and Noel Odell, and the geographical academic upper echelon from Britain, including S. W. Wooldridge, David Linton, Sir (later, Lord) Dudley Stamp. Among others, a large contingent of American servicemen appeared as eager students.

At the same time as these arctic and subarctic developments were unfolding, a group of U.S. and Canadian citizens were in the process of establishing the Arctic Institute of North America (AINA), a binational institute. Almost concurrent with Hare's initial arrival in Montréal, Dr. Lincoln Washburn became the executive director of AINA with its head office at McGill and subsidiary offices in New York and Washington. Lt. Col. Patrick D. Baird, who had extensive arctic experience, was later appointed director of the Montréal office. There followed a series of joint McGill-AINA ventures in quick succession: involvement in the joint Canada/U.S. meteorological stations in the

High Arctic, and two expeditions to Baffin Island (1950, 1953) led by Pat Baird. Graham and Diana Rowley were strong supporters of the AINA while Diana was involved in the development of its quarterly journal, *Arctic,* launched by Professor Trevor Lloyd, its founding editor. Graham Rowley, from his senior position in the newly established Canadian Defence Research Board, had been instrumental in obtaining official approval for the Hare-Wilson venture to check the validity of an unfrozen Hudson Bay.[18]

Following the success of the Stanstead-McGill Summer School, Hare was again approached by the Carnegie Corporation of New York. The corporation proposed financing a succession of joint McGill-AINA scholarships and senior fellowships to encourage recruitment of highly motivated graduate students. Although geographers were the principal beneficiaries, the McGill-Carnegie-Arctic fellowship/scholarship program became interdisciplinary and included geologists, zoologists, botanists, and anthropologists. Max Dunbar's marine biology group became a major participant. The 1950 and 1953 Baffin Island expeditions benefited greatly, as did the McGill Sub-Arctic Research Laboratory. The overwhelming majority of scholarship recipients were from Britain and Europe, thus bringing into Canada an infusion of competent young academics, mainly, but not entirely, male.

The decade 1945 to 1954, at McGill at least, appears as a time when everything came together. Certainly Hare was a principal influence, and it seemed almost inevitable that the McGill Sub-Arctic Research Laboratory would follow in this series of successes.

The establishment of the Lab, close to the geographic center of Labrador-Ungava, was essentially the natural outgrowth of the burst in arctic and subarctic research and teaching activity at McGill. The various developments already outlined converged on the railway northward from Sept-Îles and the opening of the iron mines at Knob Lake. At this point it is necessary to introduce George Jacobsen.[19] Jacobsen, president of the Tower Company, was one of the AINA pioneers and yet another close personal friend of Hare. His business centered on the design and prefabricated construction of buildings in the North, including weather stations. He was well aware of Hare's aspirations and was already involved in construction for the IOCC. Jacobsen offered to build a laboratory at Knob Lake with living quarters for four or five assistants and a small apartment for a director. He would charge the incredibly low sum of $17,000 for this. McGill principal, Cyril James, was easily persuaded to approve the funding. The ultimate source of the $17,000, however, was J. W. McConnell, McGill's chief benefactor at the time.

Yet, despite the dovetailing of all these events, there were serious obstacles. A schism developed within the AINA hierarchy and between the McGill/AINA thrusts into the Arctic and Subarctic and vested interests in Ottawa. In Hare's own words:

> But it was disconcerting that so much of our support came from the U.S., and so little from Canadian agencies. Later I was to experience an even more disconcerting problem: that powerful agencies in Ottawa were actively trying to block such aid on the grounds that it infringed Canadian sovereignty.

On the former "front," and according to Hare:

> Some members of the Arctic Institute's Board felt that we were doing an end run round them in setting up such facilities [the Lab]. The National Research Council said that permanent field facilities always failed because there was nothing to do in winter which I confess I thought was proof of their failure to face up to Canadian realities.

The concern over winter activities was a major issue with Hare, who was convinced that the routine hourly recording of weather elements in such a little-known location as central Labrador-Ungava was a worthwhile research task in itself. This issue will be discussed later on. Nevertheless, his assessment and his climatological and meteorological interests were reflected in the next vital step in founding the Lab. He prompted McGill University to sign a contract with Canada's Department of Transport (specifically, with its weather service, through another of his special personal contacts, Andrew Thompson, its director). It committed the nascent Lab to operate as a year-round first-order weather station. Although other observational programs were added later, the Lab's financial basis proved to be its function as a weather station, and it was a major determinant of its viability for years to come.

Despite the tangle of opportunities and obstacles, the Lab began recording weather observations on schedule on 1 October 1954. As related above, I spent the academic year 1954–1955 on the McGill campus, which enabled me to proceed rapidly with my doctoral dissertation and led to my appointment as acting field director of the Lab for the 1955 summer. In Hare's own words:

> The success of the McGill Sub-Arctic Research Laboratory illustrates the triumphs of poverty-stricken optimism and ambition over the scepticism of others. We did it on a shoestring, and it paid off.

It should be noted that the McGill Geography Department's direct financial base was abysmally slender.

The following narrative has been prepared to illustrate how well founded the above quotation proved to be. Even so, I will record only the Lab's first decade and place most emphasis on how I was able to use the outstanding opportunity that Ken Hare placed in my way.

Chapter Two

Knob Lake and the Lab: Summer 1955

As outlined in the prologue and chapter 1, the Lab was in full operation from 1 October 1954, onward. It was the first summer, however,
that witnessed a large increase in activities and responsibilities when the
Labrador-Ungava sector of the Mid-Canada Line was under rapid construction. A Royal Canadian Air Force base had been set up between the Lab
and the expanding IOCC town site. In terms of the number of landings
and takeoffs, the airstrip facing the Lab became the third busiest airport in
the whole of Canada after Dorval (Montréal) and Toronto. Manned radar
sites were being constructed at 50-mile (80 km) intervals across the 1,000-
mile (1,609 km) distance along latitude 55° N between Hudson Bay and the
Atlantic coast of Labrador.

The entire route of the Mid-Canada Line lay across hundreds of lakes of
all sizes so that the radar sites were accessible by floatplane, which greatly
facilitated delivery of men and supplies. The Knob Lake airstrip experienced
almost continual landings and takeoffs throughout the daylight hours.
Canso amphibious flying boats, capable of landing on wheels on the run-
way and on water at the radar station construction sites, were in constant
use. These activities greatly increased the demands on the Lab for aircraft
briefings and special weather forecasts, especially with the very changeable
weather conditions of a central Labrador-Ungava summer. The Department
of Transport (DOT) was prompted to allocate a senior weather forecaster to
help us out, and so Art Morris became an essential member of the team and
a personable and enthusiastic contributor to the maintenance of our sanity.
He provided me with much-needed assistance as I was tentatively feeling
my way forward as acting station chief and field director. We also had three
summer relief observers, McGill graduates and undergraduates, whom Hare
had recruited so that the winter crew, Les, George, and Jean-Claude, had
free time for their independent research. Thus we welcomed to our motley

crew a very shy, highly intelligent Jock Galloway; a rambunctious Cyril "Cy" Lewis, who insisted that he hated every minute away from his flaunted low-life Montréal haunts yet did a very passable job; and Jim Lotz from Liverpool, England. Jim had a Liverpool and Scottish upbringing and BA in geography, which he followed with a stint as a trader in West Africa. He was a very jovial and willing addition, despite his theatrical reaction to mosquitoes and black flies, tents, rain, and the prospect of being lost in the "bloody bush." (More about Jim will be related later.)

I experienced a hectic and very fulfilling summer. First, there was responsibility for the Lab and, aided by Art, for the weather routine, while based at the camp on John Lake with Pauline, Les, and Teri. I took short excursions by four-wheel-drive jeep—which I first had to learn to drive—and on foot. There were also short weekend camps at the limit of our jeep-plus-foot capability and a substantial canoe trip in August, succeeded by longer camps and hikes as far as Pauline and I could reach.

The opportunity to see an entire cross-section of Labrador-Ungava, however, came from a chance friendship with one of the Mid-Canada Line Canso pilots who was a regular visitor to the Lab's weather office. Illegally, Jules would sneak me onboard his Canso and so enabled me to conduct my own aerial reconnaissance from the Atlantic coast to within 50 mi (80 km) of Hudson Bay—that is, until we were caught and reprimanded by an officer of the RCAF. Until that embarrassing late afternoon I had been able to make a dozen flights along most of the line of radar sites. I plotted the distribution of burned-over forest and the wide areas of trampled Cladonia lichen (caribou moss), interspersed with winding caribou trails (but with few sightings of caribou). I roughly recorded numerous glacial drainage channels (appendix I) and what I thought must be the shorelines of former lakes that had been dammed by the last great ice sheet as it progressively melted away. While this record was impossible to reproduce adequately because of the scale and poor quality of the base maps, it became of great value in my later attempt to formulate a peninsula-wide research program. Finally, during quiet periods (usually between midnight and 5 a.m.) while on weather-observing duty at the Lab, I was hastily drafting maps and graphs that would ultimately go into my doctoral dissertation on southeast Iceland. I was determined to complete this during the following academic year in Montréal.

The northern Labrador coast and especially the Torngat Mountains had been fixed in my mind from undergraduate reading at Nottingham University. The 1955 summer proved invaluable for the first flimsy formulation of what turned out to be a long-range field research plan. My 1951 summer in arctic Norway and Sweden and especially the three summers in Iceland had led me to read the most recent Swedish and Norwegian research publications in glacial geomorphology. And so I became familiar with the innovative work of Professor Gunnar Hoppe and Dr. Carl Mannerfelt. In particular, I learned of Mannerfelt's interpretation of the myriad glacial drainage channels, now abandoned, across wide areas of the mountains of central and arctic Scandinavia. Thus my initial identification of what appeared to be similar features in the Knob Lake area and much farther afield sent a pulse of excitement through my system. When I was able to follow up the airborne reconnaissance with extensive hiking, I realized that the Lab had been located in the middle of hundreds of now dry channels, often in subparallel flights of twelve or more sloping down entire hillsides. I could only assume, from their similarity to landforms that had been pivotal to the Scandinavian research, that these channels represented the margins of lobes of ice that had been formed by glacial meltwater during the final stages of the Ice Age Laurentide Ice Sheet as it rapidly melted away some thousands of years ago.[20] This was all the more exciting and remarkable because the Geological Survey of Canada had fielded research parties in 1953 and 1954 to investigate the glacial geology of the Knob Lake area and, in my new understanding, these critically diagnostic features had been misinterpreted (see pages 55–56).

In the vicinity of Knob Lake these flights of channels sloped down in a general southerly direction, indicating that the southern margin of the last great ice sheet had retreated northward across the area. It seemed too much to hope that we could travel far enough to the north to find a place where similar channels sloped down but toward the north. If this were the case, it would allow identification of the location of some of the last remnants of the once-vast ice sheet that had covered much of Canada and a large part of the northern and northeastern United States. But it was well worth the search and it fit into my evolving plan of maximum familiarization of the interior of this enormous stretch of wilderness.

Therefore, as time permitted, we began to push as far northward as possible up the tortuous and largely abandoned IOCC exploration trails with the wretchedly unreliable Willys jeep. (Les warned that we should always park facing down a good long hill, to improve our chance of starting the engine and so avoid a long walk back to the Lab.) In late August we reached a point about 30 mi (48 km) north of the Lab and were able to prove that my hunch was correct. In the area just north of Kivivic Lake and Sunny Mountain we discovered the first channels that sloped down toward the north. We had found what appeared to be one of the final ice divides and melting locations of the Laurentide Ice Sheet, and this set the stage for a subsequent influential academic publication (Ives 1959b).

The other exploration of more-distant locations was by canoe to the southern end of the series of lakes (Astray, Dyke, Marble lakes) that flowed into the upper Hamilton River and so over Grand Falls and eventually into the Labrador Sea. This adventure so aptly characterizes an example of English neophytes let loose in the Labrador-Ungava wilderness that it deserves its own section.

Astray Lake, 1955: Our First Canoe Trip

Les Viereck and I had installed ourselves in the bush camp we had established on the edge of John Lake a couple miles through the spruce forest east of the Lab. Teri and Pauline, our wives, joined us a few days later. The camp was set up in grand style, reflecting Les's skill as an experienced woodsman. It was to be shared with our wives and, regrettably, with swarms of mosquitoes and black flies that arrived uninvited. Les was a former captain of the Dartmouth College Outing Club. Tough, competent, and a tower of strength, Les had nothing little about him, and his excellent physique went with a very sensitive and gentle personality. Teri was blond, beautiful, and elegant—there were occasions when three of us, behind double mosquito nets, glumly eyed a bikini-clad Teri stretched out on a rock after an energetic swim in the lake, totally ignored by mosquito and black fly alike.

Then there was the Lab summer relief crew—Jock Galloway, Cy Lewis, and Jim Lotz. We had occasional visits from Dartmouth College: Huntingdon "Curt" Curtis, professor of engineering; Erv Bentley; and very occasionally, Millet Morgan, their team leader. The three of them constituted Dartmouth's Whistler—Northern Lights—research program. All in all, we had an interesting group of regular and visitor staff and two wives, as well as Les and Teri's giant malamute, Kobuk, and Cassie, a black spaniel that Norm and Pat left in our care.

A handsome new orange canoe arrived on the train with Teri in early June; it was 18 ft (5.5 m) long and had a square stern, and thus was a boat. I thought that we would have to portage down at the southern end of Astray Lake, so-called because the famous Canadian government geologist, A. P. Low, had lost himself down there for a couple of weeks in 1894, even though accompanied by Montagnais Indian guides. So I suggested that Pauline and I should start our training course by trying to carry the canoe while we were still at our home base. This involved swinging it over our heads and onto our shoulders, ready to march.

Eyed by Jim and George, I took the center, Pauline the stern.

"One, two, three, lift!" I cried.

We both lifted.

Pause, over our heads, pause.

Pauline collapses; I collapse.

"Let's try again," said Pauline.

"It's just a matter of getting the swing right," said I.

"It's heavy!"

"Well, Hubbard and Dillon Wallace did it, so we will succeed if we keep trying."

"I don't think so," said Pauline. "What about the outboard?"

"Wallace and Hubbard didn't have an outboard."

"Hubbard died of starvation and hypothermia, but even if you were born in Grimsby, greatest fishing port in the world, that will not enable you to be a better fisher for trout than Hubbard."

"Perhaps we had better avoid portages," I suggested.

"Then you'll have to swim the next lake," said Jim, "and the water will be damn cold."

"Don't worry," replied Pauline, "Jack can't swim."

"My God," said Jim.

I obviously needed a new tack. So we transported the canoe, on the roof of the jeep station wagon, over to John Lake and, with Jim's incompetent help, set in place the outboard motor. After supper we would have our first test run on the lake—great excitement and anticipation. Very unfortunately, for us at least, Les and Teri were away camping on Sunny Mountain, trapping small mammals for Teri.[21]

Jim had supper with us in the big tent on John Lake—he was excited to be in a tent for the first time, and he had never seen so many bloody mosquitoes and black flies, trees and lakes. By the time we had finished supper, the weather was looking much worse. Still, cheerful with our new toy, we pushed off and Jim and I zigzagged up the lake a couple of miles as Jim plunged from side to side. Pauline, in the center, watched, half amused, half anxious. We decided it was time to turn back, so we swung around into a steadily increasing wind, with rain, on the port bow. It had become apparent that we should start our brand-new outboard motor. We had filled it with fuel. We had put in the recommended amount of oil. So all we needed to do was open the throttle to half-lean and pull the cord. As the crew's assumed helmsman, that was my job. By now we were beginning to get wet and were being driven by the wind closer to the rocky shoreline.

I pulled.

Nothing.

Adjusted throttle and tried again.

Nothing.

"Quick, the paddles, or we will be on the rocks," said I.

So we paddled and pulled the cord, paddled and pulled, and swore.

"There must be something wrong with this bloody motor."

There was something wrong, but with me. I had neglected to open the air valve (choke). It was very simple, and Les and Teri were amazed when they learned of our exploits and incompetence a couple of days later.

By now it was nearly dark and raining heavily. So we forgot the motor and paddled and paddled. Rainwater streamed off us and lake water began to slop over the side; a pond began to grow in the bottom of the canoe. Pauline started bailing. Jim and I, in mounting desperation, continued to paddle. We could hardly see the silhouettes of the spruce trees around our camp. Jim started to sing. We were beyond care.

Pauline couldn't help laughing. "Do you really think you are going to take me down Astray Lake?"

We all began to sing—appropriately—"with a tow row, row, row, row, row, row for the British Grenadiers." But we made it back, soaked, near hysterical, hoarse with singing. We stepped out of the canoe, tied up, and went into the big tent for towels and hot chocolate. That was our first and nearly our last canoe journey. Now for the real one.

Astray and Marble lakes and the Grand/Hamilton/Churchill River basin lay to the southeast of Knob Lake at the heart of what Ken Hare called "the Labrador Lake Plateau," a trackless area in the northern boreal forest that was just beginning to be opened up with the development of a vast hydroelectricity project that would eventually cause the Churchill Falls (formerly the Grand Falls on the Hamilton), nearly twice the height of Niagara, to disappear. Some 30 percent of the plateau is open water, 15 percent muskeg, and the rest almost impenetrable taiga, with black and white spruce dominating. The area, part of the hunting territory of the Montagnais Indians, had been explored by the Canadian government geologist A. P. Low. The area chosen for our first real canoe venture included parts of Astray Lake and Marble Lake, and the muskeg to the south. It would give us access to a large area of the so-called rippled till ("ribbed moraine" in some publications), a spectacular and unexplained pattern of glacial ground moraine that had been mapped from air photographs by Norm Drummond. The difficulties experienced by Low did not alarm us, as our area was covered by new topographical maps on a scale of 1:50,000. Nevertheless we had a sense of high adventure fueled by our total inexperience. There is only one sure way of transforming inexperience into experience: do it!

On a bright sunny afternoon we laboriously drove the jeep down the deeply rutted Iron Ore Company exploration track the 20-odd mi (32 km) from Knob Lake to the northwestern arm of Astray Lake. The great orange monster was strapped on the roof, Les was driver, and Teri cheered us on. After two hours of tedious driving we emerged from the forest and sidled down to a pebbly beach giving on to a broad stretch of beautiful calm water. We lifted the canoe off the jeep and set it in the water looking across to Autumn Island, a little to the south of us. We had loaded the outboard motor, tent, rucksacks, sleeping bags with waterproof covers, five gallons of outboard motor fuel, and fishing rods and gill nets, as well as a spare paddle (urged on us by Les, who was convinced that we were bound to lose at least one). There were also a stove and cooking pans and a stack of food (in the event that the fish were smarter than we were) and, given the luxurious size of the canoe, even six grapefruit (always my favorite for breakfast), to the amusement of Les and Teri.

"You English are hopeless in the bush!"

To which I replied: "Well, we did establish a couple of empires."

By 3:30 p.m. that day, life belts adjusted, we were ready. We pushed off with waves and shouts from shore to canoe and back. This time the motor started on the first pull, and its low rumble generated a crescendo of good wishes. At half throttle we gently coasted down the northwestern arm of this vast intricate stretch of water. We now began to understand why Low had chosen the name "Astray." The myriad lakes, islands, and peninsulas would have made it impossible to select a course in the 1890s, but in 1955 we could negotiate with relative ease aided by our new 1:50,000 scale maps.

We are about to depart on our first canoe trip. Astray Lake, central Labrador-Ungava. August 1955.

We felt ourselves totally alone in the world, so we turned off the motor and took to the paddles. The experience was unlike anything we had ever known. The surface of the lake was limpid with the reflection of high, scattered cirrus clouds and the deep blue of the sky and, closer to land, the sharp spires of the spruce. By peering straight down into the water we could see the bottom far below, sharp and clear, and the occasional trout gliding under us. We paddled for a couple of hours until the high clouds began to turn pink and the reflecting lake surface deep purple, still like glass. We pulled into a small cove and prepared to camp for the night. A lone campfire on the shore and the great expanse of water before us created a sense of remoteness and completeness. To this was added the eerie cry of a loon from far across the lake that eventually reflected a nearly full moon (see Plate 1).

The repeated call of the loon, known to us from Iceland as the Great Northern Diver, seemed to beckon us onto the lake. We threw another piece of wood on the campfire and gently pushed off, our slow paddles producing the only additional sound to that of the loon. Three hundred yards across the placid surface was enough, our fire now a tiny flickering beneath the black curtain of spruce. We brought the paddles inboard and sat in silence. The eerie bird call continued intermittently. We spotted circular ripples some 50 yards ahead; our mysterious new friend emerged to inspect us.

After sunset the air temperature had dropped and layers of wispy vapor had begun to form above the surface of the still water. The intermixture of purple, mauve, and the lunar reflection was entrancing. I was caught in a profound introspection: marriage to Pauline and emigration to Canada less than a year ago, together with this penetration of the vast and lovely emptiness of interior Labrador-Ungava, combined into a sense of adventure. In a real sense we were alone in the world, dependent on each other for survival, if only for the short space of a fortnight. It was a delicate circumspect beginning to our Labrador-Ungava mission.

Already I was thinking about the next summer and the prospects of reaching the Torngat Mountains far to the northeast. Then our rather gentle experiences in the center of the great peninsula set between Hudson Bay, the Atlantic Ocean, and the Gulf of St. Lawrence would be put to a more serious test. How would we overcome the logistical challenge of getting there in the first place, given our very limited financial resources?

The loon emerged once more, even closer this time, and called into the spreading layers of mist, bringing my thoughts back to the present. Picking up the paddles, we coaxed the canoe back toward our nearly extinct fire, pulled it well up onto the narrow cobbly beach, turned it on its side, and looped the painter around a nearby spruce tree. We doused the fire and crawled into our compact mountain tent. Then we were off to bed on the wonderfully scented spruce boughs we had carefully inserted into the mossy ground surface as Les and Teri had shown us at our John Lake camp.

The next morning dawned bright with a light westerly breeze so that the lake surface in front of us remained unruffled. We breakfasted on grapefruit and porridge laced with sugar, butter, and raisins, the whole washed down with instant coffee.

Tent and sleeping bags were soon packed and the canoe loaded, and we were away, heading eastward across Astray Lake. We had decided to test our navigation capabilities and examine one of the two outlets into Dyke Lake, about 7 mi (11 km) to the east. We skirted an array of islands and peninsulas, coming ashore repeatedly so I could measure the directions of glacial striations at many points along our serpentine route. Since the day was long and the lake calm, we used our paddles for most of the trip, thus saving our small supply of outboard motor fuel. Out on the water we were largely free of the mosquitoes and black flies, but as we came into land we were almost suffocated and quickly donned our head nets.

By early afternoon we had rounded a large island and began to head northeast to the southerly of the two broad channels that led from Astray into Dyke Lake. From our maps we had assumed that we would find still water in the channel that was about 30 paces wide. But as we approached we were caught by surprise in a strong current. We soon found ourselves in a precarious position, moving rapidly broadside into what had become significant rapids with a scattering of huge boulders breaking the surface. After some hefty paddle strokes we righted ourselves and ran ashore on an attractive gravel beach on the south side of the channel. My first reaction was that we now had an excellent prospect for bagging some trout for dinner, so we unloaded, secured the canoe, and rushed for the fishing kits.

Soon we were pulling in big fish fast and furiously—lake trout, brook trout, and two splendid land-locked salmon (ouananiche—*Salmo salar ouananiche*). The total catch was more than twenty in barely two hours. The lake trout were easy to secure, but some of the brook trout were quite feisty. Our two salmon, however, put up a tremendous fight, leaping well clear of the water only to dive back again and go deep. Fortunately I had landed mine before the second salmon began to challenge Pauline's newly acquired skills, so she handed me her rod. After a fight, I brought the fish ashore. All the trout were carefully released. One of the salmon was roasted in the embers of our campfire and provided a meal that became a lifelong memory.

By the time we were finished angling and after the feast from a 10-pound (4.5 kg) fish, a moderate onshore breeze had sprung up. We laid out on the beach, our fingertips lightly touching across our gently aching tummies, with the breeze keeping at bay the airborne carnivores. Paradise!

The next morning we headed southward along the east side of Astray Lake. By late afternoon we crossed over to the opposite shore and so reached the connecting channel with Marble Lake. Here we camped; we had covered about 18 mi (29 km).

Our location between the two large lakes was similar to our previous night's campsite, although there was no discernable current. We thought that after breakfast another assault on the local fish population would be in order. Our second ouananiche had been devoured the night before, so it was time to renew our larder. We caught nothing but pike: in fact, as many as we could bother to heave ashore. And although I was well aware of their good taste, my recollection of their bone structure encouraged me to put them all back.

The day was spent meandering to the south end of Marble Lake with the intent of entering Esker Lake, a string of three small lakes, each less than a mile long and separated by short narrow channels. As we entered the first of the three lakes, our canoe scraped the bottom and we sensed that we had run aground. Our canoeing strategy needed a dramatic change of focus.

Stepping out of the canoe, I realized that we had entered a very shallow lake with a bottom of fine sand and mud. To float the canoe, Pauline also had to wade alongside me while I pulled on the painter. Thus, feeling rather ridiculous, and relieved that Les and Teri were nowhere in sight, we plodded onward in calf-to-knee-deep water. The predicament caused us much laughter as we recollected our first experience with the prospect of what to do in the event

We strike the very shallow "Esker Lake I" and barely avoid a heavy, wet portage. August 1955.

of having to portage. So far, however, we had not needed to carry the orange monster. We proceeded with caution, probing ahead with a paddle to make sure that we avoided any deep holes concealed by the opaque muddy water: a fine kettle of fish, absence of trout not withstanding! At least we had reached our objective—rippled till terrain.

Esker Lake II was deep and transparent, offering the prospect of trout. There was a small steep-sided island close to the north end, so we paddled toward it, beached the canoe, and found an ideal campsite on the crest of the island amid a thick cover of Cladonia lichen and scattered spruce trees (see Plate 2).

We had a perfect island setting (see Plate 3), although the insects were almost insufferable during periods of calm. We were about 60 ft (18 m) above lake level and looked westward onto the flank of a large north-south trending esker that gleamed Cladonia yellow where it emerged from fairly dense spruce. To the east and south we could see all the rippled till we thought we would ever need.

We spent seven nights on this hospitable island. During long days we walked along the crest of the esker, descended and scouted the shores of Bray and Shoal lakes, digging dozens of soil pits as we progressed. Except for enabling us to

The "Labrador Lake Plateau," where a canoe is of limited use and the black flies and mosquitoes are a torment.

cross dry shod onto the flank of the esker, the canoe was of little value on our island sanctuary. Off the esker, the going was very rough: wet ground, marsh, bogs, small ponds, and lakes all around us. The esker crest carried a well-marked but rather old and unused trail. We quickly learned to appreciate the efforts of former generations of caribou, although we sighted none.

The black flies and mosquitoes continued to torment us, but the weather remained mostly favorable. The occasional shower soaked us. Long after the rain stopped, too, dense alder thickets brought down torrents of water upon us as we forced our way through them. Nevertheless, our lake provided ample trout for supper. And the flickering glow of a campfire in the evenings as daylight paled into a gentle gloaming, followed by a fading moon and starlight, caused our thoughts to drift back to the turn of the century when, almost equally unprepared, Hubbard and Wallace lost themselves in such a setting. Not that we were tempted to make a comparison, but rather to contrast the Labrador interior of the midcentury with that of its beginning.

We packed up our tiny camp after seven nights on the island and started back toward our northern road access. We waded back along Esker Lake I and, after two more camps, reached the roadhead north of Autumn Island by early afternoon on the third day. We had debated with Les and Teri the problem of being picked up, because we did not want to propose a definite time and then be unable to make it. We had decided that, if no assistance was to hand, we could cache the canoe and our heavy baggage and walk back. As it happened, fortune continued to smile on us and we ran into a group of Iron Ore Company employees who had driven down from Knob Lake in two trucks on a pleasure outing. They took both of us back to the Lab with all of our equipment, except the canoe. That we retrieved the following week during the first snowfall of the autumn. Les and Teri marveled at our adventure, relieved, they said, at not needing to organize a search party for the two incompetent Brits.

Summing Up: First Summer

The activities of the first summer set the pattern for the next decade. However, there was an important exception. So far, little thought had been given to outfitting and provisioning the Lab winter staff for summer fieldwork in the more distant parts of the immense expanse of Labrador-Ungava. (This will be taken up in the following chapters.) However, this first summer had been experimental, and fieldwork was largely restricted to those relatively nearby areas that could be reached by four-wheel-drive jeep, the canoe, and on foot. It was remarkable, for the predominantly geography-based enterprise, that the human geography of Knob Lake, the new mining town in the wilderness with no road connection with the outside, received nothing more than incidental attention. This was most likely due to a lack of clear field research direction. In this sense the individual graduate students were left to their own devices, a reasonable strategy under the circumstances for the early years of operation, but one that needed rectification.

Able to combine their botanical and zoological interests, Les and Teri were among the first to focus their research on these then relatively unknown arctic and subarctic ecosystems located between the northern boreal forest and the full arctic tundra. The local relief of 1,000 ft (300 m) or so provided an alpine,

Retrieval of the canoe during the first "winter" snowfall. Late August 1955.

or altitudinal, component so that there was a range of vegetation types from closed-crown spruce forests, string bog, and lake in the broad valley bottoms, open lichen woodland at midelevation, and arctic tundra along the ridge crests and on the upper plateaulike highlands.

The summer also saw the beginnings of instrument-supported climatological vegetation research. This was one of Ken Hare's primary research interests and attracted the attention of Svenn Orvig, who drew from his glacioclimatological and meteorological experience on the Baffin Island expeditions of 1950 and 1953. The theoretical collaboration between Ken Hare and Professor Warren Thornthwaite (the preeminent geographer/climatologist of that period) provided a platform for the systematic study of the albedo (reflectivity) of the variety of cover types and their associated rates of evapotranspiration. This project, however, had to await its full development in subsequent summers when additional funding became available.

George Michie had originally intended to undertake a self-contained overland vegetation and landscape traverse of the 250 mi (402 km) of trackless terrain between Knob Lake and Fort Chimo. However, without adequate financial backing for pontoon plane support, George eventually settled on a study of the founding and development of the port and town of Sept-Îles. Jean-Claude Langlois wrote about the formation of mining towns in the wilderness, and the summer student visitors were fully occupied as the "laborers" of the demanding weather-observing program.

One other highly specialized research project had a major impact on the Lab for the following five years. The link with Dartmouth College, NH, had been established by Ken Hare through his association with Professor Millet Morgan of the Thayer School of Engineering at Dartmouth. Professor Morgan was a "northern lights freak," and Knob Lake lay athwart the zone of maximum aurora borealis intensity that swept west-southwest from Iceland into central Labrador-Ungava before veering away northwestward into Alaska. Instrumentation was set up at the Lab to record electromagnetic ionosphere fluctuations and, while Millet Morgan proved to be a rare visitor, his colleague, Dr. Huntingdon "Curt" Curtis, made short visits throughout the summer. The arrival of Curt, ostensibly to set up and tune a highly sophisticated array of instruments that we learned to refer to as the "whistler" array, was invariably met with enthusiasm. Curt exuded fun, intelligence, curiosity, and bonhomie. Above all, he fixed everything: the wretched Willys jeep, the Lab electricity and sewerage systems, the DOT teletype, and the newly introduced Weatherfax equipment. He described his approach to the teletype and the Weatherfax as "kick it on the left side and throw sand over it," and he always succeeded in getting them to function. He was a keen angler and accompanied us on trips up the IOCC prospecting trails northward, teaching me refinements of off-the-road driving en route, and the fine art of winching the green monster across washouts in the trail. Curt was an all-around inspiration, although later on, as the whistler project expanded, he was replaced by a full-time technician, Erv Bentley, also a man of many parts.

The experiences of the 1955 Lab summer had unfolded as a serious and successful beginning to what came to be regarded as a "permanent expedition to the subarctic"; it entailed a series of enjoyable events that laid the foundations for an integrated and far-flung field program. It was also great fun for most of those involved, with much amusement centered on Les and Teri's giant malamute, Kobuk. He was an admirable canine specimen, a physical powerhouse, although the dumbest dog I have ever known. Under mischievous coaxing he would laboriously search all the corners of a pond of clear water for nonexistent fish that Les had prompted him to believe were there. While we were hiking across Sunny Mountain, some 30 mi (48 km) to the north, Kobuk would mistake a distant, low-flying Canso for a caribou and chase it for miles, leaving us perplexed and anxious. But above all, he loved bacon and butter and was addicted to porcupine.

During one weekend camp on Sunny Mountain with Les and Teri, Kobuk set off an evening's entertainment by first finding and then devouring our well-concealed supply of bacon and butter. Later he cornered a porcupine and managed to fill his mouth with quills. It required a coordinated effort by all four of us to extract the quills: Teri, Pauline, and I lay across his great girth and attempted to immobilize his head; Les pulled the quills, one by one, using a pair of pincers and thick leather gloves. After the sad yelping and whining had died down, Les buried the porcupine corpse at the bottom of a 5-foot-deep mining exploration hole, carefully loading large rocks on top. By 3 a.m. we were all awakened by a fresh outburst of cries and howls. Kobuk had unearthed his nemesis and had filled his already badly torn mouth once more with quills. Another major operation was required.

The saga of Kobuk went on all summer. Les and Teri had seriously discussed becoming members of our planned field adventure in the Torngat Mountains during the following summer. Pauline and I were very keen about this, both because they were great friends and companions, and a four-person expedition would be a much safer proposition than two, as well as much more convivial. Nevertheless, Les's efforts to train Kobuk as a pack animal for the Torngat venture filled Pauline and me with a sense of mild dismay. Regrettably, these tentative plans failed to materialize. Les and Teri found that the University of Colorado led to much more secure funding prospects that reinforced their attraction to Alaska, a combination that they could not refuse.[22]

The 1955 summer helped to clarify a number of operational problems. A firm field research plan was needed, one that would complement research within easy access of the Lab with field parties spread across the much wider area of the Labrador-Ungava peninsula. The possibility for tension between winter and summer staff, and the winter graduate assistants and a married Lab director, needed careful attention. Certainly, it was not ideal to have a summer acting director obliged to camp 2 mi (3 km) away in the bush because he was married and his wife was a competent field assistant or independent researcher.[23]

The personality problems were closely related to the very limited Lab accommodation of the first year, which, in turn, was a result of financial limitations. Furthermore, in my estimation, a three-man winter crew was inadequate. However, all these problems, excepting lack of a broad field plan, were about to be alleviated. The 1955–1956 winter's crew was to be increased from three to four. Plans were afoot for a second building that would include living accommodation for the field director and his family. Nevertheless, reliable motorized local transport and funding for pontoon plane support for distant field parties remained as challenges. I believed that the latter would be met once a firm field plan was in place. I also felt that I was on the verge of being able to formulate the initial outline for such a plan, at least in terms of Ice Age history and geomorphology. However, with an incomplete doctoral dissertation, I was not in a particularly strong position to initiate any detailed program.

Ken Hare's remarkable venture into central Labrador-Ungava seemed to be succeeding beyond expectations, although there were still undercurrents within the Geography Department arising from the perceived dangers of a fixed location and long confined winters. These undercurrents were similar to the original opposition to Ken Hare's concept that came from several Canadian government institutions in Ottawa—how would graduate students handle the potential boredom of long winters punctuated solely by routine and repetitive weather observations?

Nevertheless, Pauline and I had an exhilarating summer and I had become fully committed to the Lab and to a better understanding of the geography of Labrador-Ungava. However, there were two more years before I would learn whether the Geography Department was prepared to give me the responsibility to carry through on such tentative ideas. This would coincide with the expiration of Norm Drummond's three-year appointment as field director.

Chapter Three

The Torngat Mountains: 1956–1957

The 1955–1956 winter in Montréal turned out to be one of the most hectic in our lives. Pauline no longer had her job with CIL, as she had resigned to spend the previous summer with me at Knob Lake. Our financial situation obliged her to take up the less-than-ideal job of teacher of geography and English at a private girls' high school. I had to divide my time between completing a doctoral dissertation on the Skaftafell area of southeast Iceland and finding a way to get the two of us to the Torngat Mountains the following summer, adequately supplied with food and equipment.

Our choice of field area, at least from a theoretical point of view, presented no problem. We chose the area between Kangalaksiorvik Fiord on the Atlantic coast and the head of Abloviak Fiord that leads into Ungava Bay, accessible through one of the great Torngat passes (see sketch map, page 45). The pass runs through a pronounced U-shaped trench carved by Ice Age glacial erosion. Sea Plane Cove, about 60° N, at the entrance to Kangalaksiorvik Fiord, had been the major base of the Forbes/American Geographical Society expedition of 1931. The fiord and pass led westward via the Kangalaksiorvik lakes through some of the most impressive mountains: the Four Peaks to the north and Mount Tetragona to the south. Upper Kangalaksiorvik Lake opens southward through a broad structural valley between Odell's "coast range" and "interior range." It provides easy access to the Komaktorvik lakes, which occupy another great trough cutting through the mountains. From the air photographs of the Forbes expedition, this was clearly attractive mountain country, open to apparently easy long-distance backpacking, a potential joy for camping, fishing, and hill walking. (It now forms part of the Torngat Mountain National Park, established in 2006.)

The area had been the most intensively studied in 1931 by members of the Forbes expedition, especially Odell, who had climbed most of the prominent peaks. Yet their research had provided rather ambiguous results. In addition, the eastern section was covered by the excellent 1:100,000 scale Forbes maps; the western section was a virtual blank.

Thus there were ample reasons for choosing this area. But why attempt to study the rather inaccessible Torngat Mountains in the first place? Apart from a BRINEX geological reconnaissance (with pontoon-equipped planes and a small helicopter) the previous summer, and with the possible exception of Inuit hunting parties along the coast north from Hebron, there had been no visitors since Forbes/Odell in 1931.

The choice of the Torngat Mountains was related to my schoolboy fascination with Sir Wilfred Grenfell, the Moravians, and Labrador, and to my reading of the account of the Forbes/Northernmost Labrador expedition while an undergraduate at Nottingham University. These impressions were reinforced by my later assessment of the prevailing views on the glaciation and deglaciation of the Labrador-Ungava peninsula and, indeed, of eastern and central Canada as a whole. While Forbes had produced maps that provided accurate topographical data (very unusual for any area of Arctic Canada at that time), the Labrador-Ungava peninsula in general remained little known. Sources, ranging from the then current edition of *Encyclopaedia Britannica* to the publications of Richard Foster Flint, presented the regional relief as a mountain range extending along the northern half of the Labrador coast backed by an undulating but much lower plateau interior and lowland fronting Ungava Bay. The *Encyclopaedia Britannica* recorded the mountain range as exceeding 7,000 ft (2,100 m), and possibly up to 9,000 ft (2,800 m)—this was a gross exaggeration and an indication of how encyclopedias can provide out-of-date information.

It was also remarkable that the notion of a coastal range had clearly influenced Flint's hypothetical construct of the mode of initiation, growth, and eventual decay of each of the four Laurentide ice sheets that were then assumed to have characterized the Pleistocene Ice Ages (Flint 1943). Flint had taken research on Ice Age history in Scandinavia and applied it as a mirror-image model to the opposite side of the North Atlantic.

In brief, Flint's argument predicted the initial development of glaciers at the onset of each ice age on the highest elevations in the coastal range. As the glaciers thickened and expanded, on the eastern (Atlantic) side they would eventually calve into the fiords and so into the ocean, thus attaining a form of stability—the outflow of icebergs would offset the accumulation of ice and snow at the higher elevations. Flint envisioned that the expanding ice masses would also flow down the western slopes of this hypothetical mountain range and accumulate as vast piedmont lobes on the lower land farther west and southwest. It was also assumed that the major source of moisture nourishing the expanding ice sheets was derived from deep atmospheric depressions that originated in the Gulf of Mexico. Thus the growth of the ice sheet toward the southwest would be enhanced as it advanced into the moisture source. Eventually, it would thicken until the surface was higher than the mountain crest and cause a reversal of ice flow back across the mountains and into the Atlantic. The continued southwestward growth of the ice sheet would eventually overwhelm the entire Labrador-Ungava plateau, engulf Hudson Bay, cross the prairies, and push up against the Rocky Mountains. This had become the widely accepted interpretation of Quaternary history from the 1940s to the 1970s.

Flint hypothesized the total reversal of this scenario as the closing phase of each of the four ice ages so that the thinning ice mass would be progressively reduced to local glaciers and small ice caps within the fastnesses of the coastal range (that is, Torngat Mountains), where small glaciers persist today.

Flint published many papers and two major textbooks (in 1947 and 1957) and his hypothetical construct became the glacial paradigm of the day. It was well argued and seemed eminently logical, although there was scarcely any field evidence to back it up. Odell alone had provided supporting field data from the Torngat Mountains, but nothing from the western slopes. Odell's interpretation had been readily accepted by Tanner, and together they had swept under the carpet the "scientific truth" of the earlier conclusions drawn by Bell, Daly, and Coleman.

This predominant scientific contention of the early 1950s had increased my curiosity about the Torngat Mountains. Here would lie the evidence to support Flint's hypothesis. He had himself indicated that the western "flank" of the Torngat Mountains would most likely provide essential supporting field evidence: thus the appeal of the Kangalaksiorvik-Abloviak transect. All we had to do was cross the mountains and record the direction of final ice movement west of the divide, thus confirming his presumed late-glacial westerly ice flow.

There was a complementary problem—the determination of the greatest thickness of the ice carapace at the maximum of the glacial period(s). This, in turn, was related to research in Scandinavia, Iceland, and Greenland. A succession of biologists, from the late 1800s to the 1950s, had attempted to account for the anomalous distribution of two groups of arctic-alpine vascular plants. It had been reasoned that their present-day distribution indicated that they had survived through the maximum of the ice ages on ice-free areas high in the coastal mountains, or in ice-free sanctuaries in the coastal lee of the mountains between the great fiords. This concept, known as the Nunatak Hypothesis (*nunatak*: Greenlandic, meaning an area surrounded by ice), was hotly contested by most Scandinavian geologists and geographers and, especially, by Odell (1933), who was convinced that even the highest of the Torngat Mountains had been deeply submerged by the great ice sheets of the past.

It seemed that I had discovered an area of outstanding and relatively little-known arctic mountains, fiords, and lakes; almost undisturbed wildlife; and enough scientific controversy to keep a field research laboratory active for decades. Nevertheless, in the 1955–1956 winter there remained the formidable task of determining how to get to the Torngats. A pontoon-equipped aircraft would be essential, as would expensive camping and mountain equipment, specialized food, instruments, a rifle, and fishing gear. My McGill-Carnegie-Arctic Research Scholarship, held over from the previous summer, provided me with only $1,000 to help meet these requirements. This was augmented by a further $1,000 awarded following application to the Banting Fund, adminis-tered by AINA. But funding was still woefully inadequate.

The first breakthrough came when Ken Hare introduced me to Peter Marchant, who had worked on the Labrador-Ungava airphoto mapping proj-ect. After completing his master's degree, Peter had become an executive with BRINCO. He, in turn, introduced me to Dr. Paul Beavan, senior geologist and chief executive of BRINEX. I was surprised to find that a bedrock geologist, whose task was to discover commercially exploitable minerals, was fasci-nated with the Ice Age history of Labrador-Ungava and especially the Torngat Mountains. He was also directly interested in determination of directions of former ice flow as a possible means of detecting the bedrock source of glacial erratics that were found to contain precious metals.

After reviewing my ambitious plans he astounded me by offering to provide transport by pontoon-equipped Beaver aircraft from Goose Bay up the entire Labrador coast and into our proposed field research area. This, of course, car-ried a commitment to retrieve us at the end of the summer field season.

There were several meetings with Dr. Beavan. He remained a good friend, both to Pauline and me, and later to several members of the Lab graduate stu-dents who extended my Labrador-Ungava research. He was obviously taking on a considerable responsibility. If anything went wrong during the summer, BRINEX would have to bail us out. Dr. Beavan was worried about British stu-dents new to the Canadian wilderness. He had employed a number of them to work as field assistants in Labrador. Most of the BRINEX field exploration lay within the boreal forest and forest-tundra zones of Labrador, regions where the regular BRINEX personnel operated with confidence and ease. The forests pro-vided shelter from high winds, fuel for cooking, and building materials. But the Brits, according to Dr. Beavan, tended to become disoriented in the trackless forest, get lost, upset canoes, and inadvertently set their tents afire. One of them had managed to walk into an airplane propeller while the engine was running; he survived a split head. Dr. Beavan was also nervous about leaving the two of us alone for many weeks north of the protection of the trees, especially in the great U-shaped valleys of the Torngats, subject to sudden gale-force winds and summer snowstorms. These feelings had been reinforced during the BRINEX 1954 summer reconnaissance. The main base on Upper Kangalaksiorvik Lake had been flattened by high winds, and they had lost a helicopter.

I managed to assure Dr. Beavan that all our experience had been on wind-swept hills in unforested areas. My three summers in Iceland in small mountain tents and the problem-free 1955 summer experience in the Knob Lake area eventually set his mind at rest and he agreed to accommodate us. He also agreed to take Peter and Ellie Johnson, our most recent friends of the McGill-Carnegie-Arctic scholarship crew, to Nain at the same time. Peter was preparing to study the glacial geomorphology of the Kiglapait Mountains from a base camp in Port Manvers Run about 30 mi (48 km) north of Nain, as the basis for his doctorate.

There remained many practical details. McGill University's informal regulations proposed by Ken Hare and Svenn Orvig, the latter as director of the Montréal office of AINA, required that we take with us a radio to establish a schedule with either Hebron or Fort Chimo and that we take out substantial life insurance. This was a major blow, as we had no money! I pleaded that, in any case, we would never be able to carry with us on the several planned back-packing trips the heavy radio sets available at the time; nor could we rely on any radio contact with either Hebron or Fort Chimo—100 mi and 200 mi (161 km and 322 km) distant, respectively, especially as we would be situated in deep mountain valleys, hardly conducive to reliable radio communications. I raised the danger of setting off false rescue missions due simply to atmospheric interference with radio contact. I covered the life insurance problem by finding a Montréal insurance agent who was prepared to swear from his assessment tables that we would be at significantly lower risk in northern Labrador than if we were to stay in Montréal and be exposed to downtown traffic. This must have been a remarkable misuse of statistics because, while Montréal certainly recorded numerous accidents, the Torngat Mountains would have scored zero simply because hardly anybody had been there since 1931. Hare and Orvig were only partly assured, although they accepted my protestations.

In those days it appeared that Canada, or at least Montréal, had never heard about lightweight camping and mountaineering equipment, let alone light-weight, or at least concentrated, food.[24] We eventually augmented our limited supply of equipment by ordering directly from Black's of Greenock, Scotland, who had supplied our Nottingham University student expeditions to Iceland. We also arranged for a modest shipment of the barely palatable pemmican from Bovril, England. I purchased a rifle and ammunition locally, and a secondhand 120 camera for black-and-white photography to add to my inexpensive 35 mm camera that I used for color photographs.

The winter and spring passed, punctuated by skiing weekends at the same rented cottage of the previous winter, although this time with Pete and Ellie as members of the crew. We also attempted to procure free food for the summer fieldwork from kindly would-be suppliers as we had done so successfully in England for our student expeditions to Iceland. We requested support in this way for the entire group of that winter's McGill-Carnegie-Arctic scholars and, despite some modest success particularly with Nestlé, promptly ran into what Ken Hare had experienced earlier—the schism between Canadian and American interests in the AINA bureaucracy. The new executive director of AINA, Tom Manning, of considerable arctic fame, felt that any benefit from our attempt to obtain free food should be reserved for the Canadian members of the group.[25] I felt a sense of outrage and, despite the embarrassment of several of our colleagues, I engineered the evacuation from Bishop Mountain House and concealment of all the free food and equipment and an eventual sharing out regardless of student origin. I had anticipated some form of penalty for insisting on such democratic principles, but rather the reverse occurred (as will be related below).

During the late winter I was very excited to meet Noel Odell on one of his rare visits to McGill. He filled me in about the Torngat Mountains and assured me that the everlasting tortuous boulder fields had been worse for him than pressing toward the summit of Mount Everest, a most dubious reflection for us. He was full of enthusiasm and remained in contact for decades afterward. Another well-known visitor to Montréal was Dr. E. P. "Pep" Wheeler II, and his very elegant and charming wife, Eleanor. Pep and Eleanor arrived from Ithaca, NY, to visit BRINEX in early June in preparation for their summer geological survey west of Nain. They invited us to lunch at the Café Martin off Sherbrooke Street, far beyond our meager budget. They regaled us with Labrador lore and, above all, advised on how to cook seal meat, given our treeless location, with thin aluminum pans and a small Primus stove. If we followed Pep's advice, we would find seal meat comparable to the finest filet mignon such as we were eating as we talked—that is, rare, which meant to an Englishman of the time that it was still bleeding. The luncheon was the start of another long friendship. Pep and Eleanor loomed large as colorful, friendly, and most engaging characters. Above all, they reinforced our sense of adventure and commitment to Labrador.

A few critical details remained. I successfully completed and defended my doctoral dissertation. Reservations for our flight with Trans-Canada Airlines to Goose Bay with Pete and Ellie were easily obtained. All our worldly possessions still fit into the two cabin trunks brought with us from England nearly two years previously. These were repacked and trundled up two flights of stairs in Bishop Mountain House (demolished several years later), one step at a time, and into my student office. A letter was attached to the top of one of the trunks to the effect that we expected to be back after the middle of September. We then faced the prospect of leaving for the Labrador wilderness with no immediate openings for employment on our return and with financial resources somewhat less than those with which we had arrived as landed immigrants.[26] Looking back over the half century that has elapsed since our near-penniless departure for the unknown, I can only recollect, for me at least, that nothing seemed to matter except getting to the Torngat Mountains with Pauline. What about Pauline? She never raised any concern but, as always, provided solid support. We believed all would work out splendidly, as indeed it did.

Into the Wilderness

Late morning on 2 July we met Pete and Ellie Johnson at Dorval Airport, Montréal. Despite long delays (we did not get underway until 11 p.m.) we had a comfortable flight to Goose Bay, delighted to find that we were accompanied by Pep and Eleanor Wheeler and Dr. Paul Beavan. We reached Goose Bay at 3:30 a.m. and spent the remainder of the night in the lounge of the only hotel, nicknamed "The Golden Fleece" because of its outrageous rates. With the connivance of a sympathetic hotel attendant, we surreptitiously obtained a free night's lodging, ate our own chocolate bars for breakfast, and rashly purchased coffee. The Wheelers and Dr. Beavan were flown to North West River during the morning. Complications ensued over locating our air freight, so we were obliged to retain our tentative "camp" in the hotel lounge until midafternoon. The freight was eventually located and transferred to the Hudson's Bay Company for temporary care, after which a BRINEX Beaver aircraft made two flights to carry the four of us, with minimal personal baggage, to North West River, a distance of about 20 mi (32 km).

North West River! The place from where Leonidas Hubbard and Dillon Wallace had set out in 1903 on their ill-fated adventure into the wilderness and where the rival parties of Mrs. Hubbard and Dillon Wallace had assembled two years later. During the following days we met several of the descendants of the local heroes who had attempted to rescue Hubbard and, after his death, had gone into the bush in the late winter to retrieve his corpse. This was hallowed ground!

At North West River we were provided with a fine meal and shown to excellent tent quarters so that we soon made up for lost sleep. There followed four days during which we enjoyed the peaceful settlement. On the first day, Peter, Pep, and I went by boat under charter from one of the local residents back to Goose Bay to retrieve our equipment. Eleanor quickly displayed both her charm and iron arm. She recruited the four of us, together with Pep and as many locals as she could lay hands on, to undertake a cleanup of the settlement. There followed one of the most entrancing sunsets over Grand Lake that Pauline and I had ever witnessed—a golden-yellow sky mirrored over watery glass (see Plate 4).

The BRINEX camp was becoming crowded with newly arriving summer crews, all of whom needed to be ferried by pontoon plane to their field locations. It was decided, to my dismay, that we must be moved into the bush, but not immediately to the Torngats. Upper Kangalaksiorvik Lake, chosen as the location for our base camp, might not be sufficiently ice-free to permit a secure landing. In fact, reports from BRINEX field camps between Makkovik, Hopedale, and Nain indicated a very late breakup, with lots of snow remaining, ice on the lakes, and an unusual amount of sea ice moving slowly southward down the coast. Pep and Eleanor got away on 7 July. When their Beaver returned, the pilot reported that the northernmost point that appeared sufficiently open for landing was Webb Bay, just north of Nain, the planned base campsite for Pete and Ellie. Dr. Beavan informed Pauline and me that we would be delayed for at least three weeks. This was the first practical jolt stemming from our choice of such a remote area of study. The Beaver, a most capable and well-appointed aircraft, did not have the range to make a round trip as far afield as the Torngats without refueling, even from Nain, which was much farther north. We would depend on BRINEX fuel caches. Even so, Murray Piloski, the chief geologist at North West River, wanted to be reasonably certain that we could land on our chosen lake and so minimize the need for a second attempt. It was important to complete the mission to the Torngats in a single flight and not risk the Beaver being stuck on the coast in poor weather. This also raised the question of our pickup in mid-September, but we chose not to think about the implications of that until we were actually on Kangalaksiorvik Lake and discussing the recovery operation with the pilot.

On Sunday, 8 July, Pete and Ellie had all their equipment on the seaplane jetty, ready to go, when the latest report about ice conditions around Webb Bay caused a postponement. Instead, departing at 3:15 p.m., Pauline and I were flown about 60 mi (96 km) to the northeast into an area of rolling hills that extended above the local treeline, dense forest, and many scattered lakes. We were approximately due west of Makkovik, although we had no maps and were truly entering the unknown. The pilot seemed to choose a lake at random, circled to examine landing conditions along the lake shore, and let down onto a gently rippling surface. The time was 4:15 p.m.

The shoreline where we landed was dense shrub with scattered clumps of spruce. We stepped off the shoreside pontoon, knee-deep into very cold water, and began hastily unloading—our pilot had many other missions that day. He left us with a great pile of equipment scattered about, with the promise that he would pick us up in about a week, provided ice reports from Nain and Hebron were favorable. He was trying to keep our spirits high as we were well aware that the delay would be longer.

As seemed standard practice, once in the air, the Beaver circled to fly low over us, waggling his wings. It was late afternoon. As the drone of the Beaver faded, a deafening hush descended, accentuated by the gentle ripple of waves on occasional rocks that projected along the lake shore. We cleared space for our two tents, from Black's of Greenock: a golden-yellow Arctic Guinea mountain tent for sleeping and backpacking, and a very sturdy Nijer, floral green with stout upright poles and a strong ridge pole. The Nijer was to serve as our base tent, for working and cooking. From experience in Iceland, we were confident that it could withstand any blow. We had also packed a spare mountain tent.

By the time the camp was shipshape and the equipment under tarpaulin, we were ready for supper. Next came a reassuring wilderness campfire as dusk descended and streaks of mist partially enshrouded our lonely subarctic lake. A pair of loons, calling and echoing across the water, provided the final good-night to an entrancing evening (see Plate 5).

And so to bed. But we were in bear country. What if a bear approached? And with those thoughts in mind, and our bodies protected from the very rocky ground by air mattresses, we must have drifted into heavy sleep. At some unknown time later, I was awakened by ominous tearing and clattering sounds.

I whispered, "Pauline, are you awake?"

"Yes," she said, "what is it?"

I decided that it must be a bear attacking the Nijer. Instant alarm! We could not risk having our food supplies plundered or the Nijer destroyed. The rifle is in the Nijer. Damn! I unsheathed my knife.

"Don't worry; I can handle it," I said to Pauline.

"But you are trembling," she replied.

How could she infer that I was afraid?

"Well, your air mattress is shaking so much that it is wobbling mine."

With that slur on my masculine prowess and ability to defend my wife against anything—anything!—I emerged quietly from the tent, the knife clasped in my right hand and a flashlight in my left. Holding my breath, I circled the Nijer. The noise had stopped and there was no sign of damage. I gently opened the drawstrings and entered the tent. Relieved and bewildered, I looked around the tent interior, which was covered in what appeared to be white confetti (lacerated toilet paper). Lids from our metal food cans, which we had left loose, had been tipped over; hard biscuits were nibbled; and small dark droppings scattered across the tent floor. Field mice! And so, I saved my dear wife of less than two years from our first wilderness life-and-death threat.

We spent the next sixteen days feeling frustrated and anxious in what would have been the last place on earth that I would have chosen for fieldwork. Due to the late season, the frequent patches of dense forest were deep in wet snow, through which we often plunged to our thighs. Many of the lakes still had ice on them. For the first half of our period of entrapment, the temperature rarely exceeded 46°F (8°C) and we were frequently hit by heavy rain. Dr. Beavan had asked me to undertake a study of the directions of ice movement that might assist in tracing the origin of metaliferous glacial erratics that had been discovered across the entire region. Certainly, it was a good learning experience and years later I came to appreciate that opportunity of becoming familiar with another area of the great peninsula. We were moved a couple of times by a small Bell helicopter to allow us to inspect a much larger area than we could have reached on foot alone. During the second half of the period, when day temperatures climbed into the high 60s (about 20°C), we were greeted by hordes of black flies and mosquitoes. In the best of spirits, all we could say was that we were being well seasoned to hard work and difficult conditions that would stand us in good stead when we eventually reached the Torngats.

Finally, our anguish of uncertain waiting ended on 25 July. Shortly after breakfast, a Beaver landed beside our camp and a pilot, new to us, introduced himself. Paul Saunders was to take us to the BRINEX camp close to Makkovik. There we would have a short consultation with Dr. Beavan and Murray Piloski, and then leave for Nain and points north. Hurray! We quickly came to regard Paul as our pilot par excellence, perhaps because his arrival signaled that we were at last on our way. He had piloted for BRINEX last summer in the Torngats and had made many flights on to Upper Kangalaksiorvik Lake, although he admitted that he was glad that he would not be staying with us. He seemed to epitomize our notions of the tough, handsome bush pilot who could go anywhere and do anything. And that was how we proceeded.

We made a brief stop at the Makkovik camp to consult with Dr. Beavan and Murray Piloski and to drink real coffee.[27] We refueled at the Makkovik seaplane jetty, where we also learned that the remainder of our food and equipment had been deposited at Nain by BRINEX's motor vessel. Shortly thereafter we were off northward for Nain.

A ninety-minute flight brought us within sight of the small settlement of Nain, nestled at the head of a picturesque bay opposite a massive rock cliff. We circled, landing on the bay at 2:30 p.m. among a flotilla of small boats. We were quickly and expertly tied to a buoy, as it was low tide, and eagerly rowed to the town's wharf by three sturdy Inuit. It seemed that the entire town had turned out to greet us. The Reverend Peacock warmly shook my hand and especially welcomed Pauline, whom they had been enthusiastically expecting. Next, Max Budgell, manager of the government store, hailed us, then quickly disappeared with our pilot, obviously an old friend. RCMP Constable Clark, recently appointed to Nain, jokingly offered any policing duty that we might need in the Torngats—"surely the two of you are not going there alone!"

After this cheerful welcome, the Reverend Peacock took us to the Moravian Mission building, where we met Mrs. Peacock, startlingly attractive in early middle age, with intense deep-set blue eyes that I will never forget. She had abandoned her jam making to prepare a lavish spread of cakes, tea, and coffee. All in all, this was a thrilling welcome for me, which met all expectations born of my preteen Sunday School stories of the Moravian Mission to Labrador.

An overnight stay as guests of the Peacocks proved both obligatory and welcome: in part because of their enthusiasm to entertain some of their first visitors of the season; in part because there remained a long flight ahead of us and insufficient daylight for Paul to make it back the same day.

After dinner, we were taken on a grand tour. The Peacocks proudly displayed everything the mission was attempting to accomplish. This included a marching display by the Eskimo Girl Guides—in preparation for the lieutenant governor's visit—the schoolhouse, church, and nursing station. There was also a factory for polishing labradorite, a semiprecious stone that was being worked by three local Inuit, whom they were training, and a dozen houses under construction. The Reverend Peacock was working closely with the Newfoundland and federal governments to arrange for the evacuation of Hebron and the transfer of its

Nain harbor from beneath the wing of the Beaver floatplane. A supply of logs is being towed across the harbor. 25 July 1956.

200 to 300 Inuit to Nain. Sixty had already arrived and were being settled. We were introduced to the impact of a political decision that became the source of a major controversy that rages to this day. When we reached Hebron, we found that Seigfried Hettasch and his sister Katie, the custodians of this northern-most Moravian outpost, had a very different point of view. They argued that the Hebron Inuit were the best placed on the coast for maintaining a near-traditional way of life. In particular, they could sustain themselves by hunting and fishing, which would be impossible if they were crowded into Nain. They believed that the move would result in even more Inuit being forced onto government welfare and the unhealthy European food that would go with it. In retrospect, it would appear that the Hettasches were right.

Later in the evening the Reverend Peacock took us into his office, where he maintained a transmitting radio and recording equipment. He explained that he taped his church services, as well as Eskimo singing and other events, and sent them to St. John's. Sometimes they were broadcast on the local Canadian Broadcasting Corporation (CBC) service, occasionally nationwide. He explained that, while in England earlier in the year, he had given an interview as part of the very popular British Broadcasting Corporation (BBC) program *In Town Tonight*, for which he (or the mission) was paid £6 Sterling. With that he pressed us for a recorded interview, to which we could hardly refuse. Putting on his best BBC accent, he began: "Now let me introduce to you two young scientists who will be Labrador's northernmost inhabitants this summer. . . ." We never heard whether this was broadcast, although it sent us to bed with an inflated sense of our own importance.

Next morning Nain was beset by low clouds and an uncomfortable wind. The hearty Moravian breakfast was preceded, as on all occasions at mealtimes, by the charming custom of holding fingertips raised in a circle around the table while grace was said. After breakfast we had doubts about being able to take off in such weather. Nevertheless, Paul decided to make the attempt. We had to cover a total distance of about 220 mi (354 km) in a direct line along an increasingly precipitous coast with several inhospitable mountain passes. Hebron, where we would make our last refueling stop, was about 120 mi (193 km) north of Nain.

Once the tide was high enough, Paul taxied the Beaver over to the wharf and tied up for our loading operation. We had to add all the food and equipment that BRINEX had sent from North West River to Nain by sea. This presented a space and weight problem because we also needed full fuel tanks. We had already jettisoned the two rear passenger seats at Makkovik. Even so, the space behind the pilot's and copilot's seats became crammed full. We could hardly leave Pauline behind! In the end, after considerable rearranging, she had to be squeezed on top of the baggage and stuffed in horizontally, with her nose almost touching the cabin roof. Why would any young woman let herself in for experiences such as this? Of course, it was necessary for me to take the copilot's seat. I needed access for photographing the splendid glacial features we were certain to pass en route, and we could hardly take turns and change places while airborne.

After warm good-byes in Nain, we taxied into position and lifted off at 11:40 a.m. Low cloud banks obliterated the outer islands and the many promontories, although we saw an abundance of rugged topography as we headed north. Passing over Webb Bay we spotted Pete and Ellie's tent, then skirted the western flanks of the Kiglapait Mountains that rise to about 3,000 ft (900 m). We were startled by the amount of ice and snow so late in the season. Even quite large, low-lying lakes were almost completely ice-covered. This caused concern; what would confront us much further north in the Torngats?

By 12:20 p.m. we were passing over Nutak and approaching the impressive Kaumajet massif that rose almost sheer from the sea for over 3,000 ft (914 m). Half an hour later we were tied up to the Hebron wharf and were greeted with another boisterous welcome—at least a hundred Inuit families with small children running around in circles. Among this throng we met Seigfried Hettasch, the Moravian custodian, and Mr. Pilgrim, manager of the government store.

The large crowd appeared to push-pull us up the slope to the amazing elongate structure that housed the mission, church, schoolroom, government store, and living quarters (see Plate 6). In the confusion I found myself with Paul

Nain and the Moravian Mission church. 26 July 1956.

seated at the dining table of Mr. and Mrs. Pilgrim. Pauline and the Hettasches had apparently disappeared. We learned later that the traders in worldly goods were not on speaking terms with those offering spiritual services. It had been a long winter and a number of items (such as sugar and coffee) had long since been exhausted. This had exacerbated the tensions that had arisen over the proposed evacuation of Hebron (see page 40). In addition, even as late as 26 July, we were the first visitors of the season. Since both families thirsted for news from outside and fresh conversation, Pauline and I had been surreptitiously, perhaps subconsciously, separated so we could be shared equally between our two groups of hosts. We also realized that Katie Hettasch was the dominant personality who had launched a campaign to prevent the abandonment of Hebron; regrettably, she did not succeed.

After lunch I recovered a bemused Pauline and we once again "stood in" for the lieutenant governor and experienced a "command performance" by both Girl Guides and Boy Scouts. Mr. Hettasch approached a conspicuously nervous Boy Scout: "Here, Ogiloik [attempted Inuktituk for Tommy], shake hands with Dr. and Mrs. Ives and say 'How d'ye do,' like you're going to later for the lieutenant governor." After the delightful performance we duly praised the children's big display in the schoolroom, readied for the lieutenant governor. Regrettably, the very late season and continued bad ice conditions prevented the much-anticipated important visitor from getting any farther north than Makkovik.

The entire Hebron crowd reassembled for our departure and we all walked down to the wharf. We extracted from our baggage small amounts of our precious sugar and coffee as a token of our appreciation. The gleam in the eyes of our new friends indicated more than their enthusiastic thanks that we had hit on the best possible gesture. Paul refueled for the last time (see Plate 7). Pauline was carefully reinserted on top of the baggage, and by 2:30 p.m. we were in the air. Hazy weather spoiled the opportunity for some fine photography, although my pulse was racing as we passed over Saglek Fiord and entered the Torngat area proper. I was able to recognize many of the prominent landmarks, committed to my memory from scrutiny of the Forbes/AGS photographs. It was almost as if I had been to the Torngats before. Here was a geomorphologist's paradise of glacial landforms: fiords, knife-edged arêtes, finger lakes, cirques, jagged peaks, and small glaciers. We flew past Nachvak Fiord, Chasm Lake, the Komaktorvik lakes, and Odell's Precipice Mountain. Finally we sighted the Four Peaks, Mount Tetragona, and Upper Kangalaksiorvik Lake. We were amazed and relieved to see that not a sign of ice marred the beautiful blue-green of the water.

Paul obviously knew where he was going. Without hesitation, he landed and quickly beached the floatplane on a long, narrow sand spit that extended into the lake from the midsection of its south shore. This had been BRINEX's base of operations the year before, ideal for a floatplane as it provided both east-facing and west-facing moorings against the prevailing wind directions, although it was rather exposed and offered a breezy challenge for tents.

Awaiting us was a gift from the gods in the form of a 17-foot (5 m) canoe that had been left behind by BRINEX the previous summer. We quickly unloaded most of our food and equipment, leaving in the plane supplies for three caches that we wanted set out for us by the Beaver. Next we tied the canoe onto one of the Beaver's pontoons and took off for Komaktorvik lakes, about 20 mi (32 km) south of us.

The general field plan had been to attempt two separate transects across the Torngat Mountains: the first from our base camp on Upper Kangalaksiorvik Lake to Abloviak Fiord; the second along Komaktorvik Lakes and across the watershed to a small lake on the Québec side where we would need the Beaver to put down a cache for us. We would also need a cache as far west as possible from base camp toward Abloviak Fiord. As it turned out, the small lake, which we informally named Essay Lake (to become Lac des Essais on the official topographic map sheet decades later), west of the head of the Komaktorvik drainage was frozen solid, so we left the cache with the canoe on Lower Komaktorvik Lake. At the time we hoped that it would help us to reach Essay Lake by paddling the length of the lakes and then walking. We did find a partially ice-free lake west of the divide in the upper Abloviak drainage and so were able to land and place a cache there, even though it was not as far west as we would have hoped.

Kangalaksiorvik Lake, Torngat Mountains: setting up base camp. 27 July 1956.

After setting out the caches, we returned to our base campsite where Paul gave us last-minute instructions. We should regard 10 September as the first day to expect the Beaver to return to collect us. He would make attempts during the following five days if weather prevented a successful flight on the tenth. Beyond that, he jested, we should prepare for a long, cold, and hungry winter. We should be ready for immediate evacuation from the tenth onward. Any further delay would be considered an emergency as we could expect snow and freezing temperatures after the middle of the month.

We scribbled hasty notes to parents in England, shook hands with Paul, and watched him taxi out onto the lake and prepare for takeoff. So ended our last contact with the outside world. We had indeed reached our mountain objective and were thrilled with the thought that for the next seven weeks we would be without a sign of civilization.

The period from 27 July to 10 September proved both exhilarating and challenging. At last we were in pristine arctic mountain terrain and dependent entirely on our own resources. Our base camp sand spit was regularly surrounded by curious seals, and fish were plentiful. I proved to be a fair marksman; one of the seals met with an untimely fate and we were able to test Pep Wheeler's recipe. The lean meat equaled the best filet mignon, and the liver and heart, fried for breakfast, lasted many days. The lack of cabin space in the Beaver had limited our rations, so the seal meat was a welcome supplement. This was especially so as the corned beef we had ordered from the Hudson's Bay Company at North West River was found to be Argentinian, dating from before the war. Some of the cans had rusted through!

Lemmings were numerous, so much so that they proved to be our most dangerous threat of the summer. They made a concerted effort to eat everything: clothes, food, tent canvas. This was most obviously a lemming peak year. They did everything legend accorded them except, unfortunately, rushing en mass into the lake and drowning themselves.

One lemming tale is worth recounting in full. Lying beside Pauline early one morning in our orange mountain tent, I slowly emerged from sleep as the sun began to illuminate the canvas. Still in a befuddled state, I noticed something small slide down the outside of the tent from the center of the ridge: then another, then yet another. While this was going on Pauline awakened and, placing one finger on my lips, I indicated the strange performance to her. What on earth could it be? My fertile mind conjured up a queue of lemmings patiently waiting their turn at the base of one of the main guy ropes, then, one by one, climbing onto the tent along the ridge to the midpoint, to enjoy the slide down. At least seven of the blighters were doing just that trick. The eighth got more than he had bargained for, since I clouted the moving, sliding shadow with the

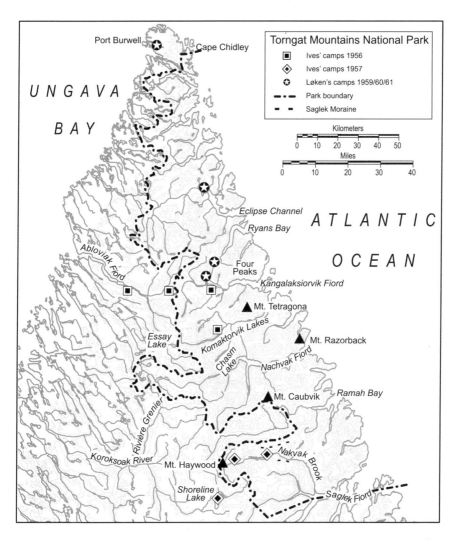

Top: Sketch map of the northern Torngat Mountains, showing campsites and prominent features relative to the 1956 and 1957 (Ives) and 1959–1962 (Løken) summer fieldwork.

Right: The essential business of adding to our larder. This is one of our many base camp seals about to lose his coat, heart, and liver. 30 July 1956.

back of my hand, which, if my conjecture was correct, must have sent him flying through the air. Despite rushing out of the tent, I saw nothing untoward.

During our field studies our most serious obstacles were the rivers—like
wine to drink, but fast, cold, and often challenging to ford. We made several
precarious crossings, using our climbing rope, but our attempts to cross the
main river flowing into the head of Upper Kangalaksiorvik Lake were unsuc-
cessful. Nevertheless, we completed our trek through the mountains to the
head of Abloviak Fiord. This was our primary objective. Next we walked to
the cache and our canoe on Lower Komaktorvik Lake, some 20 mi (32 km)
south of us. In this instance, our arrival on 19 August coincided with a twenty-
four-hour snowstorm that left the mountains above the 500-foot (152 m) level
with a white mantle. We had to abandon our plan to canoe to the west end of
the Komaktorvik Lakes after two thwarted efforts, defeated by heavy waves
that even a light breeze could produce in the 2,000-foot-deep (610 m) trench
that cut through the highest mountains in the vicinity. We climbed many of
the surrounding peaks and enjoyed good weather after the introductory snowstorm. The planned trip from base camp to Mount Tetragona and Bryants
Glacier was severely curtailed by heavy winds, torrential rain, and snowstorms
in early September. An ascent of Mount Tetragona was out of the question and

*After backpacking through the Torngat Mountains to Abloviak Fiord, we find our
first absolute evidence that the Laurentide Ice Sheet withdrew westward from the
mountains. The pronounced delta and the lake shoreline beyond demonstrate that
the ice sheet dammed up lakes in the westward draining valleys and caused water to
spill across the lowest passes into the Atlantic Ocean.*

After a snowstorm on 19–20 August 1956, the Komaktorvik Lakes emerged calm and serene. The planned canoe journey to the far western end of the lakes through the gigantic rock-walled chasm was prevented by wind and heavy waves.

Below the rapids in the Komaktorvik River, the water is full of arctic char fighting their way upstream to their breeding grounds. Noel Odell maintained that the only chance of taking any was to use a rifle. Precipice Mountain forms the right hand trough wall. We climbed the snow-covered 4,000-foot (1,220-meter) summits on the far side of the lake. 23 August 1956.

we became very conscious of the gradual approach of 10 September, the first of the allotted days for the Beaver's return.

BRINEX personnel had warned us that we would have a windy time, and they were correct, certainly in September. We were almost blown away. Yet despite very heavy westerly squalls that carried waterspouts and occasional torrential rain and snow along our lake, we managed to hold down our tents. In fact, our sleeping bags were never wet, a feat I largely put down to the excellent equipment that had been supplied by Black's of Greenock and the camping precision I had learned from contending with similar buffeting in Iceland.

The days beyond 10 September continued very stormy and cold. The eleventh, our second wedding anniversary, was celebrated amid snow squalls and high winds, toasted with countless cups of Nescafé. As we reached the fifteenth of the month without sighting the Beaver, in conditions that we realized would have been impossible for a landing for much of the time, our apprehensions grew. Then, midmorning on the sixteenth, the Beaver landed in a snow squall without our realizing. We eventually heard its engine and then saw it emerge, miraculously, from a curtain of snow and spray. A couple of minutes later Paul stepped off the pontoon to hand us exotic presents—four oranges, surprise gifts from our friends at Hebron, where Paul had spent the preceding night.

By noon, after a hasty coffee with Paul, we were packed, loaded, and skimming across the lake into a heavy wind for a very short takeoff. We made a quick stop at our Komaktorvik campsite to retrieve a box of rock samples and then had a turbulent flight low through the mountains to reach Hebron by 1:30 p.m. We refueled with the utmost speed; Paul could allow us little more than an hour to exchange greetings with our Hebron friends, drink coffee, and answer all their questions about our stay in the Torngats. We were very sorry to push off from the wharf amid the protestations from both missionaries and storekeepers, now in apparent harmony again.

We had the same experience at Nain, where Paul allowed only thirty minutes to embrace the Peacocks, as he was anxious to reach North West River before dark. By 7:15 p.m. we had touched down on Grand Lake and were being welcomed back by Murray Piloski and his wife, Edna, who immediately took charge and provided a delicious meal of roast caribou followed by bowls of "bakeapple" (Newfoundland-Labrador term for cloudberry, an herbaceous raspberry) gathered from the nearby wetlands.

The rest of our stay was routine: report writing for Dr. Beavan, packing, good-byes, a boat trip on BRINEX's MV *Earl Keith* to Goose Bay, and a flight the following day to Montréal via Moncton, courtesy of Trans-Canada Airlines. We reached Dorval Airport by 10:30 p.m. on 19 September. We took a taxi

Panoramic view from the summits shown in Figure 17, looking down onto Komaktorvik Lakes. Our campsite is marked by the cross. Snow-clad mountains in the distance are part of Odell's "Coast Range" and include Mt. Tetragona, and the Four Peaks beyond Kangalaksiorvik Fiord. 24 August 1956.

Heavily burdened and ready to return to base camp on Upper Kangalaksiorvik Lake at the end of August 1956.

into the proximity of the McGill campus and found our way to Bar Battle's apartment, spending the night on her floor.

So ended our first summer in the Torngats. Our high expectations had been realized or surpassed. We had been able to examine a critical section of the western "flanks" of the Torngat Mountains, climb more than a dozen of the prominent peaks. I brought back with us more than enough field notes to form the basis of a useful scientific paper (see Plates 8, 9, and 10).

Results: Summer 1956

The reconnaissance nature of our first venture to the Torngats yielded somewhat surprising results. We appeared to have proven the reverse of what we had set out to do. We had countered rather than confirmed, as I had originally expected, much of the paradigm of continental glacierization proposed by Professor Flint.

From the crest of the Kangalaksiorvik/Abloviak pass westward to Ungava Bay tidewater, we had demonstrated that the final movement of the Ice Age glaciers was eastward through the mountains toward the Atlantic Ocean. This conclusion was further supported by the discovery of perched lake deltas and shorelines in the valleys of streams that flowed westward into Ungava Bay. It

Komaktorvik Lakes from the air looking eastward onto the "Coast Range." "Essay Lake" lies directly beneath the plane and out of sight. July 1978.

View northward from the same summit as in Plates 8 and 9 along the eastern side of Noel Odell's "Interior Range." The Four Peaks form the right-hand skyline; Komaktorvik and Kangalaksiorvik lakes are hidden by the mountains. July 1978.

indicated that the former lakes had been dammed by continental ice that was withdrawing westward from the Torngats after the mountains had emerged from the ice mass. Flint's hypothesis of a coastal mountain range as the locus of the last remaining remnants of the Laurentide Ice Sheet was untenable. In some places, local cirque glaciers had expanded across the paths of the major outlet glaciers after the latter had melted and retreated westward. Small local ice caps may have formed or persisted, but these ice masses would have been insignificant in the overall pattern of deglaciation. Odell himself had raised the possibility of a late-glacial continental ice sheet withdrawing westward from the Torngats, but this notion had been entirely hypothetical and had been ignored in subsequent publications.

In broad geographic terms, and to our surprise considering the many assertions to the contrary, the Torngats were not a coastal mountain range with a pronounced western flank. Rather, they were the deeply eroded (glaciated) eastern edge of an uplifted and tilted plateau. Thus there was no western flank (see Plate 9) down which Flint's hypothetical glaciers could flow and coalesce. Instead, the highland sloped very gently down toward Ungava Bay. Farther south, it became part of the vast Labrador-Ungava plateau. This led to our speculation that the onset of each ice age would develop as the rapid buildup of great masses of ice on the plateau, thereby initiating the Laurentide Ice Sheet that eventually flowed through and engulfed the Torngats. I described this as "instantaneous glacierization across wide areas of the plateau." No doubt, cirque glaciers, local ice caps, and valley glaciers accumulated early in the Torngats, but in terms of timing and total mass, they would have been insignificant in the overall buildup of the Laurentide Ice Sheet.

There remained the question of the frost-riven block fields (felsenmeer) described by Odell, and his insistence that the highest summits of the Torngats had been completely submerged by the ice sheet. The one mountaintop that Odell had identified with sufficient precision to allow us to examine produced ambiguity. His glacial striations on a few small exposures on the summit seemed rather to be weathered bedrock lineations. Nevertheless, we did conclude that a stream of large anomalous blocks that we traced up the western slope and onto a summit above 4,000 ft (1,219 m) north of the Komaktorvik lakes consisted of glacial erratics. However, the frost-shattered boulder fields at the higher levels, above about 2,000 ft (610 m), were not the result of postglacial frost action, as Odell surmised, but were much older. Obviously, much more work would be necessary. We had initiated a controversy that has continued unabated until today.

With some trepidation I sent a draft manuscript derived from this first summer to Professor Flint. He generously gave me the benefit of his expert and detailed constructive criticism and ended his letter with the admonition: "Why are you so tentative about your hypothesis of instantaneous glacierization? I think it is a lot better than the one put forward by that fellow Flint." The paper was eventually published in *Arctic* (Ives 1957) and became an important building block for my proposed field research program for the Lab.

Winter 1956–1957: Ottawa

The morning after our return from the Torngat Mountains, we awoke from the floor of Bar Battle's apartment and shared with her a hefty breakfast. We were faced with the realization that we had no apparent future accommodation and very little money. This prompted a quick walk across the McGill campus to AINA's Bishop Mountain House on Peel Street, our poste restante and depository of all our worldly possessions. Svenn Orvig welcomed us warmly and detained us over a long coffee as we gave him a detailed account of our Torngat adventures. Eventually, noting signs of our impatience, he handed us a bundle of papers from his desk drawer, saying we should check our accumulated mail. Letters from our parents took first priority, then an envelope with an official AINA imprint. Svenn was smiling. It contained a letter from Tom Manning, executive director of AINA, offering me the position of research assistant to Capt. Richard M. Southern, Royal Navy, retired, for work on the first edition of the *Pilot of Arctic Canada*. The Canadian Hydrographic Service (CHS) had contracted with AINA to undertake the extensive task of compiling data from a wide variety of sources. The work was being carried out in Ottawa at the headquarters of the CHS in Number 8 Temporary Building (a relic of World War II) near Dow's Lake. The appointment was for a year. An answer was required by 15 September. As it was already the twentieth, my anxieties resurfaced. These were quickly laid to rest by the ever-cheerful and kindly Svenn, who immediately contacted Tom Manning and handed the phone to me. Thus I committed myself to begin work at 8 a.m. the following Monday. We would transfer to Ottawa and find accommodation, come what may. And so, following the visit with Svenn, what had appeared as a chance encounter just prior to our departure for the Torngats had become a welcome rescue operation.

The appointment was not only a financial lifeline, it was highly relevant to my burgeoning arctic research career. The Ottawa location provided me with innumerable influential contacts. My working companions, in addition to the severe yet supportive Captain Southern, were Margaret Larnder (née Montgomery, of "open" Hudson Bay fame) and John Mercer, a former McGill-Carnegie-Arctic scholar. John had completed his doctoral fieldwork in southern Baffin Island on problems comparable to my Torngat investigations, but had left for Australia just before our arrival at McGill in September 1954. Pauline obtained a position as "map compiler and computer, grade II" with the federal Surveys and Mapping Branch, housed in an adjacent "temporary" building (No. 7).

With two salaries we could afford to rent the lower furnished floor of a comfortable private home, the lady-owner of which spent her winters in Florida. Its location in Ottawa South afforded us an invigorating walk along the Rideau Canal, exercise that was kept up throughout the winter, despite temperatures down to −28°F (−33°C). I recollect only a single resort to taking a bus.

The job was fascinating under the hard-driving taskmaster. Captain Southern seemed to dislike having two assistants whom, according to his strict Royal Navy propriety, he felt obliged to address as "doctor." We would sometimes hear him mutter to himself, "What on earth is a doctor of philosophy?" I reverently addressed him as Captain, responding to my early training before the skipper on a Grimsby fishing trawler, stories of which were extracted from me by an increasingly "human" Captain Southern. John had been a student of the famous public school Gordonstoun in Scotland and a contemporary there of Prince Philip (the husband of Queen Elizabeth II). Underage, he had volunteered for service in the merchant marine during the war, had been torpedoed twice in the North Atlantic, and did not appreciate Royal Navy formalities.

My work was varied. It involved the examination of all available air photograph coverage of the eastern Arctic. John was assigned the western Arctic. I had to review all the relevant literature, including the Parliamentary papers of the Franklin search expeditions, the Nares expedition, and the papers of Harald Sverdrup and Robert Edwin Peary, among others. My task was to extract any information overlooked by earlier studies for previous arctic sailing directions. I also had the task of preparing a manuscript on the general geography of the Canadian Arctic. What a fantastic opportunity: to be paid for familiarizing myself with my chosen field area! Among other things, it led to an occasional drift from my proper duties to follow the many outstanding glacial features, taking me away from the coasts and into the interior of Baffin Island, in particular. I was able to identify extensive systems of glacial moraines, former glacial lake shorelines, and some unusual features that came to be called "cross-valley moraines," most conspicuous north of the Barnes Ice Cap. Finally, I noticed and was very puzzled by an irregular pattern on the air photographs—patches of light-toned and dark-toned areas across wide sections of north-central Baffin Island. All these features became the focus of a research project in the 1960s (Ives 1962; Ives and Andrews 1963; Andrews 1963b).

A singular moment occurred in mid-January 1957 when a call came through on the only telephone in our office. It was from Dr. Erling Porsild of the Canadian Museum of Nature, chairman of the AINA/Banting Fund research grants committee. Somewhat reluctantly, Captain Southern passed the phone over to me. Dr. Porsild asked if I had lost interest in the Torngat Mountains. This question was prompted by his realization that I had not reapplied for a research grant for the following summer. In retrospect, my naïveté was astounding. I had replied that I remained fascinated with the Torngats and Northern Labrador but had not applied out of a sense of fairness to the many other applicants who had not received support in the previous year. On hearing my emphatic response, he explained that I had almost left things too late, as it was the final day for applications to be received. He then kindly instructed me to address a postcard to him, requesting $2,500 to continue my work in the Torngat Mountains. It was imperative that the postcard carried that day's postmark. He said he would speak with Captain Southern to procure a thirty-minute release of time so that I could get to the nearest post office. Dr. Porsild had a reputation based on this kind of irregular supportive procedure that has stayed in the memories of many young arctic enthusiasts of the time. Captain Southern insisted that I work an hour's overtime.

The next stepping stone en route to a Labrador-Ungava glacial geomorphology field program was a March interview with Professor Hare at McGill. I was offered and immediately accepted the position of field director of the McGill Sub-Arctic Research Lab for 1957–1960 with a cross-appointment as assistant professor in the Geography Department.[28] This latter could become a permanent tenure-track faculty position in Montréal following the three years at Knob Lake. I was able to negotiate an agreement that McGill would purchase a new short-wheelbase Land Rover for the Lab. In addition, it was agreed that one of the five graduate student weather observer positions would be redefined and upgraded to that of senior weather observer, a two-year appointment subject to renewal. I also learned that the McGill Finance Office had realized that payment of freight charges for the field director's personal furniture in and out of Knob Lake every three years was very costly. It would be less expensive for McGill to furnish the field director's apartment. This was an enormous relief, as we had no furniture and little money to purchase any. Thus, Pauline and I were allocated a very reasonable budget that gave us the pleasure of selecting our own furniture from Eaton's department store on St. Catherine Street.

Other valuable contacts made during the winter in Ottawa included Graham and Diana Rowley; Geoff Hattersley-Smith; Charles Swithinbank, who was visiting from the Scott Polar Research Institute, Cambridge; Hans Weber; and Dr. Norman Nicholson, director of the federal Geographical Branch. I also became a member of Ottawa's "Arctic Circle" and enjoyed several visits to the Museum of Nature for valuable talks with Erling Porsild and Jacques Rousseau.

A particularly friendly contact was made while I was visiting the library of the Geological Survey of Canada (GSC). Dr. Eric Henderson had worked on the Pleistocene geology of the Knob Lake area during the 1953 and 1954 summers. Eric was very interested in my 1955 work in the same area and gave me unreserved access to a nearly completed manuscript that he was close to submitting for publication (Henderson 1959). He encouraged me to feel free to comment on any aspect of it. He had obviously seen and mapped the features that I had interpreted as glacial drainage channels during my 1955 fieldwork. However, he had focused on the ridges between the channels and incorrectly identified them as glacial end moraines. Thus, his concept of the final melting of a continental ice sheet in the area was one of progressive withdrawal of valley glaciers to the highest elevations, leaving behind a series of end moraines. This was in direct contrast to my interpretation of the regional late Ice Age snow line rising above the land–ice sheet surface to create a dead ice mass that wasted away in the valley bottoms where the ice had been thickest. A few days after our initial meeting I presented Eric with a review of his manuscript in about a dozen pages of closely reasoned argument. This was most graciously received, although with surprise, and was followed by an invitation for Pauline and me to have dinner with his family the following Sunday.

I found to my astonishment that the substantial library of the GSC did not contain any of the leading Scandinavian journals in the field, and certainly not *Geografiska Annaler*. It became apparent that the geologists of the GSC Pleistocene Section of that period were not aware of the recent work of Mannerfelt and Hoppe, and the Richard Foster Flint paradigm remained entrenched. Thus began a form of competition between physical geographers and Pleistocene geologists that enlivened my research during the 1960s in Ottawa.

The Ottawa winter, in all respects, proved invaluable, much more than I could have imagined at the time; it led to my first permanent senior appointment in 1960 and even our first house the following year. Given that Pauline and I each had been able to earn a salary, we realized that we could save enough to pay for two airfares to London and visits to our families, the first since our marriage six years earlier.

In those days the flight back to Montréal from Heathrow required a refueling stop at Goose Bay. This was ideal for us. Much to the surprise and consternation of our fellow passengers on the return flight from London, we left the plane at Goose Bay. We had sent our heavier field equipment directly to North West River from Ottawa, leaving our nonfield possessions for the Geography Department to ship to Knob Lake later that summer. Our BRINEX friends flew us from Goose Bay to North West River by Beaver aircraft. So we were poised for another summer in the Torngats, with a longer-term prospect of the autumn and winter at the Lab, benefiting again from the generosity of Paul Beavan.

Torngat Mountains, 1957

The second summer in the Torngat Mountains followed a similar pattern to that of 1956. We had a long wait in the bush west of Hopedale, again due to lack of information about lake ice along the northern coast. Eventually Paul Saunders picked us up, although this time we flew over Nain and refueled at a BRINEX gas cache on a lake north of the Kiglapait Mountains. We also overflew Hebron, much to our disappointment. Our base camp was located on a 4-mile (6 km) long lake that we named Nakvak Lake in the southern Torngat Mountains. The name was taken from the cascading river, Nakvak Brook, that drains the lake to flow for about 25 mi (40 km) to enter the north side of the middle section of Saglek Fiord. We had selected this lake following information from Murray Piloski and Jacques Rousseau about an extensive linear feature that extends for a considerable distance along the north side of the main valley trough in which the lake is situated. Our impression of the research potential of this area in the southern Torngats had been reinforced by examination of air photographs in Ottawa the previous winter.

The lake was perfectly located for our purposes. It was situated on the floor of a wide valley that led westward for about 18 mi (29 km) to a pass overlooking the upper valley of the Koroksoak River that flows into the southeast corner of Ungava Bay (see map, page 45). The valley extended eastward from Nakvak Lake and curved gradually southward to enter Saglek Fiord about 25 mi (40 km) away. The landscape was much less rugged than we had encountered the previous summer, although several summits exceeded 4,000 ft (1,219 m). It appeared highly suitable for long-distance walking and backpacking, with fairly easy access in all directions.

Again we said our good-byes to Paul, our pilot. He had the same admonitions as before: "Be at this spot by 12 September, or else!" And this time we had excellent weather for our first two weeks. Our only immediate obstacle was the fording of Nakvak Brook. It descended directly from the lake over a picturesque waterfall and dropped into a deep gorge. We had to walk about 3 mi (5 km) downstream to a ford where the river, dividing into many shallow channels, ran across a wide gravely expanse. The ridge crests on either side of the main valley and the watershed far to the west could be reached easily, even when we were heavily laden with rucksacks and tent.

After Paul's departure, we used the afternoon and evening to quickly set up our base camp, well fortified against the anticipated high winds. The first full day could then be devoted to fieldwork. Our immediate objective, of course, was the distinctive linear feature that extended along the northern slope of the main valley. It was conspicuous from base camp and extended as far as we could see in either direction. Murray Piloski and Jacques Rousseau had both assumed it to be horizontal and had described it to us as either a former marine or lake shoreline. We determined that it had a distinct slope down toward the east.

The Beaver's altimeter had registered the altitude of our lake as 800 ft (244 m) above sea level. Topographical maps published in 1967 gave the height as ~793 ft (242 m). The linear feature directly upslope from the camp registered on our surveying altimeters at about 1,500 ft (457 m) above the lake, or 2,300 ft (701 m) above sea level. And it definitely sloped down toward the east and up toward the west from the point where we first reached it. The slope varied between 60 ft/mi (11.25 m/km) and 90 ft/mi (17 m/km). It proved to be a complex lateral moraine that merged into a kame terrace form and back again to a moraine form, up to 60 ft (18 m) high. It could be traced into the mouths of small tributary valleys, in some places damming lateral lakes, in others associated with the shorelines of former lakes. Looking through binoculars across to

View to the northeast from the Nakvak 1957 base camp. The pronounced linear feature crossing the center of the photograph is part of the Saglek moraine system. July 1957.

Section of the Saglek moraines emphasized by the line of snow banks. The moraine dams a small lake. August 1978.

the far side of the main valley, we could see sections of a comparable feature at the corresponding altitude. Obviously, we had discovered part of a large lateral moraine system that must have been formed when a major outlet glacier draining from the Laurentide Ice Sheet had penetrated through the Torngats to the Atlantic. By projecting an imaginary line onto the slope of the feature westward, we realized that it would pass over the highest summits. Because we did not have enough time to walk down the valley to the point where it merged with Saglek Fiord, we were not able to determine whether the outlet glacier that had formed the lateral moraine would have reached and calved into saltwater.

After completing our initial examination of the lateral moraine, we continued walking upslope across bedrock that had been eroded by moving ice, with occasional, short, indistinct stretches of lateral moraine. The products of the glacial erosion (striations, fluting, and chatter marks) had been partially obliterated by weathering, in contrast to bedrock outcrops below the main moraine system that carried glacial polish and well-preserved striations. Climbing to about 450 ft (137 m) above the lateral moraine, we came to a distinct break between moderately weathered but glacially eroded bedrock, and a complete cover of the frost-shattered, angular boulder fields that were so familiar to us from the previous summer. These were more of the interminable felsenmeer described to us originally by Noel Odell. From this point to the mountaintop at about 3,900 ft (1,189 m) we had an exasperating walk over the chaos of boulders. The highest point, however, proved to be a bedrock tor (see appendix II) capped by a glacial erratic (see appendix III) that was too heavy for me to lift (see photo, page 60). I make this remark because I was wary that Murray Piloski may have played a prank and lifted it there by helicopter, knowing my anxiety about the importance of finding glacial erratics on high summits. I was sufficiently concerned to laboriously roll the block away. We quickly determined that it had sat on clean, but slightly weathered, bedrock, in contrast to the immediately surrounding area, which had a more or less complete cover of rock lichens. This convinced me that it had not been put there by human hand and that we had made a critical discovery—it was proof that moving ice must have passed across the site and dropped a rock it had been carrying (hence the term *erratic*) on the summit. Nevertheless, it left us with the exacting task of rolling back our very heavy and vital evidence onto its former summit perch. This discovery also begged the question: while ice had moved across the highest point (that is, the summit), why had it neither eroded away the tor nor significantly disturbed the surrounding boulder field? The contemporary concepts were conspicuously inadequate.

At the day's end we enjoyed an exhilarating walk downslope and so back to camp as pastel shades of evening light gradually enshrouded us. During this

A tor forms the actual summit of a mountain at about 3,900 ft (1,190 m) north of Nakvak Lake. The perched block on the top is a glacial erratic (see appendices II and III). Late July 1957.

single day's fieldwork, the first of the summer, we had come across a series of features that has prompted more than a half century of research, ranging in extent from southern Labrador to northern Baffin Island and Ellesmere Island. Much controversy remains concerning the precise dating of what have become known in the scientific literature as the Saglek Moraines, as well as the correct interpretation of tors surmounted by glacial erratics on Torngat mountaintops. But to our immediate satisfaction I felt convinced that I now had a solid outline for a field research program for the McGill Sub-Arctic Research Lab that would provide many master's and doctoral thesis topics for years to come.

Camping on Nakvak Lake maintained a holiday atmosphere. It was enhanced by the activities of our wildlife neighbors. The innumerable lemmings provided the same threat as last year. We sighted only a few single caribou and the occasional golden eagle. Our closest friends and companions were the local wolves. Their behavior demolished our English/European beliefs derived from Little Red Riding Hood and other folk tales. The wolves seemed fascinated by us; they licked out our used porridge pans, accepted pieces of broken ship's biscuit, and followed us like pet dogs, although at a safe distance of about twenty paces. On one occasion, while we were both racing down a long mountain slope, leaping over low rock outcrops, I inadvertently landed on top of a sunbathing wolf. When Pauline caught up with me, having seen only the flash of some furry creature streaking away, she asked, "What on earth was that?" It was our first canine encounter; when I explained that I had probably kicked a great bruise in the rump of a wolf with my climbing boots, she found it hard to believe me. A few days later, when we set off to backpack westward, two wolves followed us for four days, always keeping a respectful distance. In our lonely arctic setting, we came to regard them as good friends. Farley Mowat, and Hollywood later, came to overstate the case of the essentially benign wolf in the book and movie *Never Cry Wolf.*

Paul, with the Beaver, had laid a cache of food and fuel for us on a lake at about 1,750 ft (533 m) above sea level to the west of the regional watershed and hence in Québec Province. We called this "Shoreline Lake," after the highly conspicuous feature that had attracted us to it. Its official name is Lac Tasiguluk, used on the first topographical maps published years later. It is recorded as ~1,740 ft (530 m) above sea level. The lake is drained by a steep river that flows for some 12 mi (19 km) northwest until it enters the main stream of the Koroksoak River and so into Ungava Bay. The valley in which Shoreline Lake is situated extends eastward to a pass at about 2,500 ft (762 m) in the highest mountains of this part of the Torngats, and hence the boundary between Québec and Newfoundland–Labrador. Our second major target of the summer, the conspicuous shoreline that we had used for the unofficial name of our lake, seemed to be coincident with the height of the pass, as far as we could determine at the time. This indicated that a large former lake had drained across the pass into the Atlantic.

We backpacked through the main pass at 1,050 ft (320 m) to camp by Shoreline Lake for eight days. Once established, we set about surveying the height of the main shoreline and many others, overflow channels, and related features. The landscape west of the Torngat crest line was rolling upland with summits between 3,000 ft (914 m) and more than 4,000 ft (1,219 m), sloping gently to the west. There was no trace of a western flank of the assumed coastal mountain range—rather an uplifted and tilted high plateau. The entire area was littered with the shorelines of former ice-dammed lakes that extended southwestward as far as we were able to trace them, on foot and through binoculars. The scale of these former glacial lakes was much greater than what we had discovered during the previous summer in the upper drainage of Abloviak Fiord. It was far beyond our abilities even to begin mapping their distribution, although it told the same vital tale about the pattern of deglaciation— that toward the end of the last ice age, the ice sheet had withdrawn westward from the Torngats. In fact, the shorelines and spillways of these former lakes have not yet been mapped or even investigated. Knowledge of their existence, however, added immeasurably to my plan for future fieldwork. The 1957 summer's research results again exceeded our expectations. We were impressed with how much we were able to achieve by simple reconnaissance on foot and without adequate topographical maps.

When the Beaver returned for us on 12 September, on this occasion in clear weather, Paul explained that he had time and fuel to spare and so flew us along the several arms of the massive Saglek Fiord and up and down most of the troughlike valleys into which the fiord arms extended. The aerial reconnaissance gave me an overview of an extensive system of lateral moraines, most likely contemporary with the Saglek Moraines in Nakvak Valley (see Plate 11). We then flew south to Nain for a single night, guests once more of the Moravians. Here we found Peter and Ellie Johnson awaiting us, since they had been pulled out of their field area in the Kiglapait Mountains two days earlier.

We were all in for a pleasant surprise. We could leave most of our equipment to be shipped out from Nain on the BRINEX motor vessel. To avoid a long roundabout trip via North West River, Goose Bay, and Montréal, Paul flew the four of us cross-country directly to Knob Lake. Here we all spent an unscheduled night on the floor of our McGill Lab apartment, as the new furniture had

View westward down the Koroksoak River (Rivière Koroc) from the summit that was later named Mont Haywood (about 2,400 ft or 732 m). August 1957.

The mining town of Knob Lake (Schefferville) from the air in September 1957. The McGill Sub-Arctic Research Lab lies out of the photograph, to the right.

not been unpacked. Paul took off with Peter and Ellie the next morning for North West River, leaving us to settle into our new home and prepare to take up three years' residence at Knob Lake.

Thus I entered the Lab and my new appointment as its field director in the best way possible—straight from the field. I was able to introduce myself to the newly arrived winter's crew of four graduate students and Don Macnab, straight from the Antarctic. Don was the first recruit for the new position of senior weather observer that I had requested during my appointment interview with Ken Hare. The graduate students were Roger Barry (University of Liverpool), Roger Tomlinson (University of Nottingham), Geoff Sherlock (University of Leeds), and Tony Williamson (Dartmouth College, NH). Erv Bentley had also arrived as the permanent technician for Dartmouth's Whistler Program. I learned that the pace of Lab research had accelerated considerably since our first visit in 1955. Several McGill graduate students had spent the 1957 summer on a variety of research projects: Kathleen Allington (string bogs), Walt Nebiker (albedo/vegetation survey under Svenn Orvig's direction), C. Ian Jackson (insolation and albedo), Jim Lotz (soils), and Ben Bonnlander, who was employed by IOCC (permafrost). Thus ended a highly successful summer, both in the Torngats and at the Lab; and so began our first winter in the Subarctic.

Chapter Four

The McGill Sub-Arctic
Research Lab:
Operations, 1957–1960

Our mid-September arrival proved somewhat chaotic. We had gladly accepted BRINEX's offer of the flight directly from Nain, but this meant that we arrived with little more than the clothes we had worn in the Torngats, and they had all been nibbled by countless lemmings. The bulk of our field equipment was proceeding by the long roundabout route via North West River, Montréal, Sept-Îles, and the Québec North Shore and Labrador Railway. Our usual clothes and few personal possessions were being shipped from Montréal, along with our only piece of furniture, a modest hi-fi record player that was to prove a great asset during the subarctic winters. Greeting our properly dressed graduate students (shirts and ties were still part of the uniform of Brit and Dartmouth College students) in ragged field clothes provoked some laughter. Only Don Macnab was dressed as us: we quickly learned that he always wore a navy blue polo-neck (turtleneck) sweater with ss JOHN BISCOE in large yellow letters across the chest.[29] Although even his clothes were not full of holes like ours were.

My first task was to telephone Ken Hare on the McGill University campus and report for duty. Ken's polished English accent came clearly over an often faint connection: "Great news, Jack, but where are you? We haven't seen you since early summer." When he found that I was actually "on duty," he cheerfully announced that he would be sending up several important visitors for me and Pauline to entertain. So, in our dilapidated clothes, as we scrambled to set up our own two-bedroom apartment, the first of our distinguished visitors arrived. Professor Gordon Manley, a prominent English climatologist and Pauline's professor when she was an undergraduate at Bedford College for Women, University of London, spent four delightful days with us and took part in energetic, and sometimes very humorous, discussions with our entire group. Our next visitor was Professor Hans Boesch from Zurich, Fritz Müller's doctoral adviser and the secretary-treasurer of the International Geographical Union. He also was a much appreciated guest and spent time sharing his experiences with us. Next in line was Col. Patrick D. Baird, former director of the Montréal office of AINA and leader of the two very successful expeditions to Baffin Island (1950, 1953). I had been looking forward enthusiastically to meeting him. However, he proved to be monosyllabic, extremely difficult to make conversation with. When I asked if he would give an informal talk on his Baffin Island glaciological studies, he astounded me by deferring to my "superior" knowledge of glaciology, a remark both embarrassing and absurd. This lack of communication came to haunt me two years later when he moved back from his position with Aberdeen University to McGill, thereby becoming my boss.

There were also many courtesy visits by senior staff members of the IOCC, the commander of the RCAF station, and clergy of the Anglican Church and the United Church of Canada, although by this time we wore presentable clothes and our living space was in order.

Establishment of the weather observation routine was my first essential duty. The 1955 summer as acting field director stood me in good stead here, although I quickly learned what an excellent colleague I had in Don Macnab, who had served as weather station chief on his FIDS appointment in the Antarctic. The new winter's crew as a whole demonstrated their strengths and general conviviality. Roger Barry had worked for the British Meteorological Office and proved a boon (and subsequently a lifelong friend and colleague) in every way. Roger Tomlinson (well over 6 foot, massively built, and hence known as "Tiny") was ever cheerful and ready to try anything. He was also a link with the Nottingham Geography Department. Geoff Sherlock was another delightful, willing, and energetic personality. And then there was Tony Williamson, the only non-Brit. Tony was special. He became the instant target of what he complained was a very peculiar British sense of humor and was always referred to as "The Young American Gentleman." He was indeed a gentleman in every sense of the word, and he eventually learned effective defenses against the Brits, assuming an impenetrable poker face so that we rarely knew whether or not he was serious, surely a critical element of British humor!

Roger Barry was by far the most serious and scholarly of the group. He received the title of "The Mississippi Gambler" on account of his limited success in cultivating a beard. He had brought with him his violin. Hours of practice in his small bed-study resulted in a printed notice mysteriously appearing on his door—MR. BARRY'S MUSIC ROOM. Since several of our group were classical music enthusiasts, my recordings of Beethoven, Mozart, Sibelius, and

Mahler were much appreciated. Nevertheless, Roger exceeded the limit later in the winter when using our living room for violin practice while we were out to dinner in the town. We returned earlier than Roger expected and surprised him trying to keep pace with Alfredo Campoli on a recording of Mendelssohn's Violin Concerto in E Minor, third movement—half a bar behind, at best, as we opened the door.

Don was the inveterate "fixer," especially with frozen sewer lines, a product of one of the more dire aspects of his Antarctic experience. After one particularly persistent problem he took me aside and quietly proposed that I join him in a corporate venture to be known as "Arctic and Antarctic Sewers, Inc." Our remaining, although more distant, member was Erv Bentley—more distant because he reported directly to Professor Millet Morgan at Dartmouth. His responsibility was separate and distinct. Erv, however, as the ultimate practical engineer, proved a great asset in helping keep the Lab mechanically operational.

From the foregoing it will be apparent that rapport between residents of the Lab was excellent and easily established. This may have been, at least partly, because the Lab's accommodation had been substantially expanded since that first tense winter faced by Norm and Pat. The director's apartment was at the far end of a long building separated from the main Lab building by a 60-foot (18 m) wooden walkway that opened first on to my office, a photographic darkroom, and a large room for the library and lab tables. The "boys'" quarters had expanded into what had been Norm and Pat's living room and kitchen. All of this made things much easier, even luxurious. In addition, two small two-room wooden cottages had been acquired from the McConnell construction operations and repositioned on the far side of the McGill parcel of land. They were to become important sources of income to support field research. Another major step forward was that the "boys" had been invited to take their meals in the officers' mess at the RCAF station a couple hundred yards down the road toward town. Despite this very inexpensive provision of excellent meals, Pauline and I set up regular dinner parties, usually once a week. Our student guests always came in jackets and ties and expressed their enthusiasm for eating from a table adorned with a tablecloth.

Don and I had a tense time with the first month-end (September) weather summary. After several near-sleepless nights we got the completed paperwork off to DOT-Dorval. Thereafter, the month-end rush went remarkably smoothly. However, there was an entirely new set of observations necessitated by the Lab's designation as part of the 1957–1958 International Geophysical Year (IGY) network. Our main duty in this respect was to visually record aurora borealis activity on specially printed standardized cards. Observations were required on an hourly basis throughout the long winter nights, which proved a significant addition to the workload, albeit one that was greatly enjoyed. The aurora displays were often magnificent.

During the autumn I was anxious for all the students to see as much of the surrounding country as possible, although drifting snow by the end of September seriously limited access along the barely maintained IOCC former exploration roads. Skiing, snow shoeing, and ice skating became favorite pursuits for some of us. The ice skating proved to be a great thrill for more than a week as we had low temperatures ahead of significant snow accumulation. We could cover considerable distances across clear lake surfaces. And since the freeze had occurred quickly without significant wind, skaters could see through the clear ice and look down on fish swimming beneath. This did not last long. Fall storms quickly shattered the smooth lake ice. The low temperatures occurring with the increasing length of the nights fascinated the new arrivals from England, who had never experienced more than a few degrees of frost. The real excitement of −50°F (−45.6°C), however, did not occur until well after Christmas.

One special problem I had was to induce highly intelligent English graduate students to accept some of the seemingly unnecessarily tedious Canadian weather station rules. In those days, unlike today, when I suspect that weather observers almost never have direct contact with the weather, we read thermometers and recorded incoming precipitation outdoors; we set off hydrogen-filled pilot balloons (pi-balls) to record upper air flow by theodolite tracking; and we had to ensure that, before sunrise each morning, all the hoar frost was removed from the glass mantle of the actinograph that was recording incoming solar radiation. The only practical way to do this was to use one's bare hands. In −30°F or −40°F (−34°C or −40°C), this was a delicate and painful task.

There was a special difficulty with the pilot balloon obs. From time to time balloons disappeared from the observer's telescopic sight, even in clear weather, with no apparent explanation. Eventually we found that the bright red balloons were targets used for practice by our local Naskaupi hunters. This was discovered only when the observer, usually alone and who would be wearing earphones, was accompanied by a colleague who heard the sharp crack of a rifle. It would have been somewhat embarrassing to inform DOT-Dorval on our required teletype reports that our lack of upper air observations was because our balloons were being shot out of the sky. Obviously, we needed our own "Indian treaty." Our amusing negotiations with the Naskaupi became agreeably convivial as is related below.

The only real problem, however, developed with an observer on the lonely and quiet night shifts when the weather was clear, cold, and calm. One especially inventive member of the crew realized that he could "calculate" (that is, guess) what the air temperature would be for the entire night shift.

Tony Williamson tracking a weather balloon through a theodolite. February 1958.

We were usually required to transmit all the weather observations by tele-type on the hour, every hour. But there were occasional power failures. Toward the end of one winter month I thought the records of the night temperatures looked rather odd—they were too regular. So I set my alarm clock for 2:30 a.m., got up, and quietly entered the weather room to find the observer on duty soundly asleep on the couch. The teletype was loaded with all the hourly obs from midnight to 8 a.m. (in effect, a weather forecast, entirely contrived!), with the statement that they were posted late because of a power failure. All the lights were on; there had been no power outage. The teletype, with the state-ment that power had been restored, was set for transmission just before the next eight-hour shift by the relief observer. I awakened the culprit with a piece of my mind. Once the sleep was out of his eyes his defense was that his forecast was actually better than if he had read the various sets of instruments.[30] DOT-Dorval never spotted anything amiss when we submitted that month's records. Nevertheless, I doubt it happened again. And the innovator remains nameless.

There were other elements of group rapport during our unusual and iso-lated existence. Roger Barry became a close friend of the Rev. Gavin White, the Anglican minister. One of Gavin's pastoral tasks was to minister to the Naskaupi, whose numbers were increasing and who had totally inadequate quarters on the edge of town.[31] That first winter they were beset by a particu-larly virulent flu epidemic and more than a few died. I can remember Roger coming back to the Lab, frozen after a long day with Gavin. "What on earth have you been up to, Roger?" was my anxious question. He had been helping Gavin dig graves. The frost penetration into the ground was already considerable so that crowbars were needed to reach sufficient depth for entombment. Others of the crew assisted from time to time with this charitable and very sad task.

When the temperatures really plummeted, they heralded in another personal problem. In calm, very cold weather, one could walk between the main building and the newer one containing my office, library, and darkroom, in one's shirtsleeves. A few minutes in very low temperatures were easy to endure and avoided the nuisance of dressing up. Nevertheless, as I explained to everyone, a single piece of extra clothing was advisable—one glove. That was to wear on the hand that grasped the outside door knob. It always amazed me how many times this advice was forgotten. I usually knew about it if I was working in my office that was close to the outside door—there would be a stream of obscenities. As the gloveless hand was sharply pulled back off the frozen door knob, half the skin from the palm was left sticking to it. Each member could be expected to do that once. If anyone did it twice, I felt obligated to keep careful watch, as I thought it may well be a sign that I was responsible for someone who could be classed as accident prone. This happened very infrequently.

All in all, our first winter at the Lab proved a great adventure. Social life outside the Lab was very restricted, however, simply because of the paucity of married couples in town. The overall male-to-female ratio must have been about 200:1. Our closest friends were several of the midsenior-level members of the IOCC staff, including pit foremen and wives: David and Barbara Selleck, newly arrived from what was then Northern Rhodesia; Peter and Pat Young; Dave and Liz Owen; Al and Marge Romaniuk; Carol and "Buzz" Neal (IOCC chief geologist); and Jean and Hugh Amor (IOCC chief engineer). Pauline and Jean set up a Knob Lake Girl Guides troop. Pauline helped Carol Neal create a "public library" of donated books. The books came from local donations and from as far afield as discards of the Toronto Public Libraries, with the IOCC providing free transhipment. Both these activities ran into Roman Catholic opposition. The only school in town with adequate available space was the RC school. The library was opened in its basement for two nights a week, with volunteers as part-time librarians. Our local priest, through the school principal, objected to many of the donated books, although they were reasonably well screened by Pauline and Carol. *The Merry Adventures of Robin Hood* by Howard Pyle was taboo, for instance, as it was considered likely to promote communism. Carol, to avoid a possible confrontation between the RC and the IOCC, left the project. Pauline was declared incompetent, she was told, because she lacked a degree in library science. Thus, the library closed. However, the Church could

Plate 1.   Moon over Astray Lake as the cry of the loon echoes across its placid surface. August 1955.

Plate 2.   Campsite on a small island in "Esker Lake II." Note the canoe for scale. The tent is scarcely visible on the crest of the island. August 1955.

Plate 3.   Pauline stirs the porridge at "Esker Lake II." August 1955.

Plate 4.   Sunset from the BRINEX camp at North West River. This is the legendary starting point for ventures into the then unknown by Leonidas Hubbard, Dillon Wallace, and Mina Hubbard in 1903 and 1905. 4 July 1956.

Plate 5.   Arrival at an unknown lake 60 miles (96 km) northeast of North West River, to await improvement of ice conditions farther north. 6 July 1956.

Plate 6.   The all-purpose building at Hebron, including church, school, store, and living quarters for both Moravian missionaries and government storekeepers; 26 July 1956.

Plate 7.   Preparation of the final leg of our flight to the Torngat Mountains. The Hebron jetty with our floatplane. Among the crowd are (from the left) Paul Saunders (pilot), Pauline, and Katie Hettasch. 26 July 1956.

Plate 8.   View to the southeast onto Nachvak Fiord (far right distance) across Chasm Lake from an unnamed mountaintop at about 4,900 ft (1,494 m). July 1978.

Plate 9.   View toward the southwest from the 4,900 ft summit (1,494 m). Chasm Lake occupies the deep glacially eroded trench. Note the even skyline of the Labrador Plateau. There is no trace of a steep western mountain flank as had previously been assumed. July 1978.

Plate 10.   Closer view of the interior of the Torngats taken during the ascent of the 4,900-foot (1,494-m) mountain. July 1978.

Plate 11.   One of the arms of Saglek Fiord, Torngat Mountains, showing the abrupt break in slope from the slightly dissected plateau surface to the fiord walls. August 1978.

Plate 12. The Lab buildings during the winter of 1957–1958. The low linear structure at bottom right is the water- and sewer-line insulated box, a focus for snow-shoveling and mulled wine over New Year's 1958.

Plate 13.   Indian House Lake was well named. Remnants of old deserted campsites abound. I named the ice-dammed lakes the "Naskaupi Glacial Lakes" in recognition of the former inhabitants, who must have witnessed thousands of caribou swimming across in the early twentieth century.

Plate 14.   The George River country was revisited on a return flight from the Torngats in 1978. Note the level skyline and the narrow bands of spruce forest that cling to the lower slopes projecting far northward into the arctic tundra. August 1978.

Plate 15. Forest fire to the west of Knob Lake. June 1959.

Plate 16.   A breezy crossing of Indian House Lake. August 1958.

apply only moral pressure on the functioning of the Girl Guides. This had a limited effect because the preteen and teenage girls had virtually no social outlets in town and their parents very much appreciated the volunteer efforts. This parental support extended to a request for Pauline and Jean to provide sex education, a topic that the volunteers felt beyond their remit, and more particularly that of the Girl Guides Association. Nevertheless, the Girl Guides flourished and were on hand to welcome Queen Elizabeth II and Prince Philip on an unprecedented visit in June 1959. Also, in terms of scouting, Don Macnab made a great contribution to the local Cub Scouts, while Geoff Sherlock worked with Budd Perry, the chief mine transport engineer, in developing the Knob Lake Cub Scout troop.

I felt that I was in the best career situation imaginable as Lab director, but I had so much to do in the meager three years of my appointment with a pitiful budget for field research. I had as friends and colleagues five newcomers, all very well trained, and all of us experiencing the excitement of running a first-order weather station. Temperatures were far below those any of the group had ever contemplated, with the exception of Don Macnab during his Antarctic sojourn. On especially cold nights in late January and February, in calm conditions, we would all sit up through the long night, watching the thermometers plummet. The "witching hour," if we were to break a record, was the hour before sunrise. I remember one predawn with the thermometers hovering at −50°F (−45.6°C). We were desperately hoping that the absolute calm would persist and allow for just a little more extension of the temperature inversion. A groan of anguish reverberated around the weather room as we saw the anemometer needle begin to flicker. The arrival of the slightest gentle movement of air defeated us and kept the temperature at −50.5°F (−45.8°C); the record to beat was −55.5°F (−48.6°C) that had been recorded the previous January.

Our first winter of 1957–1958 also produced a startling weather anomaly. In mid-December air temperatures rose to +41°F (+5.0°C) during a short period of heavy rain and remained above freezing for twenty-six hours. The impact on the environment amounted to a local catastrophe. Furthermore, this exceptionally rare high temperature had been preceded by two weeks of generally warm—although below freezing—weather with heavy snowfalls. The thaw caused flooding of both the mines and the town. We knew that there was much worse to come. And it did. Over a twenty-hour period the temperature dropped from +40°F to −30°F (+4.4°C to −34.4°C), freezing the standing meltwater and wet snow so that everything was coated in ice. Walking was highly dangerous. Two immense 45-ton Euclid ore trucks slid off mine roads and fell into the pits. (The drivers escaped injury because of the remarkably well-padded truck cabins.) Life was brought to a temporary standstill, including the school. Once things were partly back to normal and the schools reopened, it became a great thrill for the more daring of the kids on their iceskates to hang onto a long rope that was trailed behind the schoolbus. This would be unthinkable today, of course, in this era of overprotection.

The widespread rain and thaw, followed by the deep freeze, brought another form of life into acute danger. Our Naskaupi friends reported that a small herd of caribou, some 30 mi (48 km) to our north, would starve because they were unable to break through the iced surface to reach their Cladonia lichen food supply beneath. Sammy,the Naskaupi chief, asked if I would intervene with the senior RCAF officer on behalf of his hunters, who could not travel under such conditions.[32] A helicopter would be a great help. So a large helicopter went on a "winter training mission" carrying Naskaupi hunters. Two loads of caribou carcasses were surreptitiously deposited at the Naskaupi encampment. The following day Sammy appeared with a carefully disguised parcel: a fine leg of caribou. So we gorged on roast caribou, prohibited for whites in those days as the authorities believed that the Labrador-Ungava caribou herd, numbering over 500,000 in the 1920s, had been reduced to 5,000 and were threatened with extinction. Officially, the cause was claimed to have been introduction of the rifle to native hunting. This seemed absurd to me, although I did not doubt that the herd size was critically low. By the late 1970s the herd size was once again near 500,000 and the Québec provincial authorities were issuing a thousand hunting licenses per year! (Bergerud et al. 2007.) Much more is known today about these enormous natural population fluctuations.

The anomalous weather conditions of that first winter produced a further benefit, in addition to roast caribou. During the weeks before the mid-December thaw, temperatures had been significantly higher than average and accompanied by heavy snow accumulation. Roger Barry's initial master's thesis topic was the preparation of a synoptic climatology for Labrador-Ungava. During the winter this was extended to include analysis of the climatological conditions needed to produce "instantaneous glacierization across the Labrador-Ungava plateau." He undertook a comparison of two winters—the 1957–1958 warm winter with heavy snow accumulation and the 1956–1957 cold dry winter. He was able to demonstrate that lower temperatures in already cold regions such as Labrador-Ungava and central Keewatin are not particularly conducive to the initiation of major ice sheets. What was needed was precipitation. Roger's thesis formed the basis of an exceedingly productive climatological research and teaching career, culminating with remarkable international acclaim, including the 2007 award of the Founder's Medal of the Royal Geographical Society. Roger's climatological interests, in part, complemented those of other Lab researchers concerned with the geomorphological evaluation of evidence for

Sammy, chief of the Naskaupi Band (Innu): a good friend. February 1958.

glacierization and deglacierization of Labrador-Ungava and, subsequently, of Baffin Island.

During the winter I offered two university graduate courses to a group of highly committed students. One covered the geography of the Canadian Arctic and Subarctic, the other glaciology and glacial geomorphology. They provided a useful platform for expanding the field research program that I had been formulating since my 1955 summer at the Lab. Roger Barry's research represented the first step. The second was Roger Tomlinson's decision to extend my fieldwork in the Torngat Mountains to the Kaumajet Mountains and the coastal area farther south. Roger had married Jocelyn before leaving England. Because of the lack of married quarters at the Lab, she had spent the winter with the British Embassy in Iceland, although she reached us in time to depart with Roger for the Kaumajet Mountains. Once more, the very good offices of Dr. Paul Beavan and BRINEX came into play, since without them it would have been financially impossible for the Tomlinsons to reach such a distant field area.

Christmas was a great opportunity for celebrations, with turkey on our dining table and Gavin White, the Anglican minister, giving the blessing. We all listened intently to Her Majesty Queen Elizabeth's Christmas message to the Commonwealth. There was great excitement when Her Majesty mentioned a

Christmas dinner at the Lab, 25 December 1957. From left: Rev. Gavin White, Erv Bentley, Roger Barry, Pauline, Jack, Don Macnab, Geoff Sherlock, Roger Tomlinson. Tony Williamson is absent because he was the only member able to visit his family for the holiday.

heroic journey in almost impossible Antarctic blizzard conditions by a group of four Australians that included Malcolm Mellor, a close friend and one of the members of the 1954 Nottingham University expedition to southeastern Iceland.

Shortly after Christmas our most welcome visitor of the winter landed at the Knob Lake airstrip. I had persuaded Pep Wheeler to make a trip from Ithaca, NY. Pep arrived with an enormous piece of prime beef, which gave Pauline a case of nerves as she well knew that Pep had strict notions about cooking— there was no such thing as medium-rare, let alone well done. The roast was eventually presented and I proceeded to carve. Tiny Tomlinson called out in marked distress, "My god, it's bleeding!" To which Pep replied with a chuckle, "another minute in the oven and it would have been burnt." A delicious dinner ensued, and there followed several days of Pep's advice, enthusiasm, and sense of commitment to Labrador.

The next major event of the winter also took on a highly personal flavor. Not long after his arrival, Don Macnab had asked about the availability of one of the small cottages that had been recently acquired from McConnell Construction. I cleared this arrangement with Ken Hare and, immediately after receiving my positive response, Don commandeered the DOT weather office teletype to send a message to Kirkcaldy, Scotland. The message was short and to the point; it read something like, "Jean, will you marry me? Don." This caused excitement all around, the more so when Jean, who to that date had scarcely traveled more than 50 mi (80 km) distant from her home, sent her reply: "Yes, Jean," thereby achieving what must be a world record for brevity in a proposal and acceptance of marriage. In February a bonny Scottish lass became our house guest.

The exchange on the teletype had produced an outburst of congratulations. Preparations for the wedding were quickly set in motion. The Rev. Doug Ross, the new vicar at the United Church of Canada, took on the task of counseling and arranging the wedding ceremony. I was offered the honor of "giving away" the bride. We had no bridesmaids available and Pauline felt obliged to decline the office of matron of honor, as she was not fully recovered from a short but severe bout of influenza. Don chose Tony Williamson as his best man.

And on the very cold morning of 15 February, in −25°F and a stiff breeze, I drove the bride to the United Church. I offered my arm to a young woman clad in a decidedly nonsubarctic lightweight pink suit (Don and Jean had worried that the traditional dress and veil would not comfortably match our deep freeze). Even so, it was fortunate that there were only about twenty steps to the shelter of the church, or Don might have acquired a solidly frozen wife. But as we began our sedate walk down the aisle, Jean suddenly stopped and began to panic. She clung tightly to me and exclaimed, "Don's not there; where can he be?" She, and everyone else, except of course the best man, had failed to recognize the groom who, contrary to his stated intent the previous evening, had shaven his beard and was in complete disguise, wearing a very smart dark suit. Jean had never seen Don without his beard, nor without his SS *John Biscoe* sweater, but she effected a quick recovery and the wedding service proceeded without any further hitch. Nevertheless, we had no bridal attendant as Pauline, still with a hacking cough, sat quietly at the back of the church. What to do with the bride's bouquet? At the appropriate moment I accepted Jean's bouquet and gently nursed it through the remainder of the ceremony and took it with me into the vestry for the signing of documents. Many years later (2008), by letter from Jersey, Channel Islands, UK, and after reading an earlier draft of this text, Jean commented that we must have struck yet another world record—of having the youngest father of the bride and the oldest page boy combined in a single person.

The wedding party in our apartment was an affair to remember. There were many moments of humor. Late to arrive because of the need to close up the church, Doug and Helen Ross entered last. Geoff Sherlock approached Helen, who was conspicuously the somewhat apprehensive wife of a newly appointed vicar, and asked, "What's yours?" She hesitated; so, trying to assist, Geoff added, "We've scotch, gin, and cognac!" Pauline said she would never forget Helen's face, and quickly stepped in to offer a choice of sherry or orange juice. Helen hastily chose the latter.

The symbolic cutting of the cake also produced some moments that, with the passage of time, faded into amusement. Don had persuaded the IOCC cook to make the cake—he had won competitions for wedding cake construction. It looked magnificent; it had three tiers surmounted by a miniature bridal couple standing on top at the head of a flight of stairs, covered with red carpet to the base tier. But the ceremonial knife refused to penetrate. We quickly discovered that each tier consisted of a square cardboard box with the cake inside. Icing had been beautifully plastered onto the cardboard (we couldn't be sure whether it was edible icing or white cement), nor could we determine the best cutting implement—a can opener, a chisel, a hammer, or a blunt old field knife (the knife eventually did the trick). But the cake!—it tasted like a cross between a sponge cake and the Stone of Scone! Finally, the guests wandered away, back into town through the deeply frozen dusk, except for the boys, who stayed to consume every last sausage roll and chocolate éclair. The newlyweds offered to do the washing up, but over our gentle objections they eventually waded through deep snow to the tiny cottage, their home for the next eighteen months. Indeed, a wedding to remember.

An additional winter alarm was a power failure on New Year's Eve. Such an event was a threat to the entire town and mines, given the very low temperatures

The bride and groom: Jean and Don Macnab, 15 February 1958, happy and confident as they prepare to cut their wedding cake (photograph courtesy of Geoff Sherlock).

Consternation! The knife meets resistance. What is the impressive structure composed of—cement? (Photograph courtesy of Geoff Sherlock.)

at the time. The IOCC had three large portable generators. Two were reserved for the mines, the top economic priority. The third provided electricity in six-hour shifts for one quarter of the town in rotation, barely sufficient to prevent the freezing of water and sewerage lines, even indoor plumbing. The Lab's water and sewer lines were above the surface for a distance of some 200 yards (183 m), encased in an insulated box and heated by an electric cable.[33] We were in acute danger of a catastrophe. So we all saw in the New Year vigorously shoveling snow over the insulated box while Pauline maintained a constant supply of warm mulled wine. We had a special reward of seeing the most impressive display of red and purple northern lights we had ever witnessed. The insulating effect of the newly shoveled snow piled over the water and sewage line averted a disastrous freeze-up (see Plate 12).

While running the Lab, I also had to plan my own fieldwork for the 1958 summer. As my vision for the Lab's field program involved far-flung fieldwork, it was imperative that I played a leading role. Where to go? The 1957 discovery of extensive glacial lake shorelines stretching southwest from the southern Torngats attracted me to the possibility for further investigation. This led me to plan for a visit to the National Air Photo Library in Ottawa in conjunction with my required late winter (March) trip to McGill, Montréal, to report on progress at the Lab to the Geography Department.[34]

Throughout the winter I had been collecting every book about the exploration of Labrador-Ungava that I could locate, mainly from secondhand book stores in Montréal. These were added to the small core of the Lab library that I was keen to enlarge. The process unearthed what, for me, was a breakthrough. I had acquired a copy of Hesketh V. Hesketh-Prichard's book *Through Trackless Labrador*, published in 1911. This was an account of a desperate journey from Nain to Indian House Lake on the George River. An adventure yarn, it contained little of geomorphological interest except for two photographs and a brief description:

> This was a beach of clear gravel elevated at a height of 700 ft (by aneroid) above the present level of the lake . . . which Gathorne-Hardy [who wrote a chapter on fishing for the book] compared to *The Parallel Roads of Glenroy*.

On reading this I could not contain my excitement. *The Parallel Roads of Glenroy* was the prime British university textbook example of shorelines of former lakes dammed by the retreating last Ice Age glaciers in Scotland. How could such a discovery have remained in limbo since 1911? Was there a connection between the Indian House Lake shorelines and those we had worked on in the Torngat Mountains more than 150 mi (241 km) farther north? Here was a further incentive for my evolving peninsula-wide field program. It made a visit to the National Air Photo Library an imperative.

The air photo coverage in Ottawa was only trimetrogon, and much of it poor quality because of the weather conditions that prevailed at the time of the photography. It quickly became apparent, however, that shorelines of former glacial lakes extended across a huge area of eastern and northeastern Labrador-Ungava. Furthermore, a "late-glacial ice divide" was demarcated on the new *Glacial Map of Canada*, published by the Geological Association of Canada. It passed through the middle of the former lake systems and so was incompatible with my interpretation of the existence of large water bodies during the final phases of the last ice age. Here was an apparent contradiction that would make fieldwork in the George River basin so much more rewarding.

In Ottawa I renewed my previous winter's acquaintance with Dr. Norman Nicholson, director of the federal Geographical Branch. He not only promised financial support for a field expedition to Indian House Lake, but suggested that I apply for a permanent senior research position with his organization. More of the Geographical Branch later, but from that moment Pauline and I were set for another considerable adventure in the Labrador-Ungava wilderness.

Indian House Lake (Lac de la Hutte Sauvage), 1958

I returned to Knob Lake in late March after a week's absence. The Lab was running smoothly and Don was totally competent to manage the weather schedule. With financial backing from the Geographical Branch, I could char-ter a Canso aircraft for the following July, into which our 18-foot canoe would easily fit. I was aware that there was a first-order DOT weather station located on the southern section of Indian House Lake, which would be ideal as the ultimate jumping-off point for fieldwork far downstream. But first, permission to visit was required. Surely, all that was needed was a formal letter of request addressed to the head of the Climatological Office of the DOT to whom I reported as officer-in-charge of the Knob Lake weather station. It was not quite so simple. Once more that "problem" of women in the wilderness reared its ugly head. The Indian House weather station (long since abandoned) was a very isolated station with a crew of five. These men were confined on the edge of a wilderness lake for up to a year at a time. The first reaction to my request for permission to visit was negative—it was too dangerous for young women to visit such a place. After no little argumentation, permission was reluctantly granted. I was tempted to ask if I should go armed with hand guns as well as a hunting rifle.

On 30 June, after seeing Roger and Jocelyn Tomlinson on their way to the Kaumajet Mountains, we were ready to depart for Indian House Lake. Ken Hare had arranged for George Michie, with his new wife, Margaret, to take my place as acting field director during our absence. We prepared our apartment for them.

We loaded our chartered Canso on the airstrip only 100 yards (91 m) from our doorstep. As we expected, there was a lot of room to spare, so we invited Barbara Selleck, Liz Owen (two friends from the town), and Geoff Sherlock and Tony Williamson of the regular Lab staff along for the ride. We had daily connection with DOT-Indian House Lake by teletype so I had warned them to expect day trippers. After a comparatively short flight of 120 mi (193 km) due northeast we splashed down on Indian House Lake and tied up to a very serviceable jetty. Four of the five weather station crew were lined up to meet us—the fifth was taking the weather observations. All were wearing white shirts and neckties, obviously hastily pulled out of storage, no doubt because the visiting young ladies would expect proper dress. It was just as I had expected and we were treated royally. Our day trippers stayed for lunch and then returned with the Canso to Knob Lake. Pauline and I stayed at the weather station overnight. There followed another demonstration of the dangers of a visit by a young woman to such a place. Several of the men hadn't seen a woman for more than nine months. Although tired, Pauline and I stayed up because we realized our hosts all wanted the pleasure of talking, especially to a woman.[35]

After an excellent breakfast, two of the weather station crew took Pauline and me with our canoe some 15 mi (24 km) down the lake in the station's sturdy launch. They set us down at our prechosen base campsite just south of one of the rare named features on the very rough map—Wedge Point. On parting company with our new friends, we told them that we would find our own way back to the weather station in seven weeks when the Canso was scheduled to arrive for our flight back to Knob Lake. Thus began another period of exciting and productive field work.

The launch left us opposite Wedge Point, south of the mouth of a small stream that entered the lake from the southeast.[36] We had chosen the site because it was about midway along this 60-mile (96 km) lake expansion of the George River and close to stretches of some of the more prominent glacial lake shorelines (the "parallel roads"). Both Mina Hubbard and H. Hesketh-Prichard camped in the same locality in 1905 and 1910, respectively, although we could find no traces of their stay.

A narrow stand of white spruce bordered the lake, beyond which the land rose about 20 ft (6 m) to a small level terrace carpeted with Cladonia lichen. We had expected a beautiful as well as a practical site. It proved ideal. It was immediately apparent that we shared the same sense of esthetic appreciation as our Naskaupi predecessors, for there were abundant signs of an old encampment. We could look through the tops of the spruce across the lake to the striking esker that plunged down the far hillside into the water to form Wedge Point. The esker reemerged on our side of the lake and, paralleling the stream, continued southeastward for as far as we could see. The stream tumbled down several modest waterfalls and rapids. It provided pure drinking water and was easy to cross dry-shod. A sandy beach served as a fine pull-up for our canoe and we could almost smell the trout on arrival.

As we sat in front of our tents that first evening, I could not avoid mentally tracking back over fifty years to imagine Mina Hubbard's canoes drifting past Wedge Point on the lake below us as they began their final push to Ungava Bay. I am sure that the view would have been identical all those years ago.

Our main objective was to survey the parallel roads (terraces) that bordered the lake along its entire length, although we were aware that they extended much further north and south and far beyond our reach. Sections of the main terraces could also be seen far to the west and east of the lake, indicating the former existence of a very large body of water. We planned to make a telescopic level and staff survey of the heights of the terraces above lake level. We would also try to determine whether they were horizontal or tilted and, if the latter, the direction and amount of tilt. Because the survey had to be accurate to within about 6 in (15 cm), the farther north-south we could expand our measurements, the better. To run a precise level north-to-south across such country to encompass the 60-mile (96 km) length of the lake, however, would take far more time than we had available. Thus we assumed that the lake level itself would form an adequate benchmark and give us the opportunity of running a series of profiles up from the water line to the highest shoreline. We would

Indian House Lake. Setting up base camp close to Wedge Point. 1 July 1958.

From the air this former island, surrounded by a distinct terrace, could almost be taken for a pre-Roman encampment in southern England. Most of the area in the photograph would have been submerged by the waters of Glacial Lake Naskaupi 2 about 7,000–8,000 years ago. Note the extensive shoreline among the snowbanks in the distance. 30 June 1958.

A compound gravel spit produced by long shore currents when Glacial Lake Naskaupi 2 would have submerged most of the land shown in the photograph. Indian House Lake stretches away to the south. 7 July 1958.

record any fluctuations in lake level during the period of our survey, due to possible downstream flow, heavy rainfall, or extended periods of dry weather. We therefore placed a series of stakes along the lake at the starting points of each leveling profile to determine any change in level that might occur during our seven-week stay.

The lake was about 1.5 mi (2.4 km) wide at its maximum; the narrowest section lay immediately north of Wedge Point. We could detect a significant current in the narrows opposite Wedge Point, but assumed that any change in level would not affect our overall conclusions, or at least could be taken into our calculations. An initial survey of the lake by canoe showed that it fell 3 ft to 4 ft (or about 1 m) over its entire length. A precise survey of the entire George River by the Québec Streams Commission and the 1:50,000 topographical maps published years later gave the absolute altitude of the lake as +/–981 ft (299 m) above sea level,[37] and a 1-ft (0.30 m) change in level over the length of the lake.

During our final days at the Lab preparing for the venture, we were visited by the well-known ornithologist Dr. Roland Clement, who subsequently became president of the Audubon Society. On learning that we planned work along Indian House Lake, he explained that it was territory critical for one of his favorite research projects—the white-crowned sparrow of the Labrador coast, which differed at the subspecies level from the sparrow that occupied central Labrador-Ungava. He was eager to determine where their territories overlapped; would Pauline collect specimens for him? On agreement, Pauline underwent a crash course in shooting and skinning sparrows. It necessitated a change in armaments. We took with us a .410/.22 over-and-under rifle. The .22 was for small game such as ptarmigan. The .410 caliber included a single slug at the "top" level (for defense against bears) and bird shot (almost dust) at the other extreme, to knock down sparrows without damaging their feathers. But the gun was *always* to be left late at night loaded for bears in the event of an unwelcome visit. This led to a "tall tale" of near disaster, related below.

Following Roland's ornithological missionary zeal, we were set up as explorers of "unknown" territory in the traditional sense—observe everything and collect as much as possible! So our interests expanded to collecting spruce increment cores for Erik Mortensen, a Norwegian forest ecologist working out of the Lab that summer, and pressed plants for Jacques Rousseau, as well as recording all wildlife we saw, especially bears, wolves, and caribou.

We operated from several campsites we set up by canoe—a luxury compared with the heavy backpacking in the Torngats during the two previous summers. We precisely surveyed six profiles perpendicular to the lake shoreline along a north-south extent of nearly 60 mi (96 km), and this enabled us to determine that the three most conspicuous former lake shorelines were located at 700 ft,

500 ft, and 350 ft (213 m, 152 m, and 107 m) above lake level. We named the former lakes in honor of our indigenous predecessors—Glacial Lakes Naskaupi 1 (700 ft; 213 m), 2 (500 ft; 152 m), and 3 (350 ft; 107 m). The heights given here are averages, as we also demonstrated that they sloped up toward the south. By far the most extensive shoreline was Naskaupi 2 (N-2) and it attracted most of our survey energies. It sloped up toward the south at 1.57 ft/mi, giving a total of just over 94 ft (29 m) in the 60 mi (96 km). This was the apparent tilt; determination of the absolute direction of tilt, probably somewhat west of south, would have required a much more extensive triangular-based survey, and this would be necessary before isobases could be plotted (see appendix IV). However, the 1.57 ft/mi tilt would eliminate any small errors arising from imprecise survey or lake-level fluctuation.

We also walked as far to the east, out across the Nain Plateau, as we were able—a maximum of about 15 mi (24 km). This was part of our effort to see if we could locate the former spillways through which the glacial lakes would have drained into rivers flowing into the Atlantic. Although we did not succeed in our main task, we were able to add a lot of detail to the pattern of final ice melt and withdrawal westward from the height-of-land. Shorter hikes to the west confirmed air photo reconnaissance that a second system of large glacial lakes had existed and had submerged most of the present Whale River basin; these we named Glacial Lakes McLean (there were several at different levels)

Multiple shorelines of the Naskaupi glacial lakes on the eastern side of Indian House Lake. The three most prominent shorelines are interspersed with others that are less pronounced. These are the "parallel roads" of Gathorne-Hardy (Prichard 1911); 10 July 1958.

View along a section of the Glacial Lake Naskaupi 2 shoreline, with Pauline for scale. The distinctiveness of these shorelines, almost continuous for distances in excess of 150 mi (241 km), demonstrates the remarkable damming effects of the remnant Laurentide Ice Sheet that must have blocked Ungava Bay and Hudson Strait after the Torngats and most of the Nain Plateau had become ice-free. One can only imagine the massive outburst of water once the dam eventually burst. See photo of Icelandic jökulhlaup (page xvii) for comparison.

after the Hudson's Bay Company factor who, with Erland Erlandson, had made the first momentous traverses of the area in the mid-1800s.

The fieldwork, although arduous, proved yet another great summer adventure. Pauline knocked over more than a dozen sparrows and neatly divested them of skins and feathers. We also brought down several ptarmigan that went into the pot. We obtained more than fifty spruce increment cores for Erik and filled two plant presses for Dr. Rousseau. We feasted on easily caught lake and brook trout and returned to Knob Lake with quite a supply of unused field rations. We also saw the occasional wolf and many black bears during our daytime hikes. The wolves ignored us. The bears usually scuttled away from us.

On the day of our serious bear encounter, we had spent hours beating northward into a stiff breeze down the lake to occupy our most distant survey stations. It proved a very bumpy ride throughout the morning and early afternoon, and Pauline in center-canoe was repeatedly lifted off her knees and dumped down again. We were a little concerned, because she was two months pregnant.

However, the wind died down and we pulled into a quiet bay for a brief rest, only a mile or so short of our cache, laid out the previous week. In the bay the water was still and we glided silently toward a beckoning beach.

As we drifted in, a bear emerged from the forest and began to drink. He had not seen us. I checked the canoe's forward motion with the paddle and we watched quietly. He still failed to detect us, but neither did he go away. I began to worry. Was he too close to our intended campsite? Perhaps I should shoot him? With the thought of fresh meat uppermost in my mind, I gave the canoe a gentle push forward with my paddle and picked up the rifle. We coasted toward him like an invisible spirit over the now still water. He sensed our presence, reared up to his full height in the water. Bracing myself, barely a full canoe-length away, I took careful aim: a direct hit into his left eye. I could hardly have missed. After the loud bang, the bear simply shook his head, apparently puzzled. He brushed a large paw across his eyes, then bounded away into the forest. Shocked, I looked at the spent cartridge. On the previous night we had neglected to eject Pauline's bird shot from the rifle and reload for bear. We could have been in serious trouble, for he could have smashed the prow of the canoe in a twinkling. Luck was on our side.

Somewhat chagrined, we retreated from the bay. We retrieved our cache of food and fuel and decided that the opposite shore of the lake, here about half a mile wide, was a better and safer place to camp. To our southwest the land sloped gently up to the summit of a hill identified as Mont Kamistiuetinast on the 1983 1:250,000 map sheet.

A dinner of freshly caught lake trout was followed by a silent half hour sitting by the lake as the sun dipped below the hills behind us. In the twilight a herd of some fifteen to twenty caribou quietly picked their way on either side of us as if we were inert boulders. Such is the beauty of Labrador-Ungava.

Our seven-week subarctic venture quickly came to an end. The memories remain: idyllic sunsets over a tranquil stretch of water, battling fierce white horses on a turbulent lake, hot sunny days, periods of heavy rain, unbelievable trout fishing in this virgin lake, and suffocating clouds of mosquitoes and black flies that at times left us exhausted and Pauline with swollen glands. Above all we experienced the sense of being totally alone in an endless wilderness of rolling hills and innumerable lakes that had been visited only rarely by our several Labrador heroes: Mina Hubbard, Dillon Wallace, Hesketh Hesketh-Prichard, and G. M. Gathorne-Hardy; Pep Wheeler; and Jacques Rousseau. In contrast, the original residents of this beautiful land, and their descendents now living in squalor adjacent to white settlements, have left only remnants of their former homes along the length of the lake (see Plate 13).

On 17 August we expended the last of our outboard motor fuel within a half mile of the weather station. Our paddles managed the rest and we were heartily

Slanting Brook enters the northern end of Indian House Lake from the Nain Plateau to the east, with typical spruce forest (plus alder and willow thickets) on the lower hill slopes, merging upward into arctic tundra, and the ubiquitous glacial lake shorelines near the tops of the hills (indicated by white dots).

Precise leveling of profiles from the lake shore to the highest terraces could be tedious. Looking through telescopic sights while wearing a head net all day left one feeling dizzy. The alternative—no head net—was far worse.

welcomed to a rather late specially cooked breakfast. Our Canso touched down in midafternoon with another load of day trippers and we were back at the Lab for supper, thus closing seven perfect weeks.

Adventure aside, what had we accomplished? We had certainly not completed anything—it was only a beginning. The existence of the pronounced glacial lake shorelines had been known since the days of Hesketh-Prichard and subsequently reported in the scientific literature by Pep Wheeler (1935, 1938, 1958). Sightings had been confined, however, to the immediate environs of Indian House Lake and no attempt had been made to assess their significance. Furthermore, they were not shown on the air photo interpretation maps of Tuzo Wilson and Ken Hare. Consequently, their absence from the new *Glacial Map of Canada* left a seriously flawed view of the deglaciation of the eastern Canadian Arctic and Subarctic.

The enormous extent to the glacial lake shorelines and their multiple levels were of great significance in any attempt to understand the pattern of disintegration of the last great ice sheet across Labrador-Ungava. Most important was the unavoidable conclusion that a large mass of ice must have blocked Ungava Bay until long after the Torngat Mountains and the Nain Plateau had become ice-free. To trace the positions of the former ice dams capable of holding up a succession of such large lakes and to date that process became fascinating scientific objectives for years to come. And where were the overflow channels of the various lakes located? Given our provisionally calculated tilt of the N-2 shoreline up toward the south and the realization that the direction of maximum tilt would probably be to the southwest or south-southwest, we could at least make tentative projections and so conclude that the prominent terrace above and south of Whitegull Lake (Lac aux Goélands), more than 50 mi (80 km) farther south, was most likely part of the N-2 system.

Similarly, all three main terraces extended far beyond the northern end of Indian House Lake at least as far downstream as the Pyramid Hills over 50 mi (80 km) farther north (see Plate 14 and photo on page 91). The next important steps for future field seasons would be an investigation of the Pyramid Hills and Whitegull Lake areas, and an attempt to complete an east-west profile from the vicinity of Wedge Point or the weather station so that the relationship between the Naskaupi and McLean lakes could be determined. This should provide the actual direction and amount of maximum tilt and so facilitate construction of isobases[38] (see appendix IV). Our 1958 reconnaissance also prompted the need to search for glacial lake shorelines in other parts of Labrador-Ungava, for instance, along the north side of the Laurentian escarpment in the south and in the northwest Ungava Peninsula south of Hudson Strait. The seven weeks

The Pyramid Hills section of the George River Valley was Mike Matthew's (Lab 1959–1960) field area in the summer of 1960. This view from the Beaver floatplane shows the landscape and extension of the glacial lake shorelines for at least 60 mi (96 km) north of Indian House Lake. August 1978.

on Indian House Lake clearly had set the stage for at least a half dozen master's thesis topics for future Lab staff.[39]

One of the more curious results of the Indian House Lake work arose from the Geography Department asking if I would agree to be interviewed by one of Montréal's French language newspapers. I was duly interviewed by a journalist working for *Le Devoir*. Naturally I dwelled on my excitement that we had discovered proof of such an extensive series of former lakes up to 700 ft (213 m) above the present lake level. My interviewer was conspicuously impressed. I did not realize how impressed he was until I read the subsequent headline: *"Monsieur et Madam Yves Découvrent l'Épreuve de la Deluge* (that is, proof of the Biblical Flood) *dans Nouveau Québec."*

A good solid mix of geomorphology, history, and religion!

Helluva Lake, 1958

We returned to the Lab from Indian House Lake on 17 August 1958. George and Margaret Michie were ready to head south, and we bade farewell and expressed thanks for their having facilitated our escape to Indian House Lake. Lab summer research activities had expanded once again and the small cottage adjacent to the Macnab homestead had accommodated a succession of summer graduate student visitors. Don Macnab had done a first-class job in maintaining the weather schedule, giving me confidence that I could leave him in charge while I undertook another field trip. I chartered a pontoon plane, again using the financial support of the federal Geographical Branch, to take us for twenty-two days' camping on Helluva Lake some 50 mi (80 km) to the north.

Glacial drainage channels north of Helluva Lake, twenty years after Pauline and I completed a ground survey. Individual channels were found to be more than 60 ft (20 m) deep. From the air, their form is accentuated by variation in vegetation cover. August 1978.

Helluva Lake is about 20 mi (32 km) north of the area I had named the Kivivic Ice Divide based on field reconnaissance in 1955.[40] Since Helluva Lake was set in the midst of hundreds of north-sloping glacial drainage channels, it was an ideal location for carrying the 1955 work a step further. The three weeks on the lake would be our first opportunity for detailed investigation of these diagnostic glacial landforms (see appendix I).

The only pontoon plane available at the Knob Lake seaplane base on Pearce Lake was a Norseman. Since its capacity was much in excess of our needs, I invited Erik Mortensen and Tony Williamson to accompany us. This would give Erik an opportunity to extend his forest ecology studies much farther north. Tony, one of the last of the previous winter's Lab staff to stay on during the summer, was game to join us simply for the adventure. They planned to stay with us for nine or ten days and then walk out the 50-odd mi (80 km) to the Lab. From our point of view, this ensured a strong field group and provided us with two enthusiastic wilderness companions.

The Helluva Lake venture, although brief compared with our Torngat and Indian House Lake exploits, proved highly rewarding and most enjoyable. The actual fieldwork added greatly to our understanding of the history of the final disintegration of the Laurentide Ice Sheet. In particular, we were able to determine that the majority of the glacial drainage channels had been formed by meltwaters that had flowed directly underneath the remnant ice masses that sloped down toward the north, rather than between ice lobe margins and the adjacent hillsides. This added critical weight to our 1955 hypothesis that remnant Laurentide ice had persisted in central Labrador-Ungava long after the conventional "end" of the ice ages and that it had become climatically dead and, therefore, stagnant, with no significant motion. Furthermore, we made a unique find (for its time) of a peat bog above the local alpine treeline on the hill near our base camp. It contained embedded fossil spruce logs. Years later log samples were radiocarbon dated as about four thousand years old and indicated that a climate warmer than the 1950s had dominated central Labrador-Ungava at that time.

Our Helluva Lake base camp was close to the water's edge in a stand of large spruce trees. It afforded welcome shelter, now that a series of nocturnal frosts had brought the mosquito season to an end. And the nearby timber allowed Erik to display his forester prowess by providing abundant firewood. Thus our evenings were enlivened by discussion and storytelling warmed by a cheerful log fire.

We made only one distant excursion with our two small mountain tents. We established camp among the higher hills some 10 mi (16 km) north just before the onset of heavy rains. Dinner for the four of us in our small tent was certainly a cramped yet warm experience. Tony and Erik, well fed, eventually left us through the rain and in the dark for their own tent. We decided to scatter the utensils outside for the downpour to wash. The rain turned to snow in the early hours and, half-awakened, I remembered a strange swishing sound and the tent canvass pressing on my face. The bright morning sunlight brought us to life. Pushing my nose out of the tent, I was dazzled by the brightness and realized that knives, forks, spoons, and all accoutrements had disappeared beneath a frozen white surface. We ate breakfast as we warmed our very cold fingers on the Primus stove.

During the daily traversing through our field area, we came upon a chance meeting, much to our surprise, with Ed Derbyshire and his field assistant, hardly routine in this remote area.[41] We were able to have a full discussion in the very center of our field research area (Ives 1959b; Derbyshire 1960, 1962).

We retreated from the snowy hilltops to our comfortable base on Helluva Lake and, a few days later, Erik and Tony prepared for their long walk back to the Lab. We were sorry to see them go, although they were keen to find their own way back and not depend on the Norseman. This left Pauline and me with the remaining days to complete the precise leveling of two large sets of glacial drainage channels. Fall was clearly upon us. Night frosts occurred regularly. The birch and willow shrub was in bright color, contrasting with the almost black of the spruce. These were some of the most beautiful days and twilights of our wilderness camping: color, quiet, no insects, silence save for the crackle of the remainder of Erik's logs on our campfire. Nevertheless, we welcomed a clear morning for the scheduled pickup by the Norseman and we were home for lunch. This short field investigation was yet another demonstration of the value of a permanent research facility in the center of the Labrador-Ungava wilderness. We were able to extend our field efforts to the maximum with the knowledge that a quick return to home comfort was on call—but not literally, as we were still operating without radio contact.

Fall 1958: An Appraisal

The first four years of Lab operation had been completed and it was time to assess progress. By the beginning of my second year as field director, a pattern of routine activities had been set in motion that were maintained for many subsequent years. Norman Drummond had brought the operation to full maturity during his three-year directorship. There were now two main buildings, a large garage, two small cottages (one for summer student visitors, the other for the Macnab family, with baby John to join us early in 1959). The weather observation program was running like clockwork and we were receiving high performance ratings from DOT. This was critical because it was our financial

A perfect fall afternoon north of Helluva Lake. The low birch has taken on a striking color, causing the scattered spruce to appear almost black. September 1958.

lifeline. The weather observer team had been increased from four to six; Ken Hare's original stipulation that a heavy winter routine of observations would be an advantage rather than a burden for the graduate students was proving correct.[42] Svenn Orvig's local microclimatological research was beginning to flourish, while a small number of graduate students were acquiring modest research grants that enabled them to conduct fieldwork based on the Lab. My own push for far-flung field research to unravel the glacial history of Labrador-Ungava was well underway. Ken and Svenn seemed to have no trouble finding satisfactory summer student weather observers, critical for ensuring that the previous winter graduates had released time for their thesis research.

Relations with the IOCC could not have been better, and Dick Geren, the senior IOCC officer, had become an active father figure, so that company assistance in many areas was freely provided. The RCAF station, the Mid-Canada Radar Defense line, and BRINEX aided enormously, especially in helping place small Lab parties into distant locations, as far afield as the Torngats and Kaumajet mountains. Finally, the Geographical Branch had begun to provide vital support for my fieldwork on Indian House and Helluva lakes.

It followed that the Lab had something worthwhile to offer in return, aside from its primary official function as a first-order weather station within national and international networks. Norm had established a pattern of preparing monthly

Erik Mortensen and his instrument tower for microecological studies of white spruce in the Knob Lake area. July 1958.

climatic summaries for widespread distribution, both to our official contacts, and also to all individuals in the town who were interested. Given the severe nature of the local climate to which most town residents were unaccustomed, this proved a service much in demand. Roger Barry and Don Macnab had greatly augmented the monthly report, adding to its popularity. They also had organized specialized weather forecasts in response to IOCC requests. For instance, would tomorrow's temperature be safe for pouring tons of cement? Such forecasting was always risky, but the involvement of highly competent weather observers ensured a remarkable and much appreciated degree of success.

In addition to the Lab's direct contributions to the IOCC and the Knob Lake community (that is, more or less official), the Lab staff made important contributions to the social aspects of this very isolated township.

From the beginning, the recruitment of graduate students for the winter appointments had been based on an assumption that they would be master's-level graduates; that they would be able to save enough of their winter salaries to finance a second, final, year in Montréal for completion of their theses. However, there was no direct funding available for the intervening summer's fieldwork. In the spring of 1958 I had personally received an inquiry from a Norwegian, Olav Løken, who was completing his cand. real. degree (MS equivalent) in Oslo after a year in the Antarctic. He had also written to the Geography Department in Montréal. Ken and Svenn thought he was too senior for the Lab and should accept a McGill-Carnegie-Arctic scholarship and begin a doctoral program with them. I strongly disagreed. The ensuing contretemps was resolved by a compromise: Olav should make his own choice. He chose Knob Lake and I saw this as a great step forward for the Lab. It also heralded a change in the manner of selecting future winter staff, giving the field director a decisive role. It also led to a lifelong family friendship.

The operations of the Lab were becoming widely known and my own publications were encouraging an increasing number of inquiries, so that it became possible to have potential field research topics discussed prior to the arrival of new staff members. Thus the incoming students were well prepared on arrival at the Lab and facilitated the otherwise almost impossible task of making the fall deadlines for research grant application: for instance, to the AINA Banting Fund, the deadline for which had been advanced from its previous January date. In Olav's case it was certainly a tight squeeze for him to complete a detailed application for research in the Torngat Mountains within a few weeks of his arrival.[43]

The recruitment of the 1958–1959 winter staff, therefore, marked a significant change. The summer student replacements were appointed by the Geography Department. I felt strongly, however, that the field director should have a major say in the selection of a group of individuals who were to live and work at the Lab in very close quarters for the best part of a year. The majority of the winter staff continued to be students who worked for their master's degrees, but the selection process now tended to perpetuate and extend my own field program design. This assessment was subsequently confirmed by Peter Adams, the Lab's fourth field director (Adams 2007).

A further problem in support of such a field program remained to be solved: direct Lab access to at least a modest level of financial support. The need was partly met in a somewhat unorthodox manner. Our highly efficient, if formidable, departmental secretary in Montréal, Martha Mount, had complained that my intricate accounting of the 1957–1958 Lab operating expenses had proved too detailed (tedious) for the McGill Finance Department. Told that I was spending too much time on the minutiae of accounting induced me to devote a lot of entrepreneurial energy to raising funds locally and accounting for it locally. First, I opened an account in the name of the Lab with our local branch of the Imperial Bank of Commerce. Don Macnab and I served as the signing officers. Next I sold to the DOT radio crew the Eliason motor toboggan that had stood idle for over two years and banked the proceeds. I also began to rent out the second small cabin to local workers who could not obtain married accommodation. (The cottage had become vacant for the winter once our summer research visitors had left us.) Given the high salaries associated with the mines and the absence of rental accommodation, this provided a lucrative source of funding.

Next I sought an interview with Dick Geren, the senior IOCC officer. He gave me a good hearing and then asked: "How much?" to which I replied "Could we expect $1,000 a year?" He called in his chief accountant and had a check drawn and signed immediately. He then teased me by saying that I had been too modest. He would not increase the amount, however, and insisted it was a good lesson for me. Nor would he have the check written out to the Lab—it had to go out to McGill. Nevertheless, he told me to let him know if the Lab did not receive every penny. Subsequently, this proved good intuitive advice; Dick Geren had to telephone McGill's accounts office to insist that the entire sum was intended for the Lab's fieldwork.

With the growth of the Lab bank account and the IOCC gift of $1,000 per year, we were able to make direct purchases of equipment as well as subsidize pontoon aircraft charters. What is remarkable, in retrospect, is that I was able to accomplish such a piece of creative financing of field research. I had the good sense to continue my inclination for precise accounting and obtained statements signed by the bank manager. It was only some years after I had left Knob Lake that I learned my reputation for innovative fund-raising was not entirely appreciated in Montréal.

A further step involved my growing relationship with Université Laval (Québec City). Professors Pierre Camu and Louis-Edmond Hamelin had invited me to lecture at Laval on the work of the Lab; because of my linguistic failings, this was, somewhat embarrassingly, in English. Despite this, I was able to negotiate an understanding that one of our four Lab winter positions would be allocated to a qualified Laval student. Ken Hare heartily agreed. Camille Roy was the first to benefit from this arrangement (1959–1960), and André Grenier spent the 1959 summer with us to be groomed for the 1960–1961 winter crew.[44] This small influx of French Canadians offset the otherwise total absence of Canadian applicants after the first winter; all the others, with the exception of Tony Williamson from Dartmouth College, NH, came from the far side of the Atlantic.

The Lab in 1958–1959

The combined welcome of the new winter crew (Olav Løken, Roger Kirby, Ray Holt, and John Welsted) and send-off for the previous group was an enjoyable time. At least a few days' overlap was possible with members of the out-going group. Nevertheless, Don and Jean Macnab helped Pauline and me to provide a substantial sense of continuity. Roger and Jocelyn Tomlinson made their way directly back to the Lab from the Kaumajet Mountains and were able to spend a few days with us before continuing to Montréal. I was pleased to meet Jocelyn again after her summer in the wilderness, another example of a young woman who had not only survived a season in rugged isolation but had enjoyed

The 1958–1959 Lab staff. From the left: Roger Kirby, Olav Løken, Jack, John Welsted, Ray Holt. Don Macnab was not available. June 1959.

it. Tony Williamson was the last of my first year's crew to leave. He effected a special good-bye. His final words, with his now characteristic poker face: "If it's a boy, call him Tony after me." Our daughter Nadine's arrival the following early March spoiled the joke, but she acquired a younger brother two years later in Ottawa. He was destined to receive the name Anthony "Tony" Ragnar, after my close undergraduate colleague, Tony Prosser, and my Icelandic farmer friend, Ragnar Stefansson. The laugh was finally on Tony Williamson as we surprised him with a three-month-old namesake when he visited us in our Ottawa home.

The settling-in process for the 1958–1959 winter was routine now, for the Macnabs and Iveses were old hands. The extracurricular activities expanded, especially the snow studies and lake ice work, when the National Research Council's (NRC's) Division of Building Research became closely involved. Ever since my first 1955 acquaintance with the area, I had been intrigued by a number of local semipermanent snow patches (almost tiny glaciers) that I had recorded photographically. These were possible indications of the proximity of the area to glacierization, a proposition nurtured by Gordon Manley, Pauline's London University professor. He had compiled a record of the semipermanent snow patches in the northern Pennines and Cross Fell, England, and encouraged me to make the same approach. Our nearest and most accessible snow patch was located about 15 mi (24 km) north in a feature eponymously known as Snowy Channel. By January 1959, it was already receiving a considerable new increment, mainly by winddrift. The RCAF helped with a helicopter lift so that we were able to spend most of a day digging a long shaft through the snowbank to its base. Although the air temperature was below −25°F (−32°C) it was satisfying for me to record that the base of the snowbank was at the freezing-melting point.

During the winter of 1958–1959 the senior pit foreman at the Ferriman Mine was David Selleck, one of our close friends. Ferriman was notorious for its extensive permafrost with high ice content that created considerable operational difficulties. Frozen ore was generally blasted by using about three times the normal amount of explosives. But David had to deal with a regular series of excessive explosions that threw rocks far and wide, parts of the pit face responding as if they were not frozen. It was a serious hazard to both workers and equipment. David had the ingenuity to make a rough map of the location of the apparently unfrozen sections. From his map it was possible to define a series of narrow alignments that sloped obliquely downhill. I asked to see the IOCC air photographs of the original hill slope taken before the surface had been completely chewed up by mining operations that had included stripping off all the overburden. The air photographs clearly showed a series of glacial drainage channels that would certainly have filled with snow each winter. Hence, for some depth beneath them, the ground containing the ore would have been insulated and, I presumed, may have remained unfrozen. After some discussion, David was able to predict where to modify the quantity of explosives that he had to place in drill holes behind the working pit face.

This achievement led to another interview with IOCC chief Dick Geren. Would the company finance a renewal of the early reconnaissance permafrost research project?[45] Dick Geren's reaction to my opening request was, "Jack, why should I spend company money on an academic exercise when we already know that where the ore is frozen we simply load with more high explosive?" I responded with two arguments: first, how to account for the erratic rock bursts at Ferriman and how to predict future occurrences. Second, if the IOCC received a late-summer rush order for extra ore,[46] would he not prefer a reasonable estimate that unopened ore bodies could be placed in one of three categories: definitely frozen, condition uncertain, or definitely unfrozen? He granted me both points and agreed to authorize the drilling of holes the following summer so that I could insert additional sets of thermocouples since most of the original instrumentation had been obliterated as the mining had extended. Next he reminded me how I had asked for too little money on my previous visit. He said he had checked with McGill and found that my annual salary was the second lowest in town (after that of the Anglican priest). He insisted that, if I would take on the study, he would pay me the equivalent of six weeks' salary commensurate with my academic qualifications and residence in Schefferville. (Knob Lake had been incorporated as a Canadian town.) Together with Ben Bonnlander's earlier work (Bonnlander and Major-Marothy 1964) this led to a long-term project for the Lab. It also cemented links with the Division of Building Research of the NRC. Staff members Drs. Lorne Gold, Roger Brown, and Peter Williams became regular visitors to the Lab, lifelong colleagues, and family friends.

As winter progressed and Pauline's pregnancy advanced, I realized that life was about to change for us. We were both very fit, especially after the previous summer's rather vigorous fieldwork. Pauline, however, was so fit she was feeling somewhat "guilty"; she experienced little discomfort compared with the experience of two of our pregnant friends in town. She frequently walked the 2 mi (3 km) to and from the town post office in the late afternoons, regardless of the weather.

We had both read a revolutionary new book on natural childbirth by Dr. Grantly Dick-Read. The only doctor in town was the recently graduated French Canadian, Dr. Roy. He had never heard of natural childbirth and believed that women were best anesthetized at the time of delivery. The notion that fathers should be assistants at delivery was anathema. Thus some rather intense discussions arose. We insisted and Dr. Roy finally conceded. Once this point was passed, he proved a most helpful and supportive doctor.

At last March arrived, but still we were in the depth of a very cold winter. Stan, from the DOT radio crew, kindly offered to have on standby our old Eliason motor toboggan in case of a snowstorm at the critical moment, but he insisted that I would have to drive, as he would panic if labor were to begin en route to the hospital. Pauline and I eventually drove to the IOCC facility in the Lab Land Rover in the late afternoon, 4 March. The hospital was really a first-aid station for the miners, with Laundromat attached. In a tiny room, Pauline and I referred to our copy of Grantly Dick-Read as nature moved in its inevitable way. The nurse came in periodically—unilingual French, which was not ideal for our own limited French—and she chased me out of the room, as she felt it was not seemly for me to be present while she examined the mother-to-be.

Sometime after midnight the nurse urged me back to the Lab, suggesting there would be a very long wait so that I should not return until midmorning. I refused to leave and, shortly after, I had to make an emergency telephone call to a sleeping Dr. Roy. He was with us literally minutes later with a snowsuit over his pajamas. After what seemed like a few minutes, Dr. Roy, with my assistance, delivered a beautiful red-headed girl whom we named Nadine.

I went home exhausted, no doubt from overexcitement. The new mother fed Nadine and they both slept. Later, Pauline was awakened for breakfast and presented with a miner's cooked meal: a huge steak, two eggs, French fries, and onions. She decided she wasn't hungry! In the meantime I had returned to the Lab to find the sewer and water lines frozen and sewage backing up into our bathtub, followed by an urgent phone call to Dick Geren. It seemed that half of IOCC emergency equipment was on our doorstep within minutes. By the time I brought Pauline and Nadine home late that afternoon, everything was cleaned up. Nadine was the third baby to be born to Lab residents. John Macnab had preceded her by two weeks. Janet Drummond had been born two years earlier.

The winter proceeded with a mixture of routine and exceptional events. I became heavily involved in correspondence with potential members of the 1959–1960 winter crew. This time I successfully urged Ken and Svenn to have the new members come to the Lab shortly after arriving in Montréal instead, in my view, of sidetracking them to the McGill Geography Summer School at Stanstead in the Eastern Townships. This arrangement enabled the new arrivals to become better acquainted with the region around the Lab that would stand them in good stead for their following summer's fieldwork. In this way John Andrews, Brian Haywood, and Mike Matthew arrived at various times during July and early August, while Camille Roy worked with me for a large part of the summer. André Grenier, who had already been selected for the 1960–1961 winter, was scheduled to be at the Lab for the full 1959 summer, working on Svenn's microclimatology research (Orvig 1961).

Next there occurred a surprise: an unannounced visit from a senior DOT meteorologist (G. Salmon). He spent a week investigating our entire weather-observing operations, even staff rapport. This inspection was conducted in a most friendly manner, but it was officially precise and very exacting; I began to suspect that it was more than a routine examination. On the fifth day he requested a private interview. He told me, in the strictest confidence, that his visit was by no means routine but a response to a serious complaint that had impugned our performance. In fact, he was breaking all the rules in explaining to me the purpose of his visit because of the obvious legal implications. Nevertheless, he felt he should do this because he had been so impressed with every member of our team and the overall performance.

The inspection had been prompted by a complaint to DOT headquarters made by a Hollinger-Ungava DC-4 pilot. He had been forced to abort a flight from Sept-Îles to Schefferville because of icing conditions and had claimed that inaccurate Lab weather reports had been the cause, resulting in almost 700 mi (1,126 km) of wasted flight and a dangerous return landing on nearly empty fuel tanks.

A few months previously Québecair had begun a three times weekly commercial passenger service connecting Schefferville with Montréal, Québec City, Mont Joli, Rimouski, Rivière-de-Loup, and Sept-Îles. The airline used a Fokker-Fairchild turbo-prop that had much shorter landing and takeoff capabilities and so could effect safe landings in moderate icing conditions. The DC-4 had to make a much longer and shallower approach and was thus much more susceptible to icing. The Hollinger-Ungava crews had developed a sense of competition with Québecair. The complaint, as concluded by Inspector Salmon, was the result of the DC-4 pilot's face-saving gesture after being heavily teased for his failed bravado; our records showed that we had reported moderate icing conditions at low altitudes. Mr. Salmon assured me that his report would place our overall performance in the 100 percent category, a welcome outcome from what could have been a messy situation.

The one highly amusing and very personal episode of the winter is recounted here as a tale with a moral—to the effect that special care needs to be taken when adding insulation to the outer walls of buildings in cold climates. Roger Kirby's bed-study was on the northwest corner of the main building. He had commented that he had acquired the coldest room in the building, probably because the prevailing winter wind was from the northwest. One morning in the depth of winter he was late for his 8 a.m. weather shift. This was so unusual that one of the others tapped on his door and reported that he thought he could hear faint cries for help. I had just come into the weather room. What to do? Force the door! Immediately! So we did. There was Roger in bed in his sleeping bag with a pile of blankets thrown over him. He was frozen to the outer wall. It had been an especially cold night. Roger's breath had condensed on his sleeping bag zipper and the adjacent wall, frozen, and had imprisoned him solidly. He was pried loose with an ice ax and the zipper released by pouring hot water on it.

I retold this story to Bill Mattox some years later when he had replaced me as field director. He told me that he had had occasion to tear off a piece of the wall paneling during redecoration of Roger's former room. There he found a large gap where a section of insulation had been forgotten by the original construction worker.

By late May we had come to believe that there would be summer that year after all; the ice on our local lakes was beginning to break up and most of the snow across the town had melted. Nadine and John were growing fast and were very active, changing the entire social atmosphere of the Lab: there was an oversupply of enthusiastic babysitters.

Then came startling news. The fame of the iron ore mines in the Labrador-Ungava wilderness had reached the highest levels. We were to be favored with a royal visit. Her Majesty Queen Elizabeth II and His Royal Highness Prince Philip were including Schefferville in their cross-Canada tour.[47] Their plane landed in early June on the warmest day of the year, an exceptional 82°F (28°C). The Girl Guides were in heavy demand because of the general shortage of welcoming committees; in fact, Jean Amor and Pauline had to ferry them by the Lab Land Rover for three separate appearances. The royal day was clear and calm so that there was little possibility of the Queen's pale-blue suit becoming red from windblown iron ore dust. We were able to take closeup photographs. Prince Philip paid special attention to the young Naskaupi women and chucked the chins of several dark-skinned babies.

The main impact of Nadine's arrival for me was that I lost my precious field assistant to motherhood. However, the IOCC permafrost investigation and close involvement with the overlapping of the 1958–1959 and 1959–1960 winter crews made sure that I was not idle for long. In fact, the 1959 summer became the first "home residential" summer for me in nine years.

Much of June and July, therefore, involved working in Buzz Neal's IOCC lab preparing a series of eleven thermocouple strings, planning the locations of the same number of drill sites, and finally inserting the thermocouples as the diamond drilling was completed for each drill hole. I selected a large tract including the Ferriman mine site and the area surrounding it up to the high western ridge crest. It contained a full range of vegetation types, altitudes

Ferriman open pit mine during the discharge of a round of high explosives to facilitate excavation of iron ore in permafrost terrain. July 1959.

ranging from about 2,200 ft (671 m) to 2,750 ft (838 m), and sites that would be windswept, as well as intermediate and maximum snow accumulation sites. Drill holes varied between 50 ft (15 m) and 185 ft (56 m), irregular because of difficulties of drilling at depth. Small unheated wooden shacks were built and anchored downwind of each site to ensure a degree of shelter while reading the thermocouples during the coming winter. Two climate stations were also set up, one close to the Ferriman mine dry, the other at the highest altitude (2,750 ft, 838 m) on the western ridge. These were intended to establish a relationship with the readings from the Lab's main weather station at 1,665 ft (507 m) above sea level. The mean annual temperature at the Lab, based on ten years of observations, was 23.8°F (−4.6°C), which itself indicated a thermal climate close to the limit of permafrost occurrence, so a comparison with the situation on the highest nearby ridges would be most useful.[48] The next steps were to undertake detailed mapping of the vegetation of the chosen study site, and the pattern of snow accumulation during the following winter. Camille Roy was attracted to this aspect of the project as a good base for his proposed study for a Laval master's degree.[49]

Considerable difficulties were encountered with the thermocouple installation, although working with the drill crew was an enjoyable, if arduous, experience. Although I considered myself very fit, I was no match for a work crew accustomed to prolonged physical labor, and there was a good deal of friendly joking, usually at my expense. Most of the thermocouple strings had been

Ferriman Ridge, the highest land near the Lab. This is the site of the highest drill site for the installation of thermocouples. The small shack is to protect the winter observer from freezing. The light-toned surfaces (windswept tundra) are underlain by permafrost at least 200 ft (65 m) thick. Note the few outlying dwarf spruce trees and the darker-toned areas (dwarf willow and birch) that are winter snow accumulation sites and hence underlain by much thinner permafrost. July 1959.

installed by early August, although the final one was inserted late in the season when the ground was already white.

In anticipation of winter recording difficulties—especially making bare wire connections between the Wheatstone Bridge and the large number of thermocouples—the IOCC ordered twelve rotary switches. If these could be installed before the cold weather arrived, the thermocouple readings for each separate installation could be determined by the simple turn of a large rubberized switch using a gloved hand. Unfortunately, delivery was delayed. In effect, I received a New Year's present in the form of the twelve rotary switches. But they still had to be installed. Thus, in very low temperatures I had to make all the wire connections to the individual switches with bare hands and a screwdriver. This proved so tricky that I resorted to licking the tip of my right index finger, freezing each small screw to it in turn and thereby inventing a human screwdriver. I did lose a certain amount of fingertip: only skin. The winter observation program proved quite an adventure and the mountain snowshoes supplied by the Naskaupi, which allowed me to kick steps in steep snow slopes, proved a great help.

The advantage of having the 1959–1960 winter crew arrive early was well demonstrated. Camille had half the fieldwork for his degree completed by using the breaks in his summer round of eight-hour weather duty shifts. The second Laval student, André Grenier, selected for the following year, arrived for the 1959 summer. This enabled him to become acquainted with Brian Haywood and, by the end of the summer, it was decided that he would join Brian as his assistant in a canoe traverse along the Koroksoak River in the far northeast (but see pp. 112–125).

Arve Fiskerstrand arrived from Norway, ready to serve as Olav's assistant in the Torngat Mountains. Yet we still had time to look over the nearby glacial features before their departure. In doing so we encountered a formidable forest fire. It caused considerable excitement and we attempted to obtain impressive photographs (see Plate 15). We returned to the Lab with burn holes in our shirts. Olav and Arve left for the Labrador coast by air along the Mid-Canada line to Hopedale, where they were welcomed by BRINEX staff, who flew them to the Torngats north of Kangalaksiorvik Lake.

Roger Kirby worked on the glacial geomorphology of the local area, studying glacial till fabrics, which dovetailed beautifully with the ongoing work on the glacial drainage channels. He was able to take a respite of ten days and accompany Brian Haywood and me to Churchill Falls. This was something of a grand adventure. We took the Lab Land Rover down on the train, strapped on a flatcar. At mile 286 I had an anxious moment driving it off over a loose pile of spruce logs stacked up against the side of the flatcar, because there were no unloading facilities. We were then on the access trail to Grand Falls (Churchill Falls), mostly along the crests of eskers. We had an unusual four-wheel-drive tour to one of the world's most spectacular and inaccessible waterfalls, shortly facing obliteration in the interests of hydropower. We viewed the falls both from the lip of the cascade and from below on the far side of the Bowdoin Canyon. We nevertheless encountered the problems of foot travel through trackless forest and muskeg country. Local deposits of magnetite made our compasses useless, and in cloudy weather we were deprived of aid from the sun for navigation. This was my nearest ever to becoming lost in the bush. We arrived back at our tents well after midnight.

Ray Holt left us early in the summer for an appointment teaching high school in southern Ontario. John Welsted also left early, although he remained in Québec Province—he made a geomorphological study of the extensive Natashquan sand terrace on the St. Lawrence North Shore east of Sept-Îles. From there he continued to McGill, where he completed his master's thesis in the following academic year.

An August 1959, view of Grand Falls (Churchill Falls) on the Hamilton (Churchill) River. Today this impressive waterfall has been reduced to a trickle and the great lake, Michikamau, has been enlarged threefold to become Smallwood Reservoir, in response to North American demands for electrical energy.

A major change for my final winter as field director was the departure of the Macnab family. Don had indicated, after John's birth, that it was time to look for a permanent position in the "sunny" United Kingdom. This set in motion a lot of letter writing: applications by Don for various positions with the British Meteorological Office, my supporting letters of reference, and a search for his replacement, in addition to the responsibility of recruiting the entire 1959–1960 winter's crew.

We were all saddened by the departure of the Macnabs, because they had greatly strengthened the functioning of the Lab in every respect. Nevertheless, we were delighted to learn of Don's appointment to a weather station in the Channel Islands—a distinct change in climate from the Antarctic and the

Canadian Subarctic. A small number of applications arrived for Don's forthcoming vacancy as senior weather observer. One from Trinity College, Dublin, was both outstanding and unusual. Charles McCloughan was completing his BS in physics. His extremely wry letter attracted me immediately. Fortunately for the Lab, a "real Irish character" reached us in late August in time for an overlap with a "real Scottish character." Like Don, Charles quickly became a great team player and indispensable colleague.

The Lab in 1959–1960

I entered my final year as field director with a strong sense of confidence. For the first time the selection of the winter's crew had been largely on my own initiative: Charles McCloughan, Dublin; John Andrews, Nottingham; Brian Haywood, London; Mike Matthew, Cambridge; and Camille Roy, Laval. The 1959 field operations had been extremely successful. The new Laval connection appeared well established. And the permafrost project, reconstituted during the 1959 summer, promised a long-term future because the National Research Council had expressed interest in funding a full-time appointment for a senior research fellow. With Charles as senior weather observer and four graduate student observers, it enabled a schedule of four eight-hour shifts per week, backed by three for Charles and two for me. Thus, I was kept on my toes with this bread-and-butter operation, while gaining a generous amount of time for preparing reports for publication and maintaining the permafrost observation schedule.

The graduate students had ample time for expanding the special winter projects, reading, group discussion, and preparation for their forthcoming 1960 field research. Camille was able to undertake the winter task of regular snow depth measurements across the permafrost research test area, which I supplemented with bimonthly readings of the thermocouple installations. Brian invented an ingenious device to measure the surface heave that occurs each winter as the ground freezes, and its collapse and settlement during the following spring thaw. As each winter sets in, moisture in the ground is turned to ice and the increase in volume causes the surface to expand upward. The reverse occurs in the spring. Since the distribution of moisture in the soil is irregular, the surface movement is highly fragmented and presents a microgeomorphological problem. Brian's apparatus was nicknamed "Haywood's Bedstead" and modifications of it have been used in different mountain and arctic regions for many years (Andrews 1963a). John Andrews greatly extended the lake ice survey. He persuaded personnel at the various Mid-Canada radar sites to take regular measurements of ice thickness and send them into the Lab (Andrews and McCloughan 1961; Andrews 1962). The accumulated large data set led to a first approximation for predicting ice thickness and bearing strength on

Brian Haywood with his "bedstead" apparatus for measuring, point by point, ground heave as winter develops, and its collapse during the following spring and early summer. April 1960.

unvisited lakes as a means of aiding aircraft landings on skis.[50] Mike Matthew undertook an extensive air photo interpretation of the glacial features of the Pyramid Hills section of the lower George River. It became his area for field research the following summer and the basis for his master's degree.

The exceptional event of my final year at the Lab was the official visit to the IOCC on 6 September by Québec Premier Maurice Duplessis.[51] The major iron ore bodies were bisected by the Québec–Newfoundland border, making the calculation of provincial royalties a continual source of bickering between the premier and IOCC. His visit, with a party of his aides, induced a very tense atmosphere. This became supercharged when he suffered a serious heart attack during intensive negotiations. He received emergency medical attention in the IOCC guest house. All telephone lines with the outside were placed under strict control. The press corps attending the premier's visit quickly discovered that the Lab's telephone was the only unrestricted one in town. Some news had reached the outside because, that evening, we received numerous calls from the Montréal and Québec news media. My response was that I had nothing to report, which was true enough. I also denied requests for access to the Lab and our apartment phone by several members of the press corps. Later in the evening, information was leaked to us by IOCC friends that the premier had died.[52]

But to return to reality. The constant interchange of ideas among the Schefferville group and with former personnel who were in Montréal writing their theses led to John Andrews's selection of an area of the Labrador coast south of Roger Tomlinson's 1958 field area. Brian Haywood decided to work with André Grenier along the Koroksoak River between Ungava Bay and my 1957 research area in the southern Torngats. Olav Løken, in Montréal, was preparing for a second season in the Torngats with his new wife, Inger Marie (Løken 1962a, 1962b).

The 1960 International Geographical Congress (IGC), held in Stockholm, provided a focus for my plans. Professor Gunnar Hoppe was one of the main congress organizers. His research on the glaciation and deglaciation of arctic Norway and Sweden had given me many ideas for application to Labrador-Ungava. A major attraction, therefore, was the opportunity to join Hoppe's IGC excursion to the Abisko-Narvik area of northern Scandinavia.[53] And I was invited to give a paper in Stockholm on research across the Labrador-Ungava peninsula, the first occasion for such a presentation on the work of the Lab (Ives 1960b) at an international conference.[54] My appointment was until the end of August 1960, and I was to be introduced in Stockholm and Abisko as the Lab field director. Even so, my application to McGill University for assistance to attend the conference was rejected.

The base camp of Olav and Inger Marie Løken at the head of Eclipse Channel in the northern Torngat Mountains (photograph courtesy of Olav Løken). 14 July 1960.

View to the north across Upper Kangalaksiorvik Lake into Olav Løken's 1959 field area, Torngat Mountains. 1 August 1956.

With the Labrador-Ungava field program continuing to gather momentum, I had expressed to Ken Hare my willingness to stay on at the Lab for a fourth year, especially since no moves had been made to recruit a successor. He gently refused, explaining that the three-year term had been set to make sure that appointees did not become totally isolated in a subarctic wilderness setting and so lose touch with developing university affairs. He followed up by inviting me to accept the original offer of the tenure-track assistant professorship in the McGill Geography Department made at the time of my appointment to the Lab. Pauline and I felt that Montréal was not an ideal place for our vision of young family life. So I applied for positions at other institutions. Nevertheless, it was my earlier contact with Dr. Norman Nicholson, director of the Geographical Branch in Ottawa, that set my career course. The prospect of appointment as the assistant director of the Geographical Branch and chief of its Division of Physical Geography was altogether unexpected. In accepting I was even able to negotiate a series of expeditions to Baffin Island and continued support for the glacial geomorphological studies of Lab graduates across Labrador-Ungava. This would allow a considerable expansion of my original Labrador-Ungava program to embrace Baffin Island. It would also set up a flow of recruits for the planned Baffin Island expeditions as Lab students completed their McGill master's theses (and one doctorate—see below), and the possibility of permanent positions with the federal government for some of them.

Despite the sense of euphoria that the research momentum created, I felt a cloud forming over my relations with McGill. To my surprise, Pat Baird returned to Canada after five years on the faculty of Aberdeen University, Scotland. To facilitate this, Ken had patched together a position for him as director of field studies, and thus he became my immediate boss. From the beginning, this appointment of a remarkably uncommunicative arctic expert left me feeling uneasy. As the winter progressed, despite a trip out to Montréal to facilitate communication, my first impressions from Pat's visit to the Lab in September 1957 were reinforced. The ordering of essential Lab supplies, field equipment for the coming summer, and attempts at general coordination seemed to elicit little, or no, response from Pat. For the first time I felt that the Lab successes were being achieved in a vacuum. So I devoted myself to the permafrost research, to the planning of three graduate student expeditions to far-flung parts of Labrador-Ungava, and to a joyful home scene with a now extremely mobile infant. I was also much involved with the recruitment of the following winter's Lab crew, since no action appeared to have been taken to find a replacement for me, and Pat's attitude seemed to imply that it was not his concern. Thus, yet another group of young graduates was selected with the prospect that they would participate in research objectives that I had iden-tified. This would undoubtedly leave my successor, when he was eventually appointed, with reduced opportunity to extend his own research.

I resigned from my position with McGill effective the end of August and prepared for departure to England and Stockholm via Montréal. Apart from summer fieldwork, I had had no vacation since my arrival at the Lab three years previously, although I must admit that those early years of travel with Pauline into the distant parts of Labrador-Ungava were some of the finest "holidays" of my life.

Nadine was about to experience her first transatlantic flight and a visit to her grandparents, and I was to undergo my first significant separation from both Pauline and Nadine whilst in Sweden and Norway. I worked hard with a highly efficient and understanding colleague, Charles McCloughan, in making sure he was in as strong a position as possible to carry on with the essential Lab operations. Somewhat by default he became the acting field director following our departure. We bade farewell to the Lab and all our friends in late June with very mixed feelings. This also left Charles with heavy responsibilities, not only with the climatological operation, which I was confident he could handle easily, but also as the contact person for the various field parties and the severe dif-ficulties that were to follow.

The 1959–1960 Lab staff. From left: Camille Roy, John Andrews, Brian Haywood, Jack, Charles McCloughan, Mike Matthew. June 1960.

Death on the Koroksoak: Northeast Nouveau Québec, 1960

In early summer 1960, Pauline and I had completed our third winter in residence at the Lab. I had been confirmed in my new position with the Geographical Branch, Canadian Department of Mines and Technical Surveys, to begin on 1 September. We would leave Schefferville in late June for England, and I would attend the Stockholm 1960 International Geographical Congress, which included long field excursions in arctic Sweden and western Norway. During the 1960 summer the Lab field program was set to expand with an ambitious three-part campaign. It would be based on the planned research of Mike Matthew in the Pyramid Hills section of the George River, with Alan Strowger as his assistant; John Andrews and assistant Tim Fielding, who were to work between the Kiglapait and Kaumajet mountains on the Labrador coast; and Brian Haywood and André Grenier on the Koroksoak River. An important addition was Olav and Inger Marie Løken's extension of Olav's previous 1959 work in the Torngats north of Kangalaksiorvik Fiord. With the earlier work of Peter and Ellie Johnson in the Kiglapaits, Roger and Jocelyn Tomlinson in the Kaumajets, and Roger Kirby in the interior, this was set to result in a significant flowering of knowledge on the glaciation and deglaciation of Labrador-Ungava.

During the 1959 summer, Brian Haywood's excursion with Roger Kirby and me to Grand Falls (now Churchill Falls) had attested to his field skills, and through the following winter he had demonstrated his scholarly ingenuity. Round-faced and smiling, ruddy complexioned, inured to hardship, he had prepared for his research along the Koroksoak River with enthusiasm. André Grenier, the eldest of a large family from Québec City, was of *coureur de bois* stock, with a good deal of canoe experience in the Laurentian Mountains. They seemed like natural collaborators and, on meeting at the Lab the previous summer, they had enthusiastically agreed to work together. After the summer's fieldwork, Brian planned to return to Montréal to write up his results for a McGill master's degree. André was scheduled to overwinter at the Lab and prepare for his own fieldwork the following summer (1961).

Brian's study involved searching the valley of the lower Koroksoak for evidence of final (and earlier?) directions of ice movement. This would be followed by a traverse upstream as far as they could negotiate the river with their canoe, plus a possible short backpacking trip. Their overall objective was to ascertain the extent, and possible form, of the ice dams of the former glacial lakes that Pauline and I had discovered in 1957. I had discussed the prospects of such an excursion along the Koroksoak River with Dr. Jacques Rousseau, who had covered the same ground in 1947.

The extra funds I had raised the previous winter for the Lab field research were augmented by the Geographical Branch. All of this aided the provisioning and transport of the three research parties: essential field equipment and a chartered Canso flying boat to get them to their respective field areas and an agreement to pick them up the following mid-September. In addition, BRINEX, courtesy of its director, Dr. Paul Beavan, had agreed to provide a pontoon-equipped Beaver aircraft to take John Andrews and Tim Fielding up the coast from the Mid-Canada radar defense base at Hopedale and to collect them the following September.

Pauline and I, with Nadine, left Schefferville for Montréal with the sense that everything was in good order and that the Lab's affairs were expanding beyond our highest expectations of five years ago. In Montréal we were houseguests of Brian and Beryl Bird, then flew to England. I traveled to Sweden and Norway. Pauline and Nadine stayed in England with our families. Pauline joined me on a trip with Eilif Dahl and Peter and Kari Williams to western Norway during August.

It had been planned that the three graduate student two-man teams would leave for their field areas shortly after our departure. Mike and Alan, and Brian and André had a frustrating ten-day delay due to bad weather and the problem of finding a canoe that would fit inside the chartered Canso. John and Tim were initially delayed because of the canoe problem facing the others, but eventually flew independently with Mid-Canada Line assistance to Hopedale on the Labrador coast, from which point BRINEX flew them by Beaver to their field area north of Nain. The other two parties finally left Schefferville on 5 July. Mike and Alan were put down on a lake close to the lower George River in the Pyramid Hills section. The pilot then left Brian and André at the estuary of the Koroksoak River and returned to Schefferville. Both parties were to be retrieved by the same floatplane in mid-September.

Pauline, Nadine, and I returned to Canada in early September on the crest of a wave: a challenging new job, our first car to be shipped from England, and our first furniture (Swedish) en route on the Atlantic. The Swedish arctic excursion had sealed friendships with new colleagues—Gunnar Østrem, Gunnar Hoppe, Valter Schytt, Leszek Starkel, David Linton, Barry Bishop, Ronnie Peel, and Vaughan Lewis, among others. The Norwegian excursion to west Norway and the Rondane, which Pauline joined, cemented friendships with Eilif Dahl and Peter and Kari Williams. And all of this resulted in a further surge in enthusiasm for arctic fieldwork that influenced my career for many years to come. I had read my first paper, on the glaciation and deglaciation of Labrador-Ungava, at an International Geographical Congress. Over the coming winter I would be planning a series of expeditions to Baffin Island and assessing the results of the Labrador-Ungava fieldwork of the 1960 summer.

Within days of joining the staff of the Geographical Branch in Ottawa, I received a phone call from John Andrews in Montréal; he and Tim had been picked up as planned and were back at McGill, but he had heard that the charter aircraft sent to retrieve the other two parties had been unable to locate either.

At this point there was no reason for alarm, although there was certainly some apprehension. Charles McCloughan, acting field director of the Lab, however, had received a highly disturbing DOT teletype message from Fort Chimo (now Kuujjuaq). A canoe had been sighted, upside down and wedged between two large rocks, in rapids on the Koroksoak River. He phoned the Geography Department with this alarming news. I learned of this, in turn, by telephone from Ken Hare. He told me that Pat Baird was flying to Chimo to investigate. I immediately volunteered my services for a ground search. Ken asked me to wait for Pat Baird's report. Dr. Nicholson, my new boss at the Geographical Branch, granted my request for special leave to enable me to proceed to Chimo. He further proposed that he would support me by authorizing leave with pay. The Geographical Branch, on my request earlier in the year, had provided support for the Lab field research. This was done on the understanding that continued study of the glacial geomorphology of Labrador-Ungava was envisaged as part of the responsibilities of my new position.

On 14 September McGill received a report from the Department of Northern Affairs and National Resources (NANR). Personal belongings had been recovered over a distance of 35 mi (56 km) downstream of the wrecked canoe, together with a nearly illegible diary. This report was later found to be in error.

Pat Baird flew from Montréal to Chimo on 17 September, arriving at 4 p.m. He examined equipment brought in from the Koroksoak by the RCMP two days previously. This had been collected over a distance of 3 mi (5 km), not the previously reported 35 mi (56 km), below the canoe. It included clothing, boots, a .22 rifle, André's driver's licence and army identification card, and miscellaneous items. The diary was described as a series of loose pages, very difficult to read, although the last words, written on 12 August, were: *nous partons demain pour les rapides.* Curiously, all the equipment recovered belonged to André. Neither sleeping bags nor tent were found, nor anything belonging to Brian. This prompted my suspicion that Brian may not have been in the canoe. In fact, the mystery about his disappearance began to deepen from this point.

As I anxiously awaited more news of Brian and André, Ken Hare phoned me from Montréal. Pat Baird had completed a thorough search and indicated to the RCMP that presumption of death was unavoidable and that no further search should be undertaken. He had also drafted telegrams to the boys' parents stating that an accident had occurred and there was little chance of their survival. He would be returning to Montréal the next day.

I was shocked, especially when I realized that the search had been called off after what appeared to me as only a few hours of reconnaissance from the air. I questioned the decision and told Ken that I thought a proper ground search was imperative. Ken urged me to be patient until Pat returned to Montréal and had a chance to discuss his findings with the McGill authorities. He promised to phone me again within the next two days. My plea that precious time was being lost was disregarded, presumably in deference to Pat's formal presumption of death.

From this point the train of events became bewildering. I was told that the situation at Chimo was complicated by the fact that the RCMP was in the process of closing their station and handing over responsibility to the Québec Provincial Police. Two days later I also learned the details of Pat's mission to Chimo and the Koroksoak. Pat later sent me a copy of his report with a short cover letter dated 3 October 1960. The following section is based on this.

Weather had prevented flying the day after Pat's arrival at Chimo on 17 September. The Canso flying boat pilot, who had attempted to pick up both Mike's and Brian's parties on the twelfth, had drawn a blank in both instances. He had first flown to the Pyramid Hills area of the George River but failed to make contact with Mike and Alan. He reported that the ground had a light cover of snow and the only signs of life he could make out were caribou tracks. He had been unable to see a tent. He had then flown to the Koroksoak estuary, located Brian and André's base cache, seen no sign of life, and returned to Chimo.

Early on the next morning (6:50 a.m. on 19 September) Pat had flown with a chartered Beaver on pontoons to the Pyramid Hills area. Mike and Alan were easily located. They were picked up with all their equipment. Because this took up all available space, they were flown directly back to Chimo. Pat took off again at 12:45 p.m. with Mike. They first flew to the George River estuary and landed alongside a boat belonging to the NANR anchored just off the new Inuit community center. They were welcomed onboard by Capt. Max Budgell,[55] who was accompanied by Don Snowden, head of NANR Industrial Division, and George Koniak, an Inuit interpreter. They summoned aboard Stanley Ananek, another Inuit. Through the interpreter, they learned more about the discovery of the partially submerged canoe.

Stanley had spotted the canoe on 5 September, wedged between large rocks in midstream. He had proceeded upstream for 15 mi (24 km) to the confluence of Sukaliuk Brook and the main river. There he had found footprints and the remains of a campfire, but no further traces. He then walked back downstream to his camp at the river's mouth, keeping a sharp lookout for any signs of life.

Following this consultation, Pat and Mike reboarded the Beaver, persuading Stanley and George to accompany them. They headed for the accident site on the Koroksoak, flying directly overland in case a survivor had attempted to walk out from the rapids to the George River community center. All the rivers had been exceptionally high throughout the summer. From the air, the largest of them appeared to be unfordable.

Reaching the River Koroksoak at lat 58°38' N, long 65°15' W, they observed a series of rapids. Pat reported fast water between boulders with slight drops, although the rapids farthest upstream appeared much more turbulent—a chute over smooth rock with a total fall in elevation of about 15 ft (4.5 m) to 20 ft (6 m). The distance from the top of the chute to the point where Stanley had found the canoe was about 60 ft (18 m).

Following the aerial reconnaissance of the rapids they flew downstream some 300 ft (91 m) to 400 ft (122 m) above the level of the river, landing in a bay on the right bank at lat 58°48' N, long 65°41' W. Due to difficult beaching conditions (wind and a rocky shoreline) Pat alone went ashore and examined the site of the base cache. The cache, which contained a tide gauge, appeared neat and untouched, but there was no note.

They then flew a further 4 mi (6 km) downstream to Stanley's camp on the opposite side of the river where they left him. They immediately returned to the George River community center where they picked up Don Snowden and reached Chimo at 6:40 p.m.

Pat concluded that the likelihood of survival was zero. He had reasoned that if either or both Brian and André had survived the canoe spill unhurt, the 30-mile (48 km) walk to the Inuit camp or the 25-mile (40 km) walk on the opposite side of the river to their own cache would have been arduous, although not difficult. If injured they would surely have remained by the side of the river, where they would have been seen by Inuit who passed along the valley. Pat concluded that both had been drowned in the rapids. This concludes the section drawn from Pat Baird's written report.

The official search by Pat Baird on behalf of McGill University had been completed in a very perfunctory manner. The Beaver made two landings at the River George community center where a consultation took place, one landing at the site of Brian and André's base cache on the Koroksoak estuary, and one at Stanley's campsite. The amount of time spent actually searching took only minutes. On the other hand, Stanley had walked the length of the lower Koroksoak on 5 September between the Sukaluik Brook confluence 15 mi (24 km) upstream of the accident site and had then returned to his camp. There had also been two other flights along the river at about the same time. Nevertheless, none of Brian's possessions had been found, while numerous items belonging to André had been picked up from the riverbanks over a distance of 3 mi (5 km) below the accident site. Furthermore, the vegetation on the valley floor was a mix of closed spruce forest and open lichen-spruce woodland. From the air at 90 mph (145 km/hr) to 100 mph (161 km/hr), it would be easy to miss an injured person on the ground. This is reinforced by the occasion a few days earlier when the Canso pilot had flown to the Pyramid Hills area to pick up Mike and Alan. He had looked for them, circling for over an hour without success before flying back to Chimo. Mike and Alan had been on the ground waving to the plane, amazed that the pilot had not been able to see them or to land on the designated pickup lake. This was in stark contrast to other aircraft recovery exercises, including my own in the Torngat Mountains in 1956 and 1957.

This rationalization prompted me to question the wisdom of terminating the search for Brian and André. I was worried there had been no sighting of either of them. With the absence of anything belonging to Brian, how could the assumption that both had drowned in the rapids be rationalized? Brian may not have been in the canoe and could be lost somewhere upstream. Either or both men could have survived but suffered injuries in the rapids, as was subsequently determined in the case of André. Finally, reports of the location of a tent with André's diary upstream of the accident site remained unexplained. I was dismayed and proposed to Ken Hare that I conduct a personal and unofficial search myself. Both John Andrews and Mike Matthew, equally dissatisfied with the McGill position, offered to accompany me. I also believed that my experience in isolated parts of the northeastern quadrant of Labrador-Ungava, much of the time without any outside communication, gave me a valid claim to undertake an extensive ground search.

Ken demurred. "This is a McGill affair, Jack, and you are now federal government. Besides, I asked Pat Baird to take charge and no one is more experienced than Pat. Pat's judgment is final and absolute. No further risk of life on a pointless search will be permitted." I replied that I intended to go as a private citizen. Ken indicated that this response had been anticipated. "Jack, we do understand your feelings, and we are very sympathetic. But we have asked the Québec Provincial Police detachment at Fort Chimo to refuse you permission to land or refuel. You cannot go." At this I blew up and said that as far as I was concerned, the refusal on the part of the university amounted to gross negligence. Ken said he thought I was reacting emotionally rather than rationally and that I was making a bad situation worse. He insisted that I could not go and should not try to do anything but accept the situation as one of those things that happens in the Arctic.

In contrast to the reactions to Brian and André's disappearance was the public outcry of the loss of two young women in the Central Arctic. Anne-Marie Krüger, a McGill graduate student and personal friend, and Joan Goodfellow had perished on Great Bear Lake at about the same time, also in a canoe accident.[56] The reaction was exacerbated by the discovery of two life belts but no trace of their bodies, indicating that they had not been wearing them. The Geographical Branch was involved; Joan was a graduate student in its employ for the summer, assigned to work with Anne-Marie. Joan's father was a member of Parliament. With many other MPs he protested in the House of Commons. It was claimed that the two young women were neither experienced enough nor *strong* enough to work in the Arctic, that they never should have been allowed to go, that women must never be allowed to go in the future, and so on. I was asked to draft a report for our minister for answering possible questions in Parliament, adding to my worries about what had happened on the Koroksoak.[57] I could not avoid thinking about the difference in response; it was as if the two young men who were lost on the Koroksoak River had never existed. What happened on Great Bear Lake set me a most difficult task in my efforts to find places for women on our planned Baffin Island expeditions, but that was an issue for the future.

From October onward the Koroksoak misadventure unfolded gradually and grimly. The first weeks following the initial shock were painful. As the long dark winter settled on the Koroksoak, we presumed that the course of events would remain closed until summer, if not forever. In one of my first meetings with Dr. James Harrison, director of the Geological Survey of Canada (GSC), after expressing sincere commiseration, he told me that the GSC had lost on average two geologists or field party assistants each year in the Canadian bush and no one publicly had raised an eyebrow. He indicated that if they had been women, it would have been a different story, but the GSC was absolutely opposed to sending women into the field.

The "long dark winter" did not settle on the Koroksoak affair. To my deep chagrin I learned from my parents in England that a UK newspaper had reported the discovery of a body, believed to be that of Brian Haywood, in the wilds of northern Québec. I later realized that the report was the same source through which Brian's parents learned of their son's (supposed) fate. I had previously heard from John Andrews and Mike Matthew of rumors circulating in Montréal about the discovery of Brian's remains. This had prompted me to write to Pat Baird on 9 December 1960, requesting an explanation. While I was actually composing this letter, Pauline telephoned to tell me that airmail had just arrived from my parents with the same terrible news. So I added this information to my letter to Pat, with a strong expression of concern that Brian's parents received such shocking information in this impersonal manner.

I spent five days at the Lab at Schefferville at the year end. I had been invited by the McGill Geography Department to share my experience with the new field director, Bill Mattox, and the 1960–1961 overwintering crew of graduate students. I found Bill as perplexed as I was about the Geography Department's apparent unwillingness to keep us, and the parents of our lost colleagues, fully informed.

On my way back to Ottawa from Schefferville I stopped over in Québec City at the invitation of Professor Louis-Edmond Hamelin. We visited André's parents in Beauport, a very sad and trying experience. The Greniers were a large family; the house was threadbare, with no carpeting, only bare boards. André had been the eldest. The entire family had struggled financially so that he could attend university. Having talked with André's mother, we waited until late in the afternoon so that we could meet Mr. Grenier when he got home from work. He looked like an old man yet couldn't have been more than fifty. They had heard about the recovery of a body, and they also understood that it was Brian's. Mr. Grenier had received a check from McGill to cover some unpaid salary for work André had done at the Lab. The check was made out in his missing son's name so that he had not been able to cash it. I left the house feeling dreadful; their warm handshakes and sincere thanks made me feel worse.

On 3 January Professor Hamelin took me to the headquarters of the QPP, where we obtained access to André's belongings, recently received from Fort Chimo. My primary interest, of course, was the diary that had been sealed as confidential by the police. It was a stiff-backed notebook, not the loose collection of pages as previously reported. Because my knowledge of French was insufficient to enable me to precisely understand the content, especially as it was hand written and had been somewhat damaged by weather, Louis-Edmond spent over an hour translating for me while I made extensive notes.

It seemed that at the beginning of the undertaking, aside from the frustration of the ten-day delay in leaving Schefferville, all had gone according to plan. After an easy passage up the slack water of the lower river, aided by the outboard motor, the upstream canoe journey was much harder than expected. Brian and André had been forced to spend a lot of time thigh deep in fast water pulling and pushing the canoe, or in very heavy work portaging around rapids. However, it appears they thought that the eventual return downstream would prove an easy run. Fishing was good and they were well fed. The diary gave the impression of two friends effectively facing a trial of strength. Brian's research was going well and he was excited about the details. There were only scanty remarks about the glacial geomorphology and certainly nothing of scientific interest. Several weeks pass. André is beginning to complain—it is time to turn back. But Brian wants to reach the upper bend of the river and link up with my walking route of 1957 from the Atlantic side. The friendship comes under strain. Finally André records in his diary that if Brian would not agree to head downstream the next day, he would feel forced to take the canoe back on his own.

This was the last entry on 12 August. The diary was found in the last camp, the canoe some miles downstream, partially submerged, wedged between two large boulders in the rapids. The rest is speculation. Did André really intend to abandon Brian to a possible slow death by starvation, or merely to frighten him? Surely, the latter. Was Brian with André in the canoe so that both drowned, or were they smashed on the rocks? Unlikely, because of the position of the tent and the diary. If Brian was left in the camp and André perished in the rapids, what became of Brian?[58] His body had been identified by the police. I returned home to Ottawa feeling very frustrated and very angry, wanting to find out precisely where and when Brian's body was located.

From this point the account becomes even more convoluted. There are numerous contradictions between reports coming from the McGill Geography Department, Professor Hamelin, the Grenier family, and the Québec and Montréal offices of the QPP. In a letter to me dated 13 February 1961, Professor Hamelin wrote that the November-December identification of the remains of a body as that of Brian now proved to be in error. The body remains and personal effects, flown out from Chimo on 9 February, had been subjected to a coroner's inquiry on the following day. Both André's father and Camille Roy, one of the 1959–1960 Lab overwintering team, had made a positive identification (*ré-identifier André par son père et par Camille Roy*). This was further confirmed by a match with André's dental record. Hamelin explained in his letter to me that André had not drowned. He had escaped from the river severely injured (a badly broken leg). Nevertheless, surviving on berries, he had traveled ("crawled" would be more accurate from the coroner's certification of the condition of his injured leg) far downstream from the site of the canoe accident. His remains, found well above the river level, had been partially devoured by wild animals. Hamelin concluded: *"La mort d'André a donc été extrêmement pénible"* (André's was an extremely painful death).

At the same time rumors circulated from Chimo and in the Québec press that Brian's remains also had been discovered far downstream from the canoe accident site. It was assumed that he had drowned in the rapids and his body had been carried downstream by the river.

This account of the recovery of Brian's body, however, was never confirmed. Thus there remains the difficulty of explaining the tent containing André's diary, supposed to have been found upstream of the rapids. André's survival well into September remains as a highly disturbing possibility. There is also an indirect contradiction regarding the position of the tent found above the rapids. Surely Brian and André had penetrated much farther upstream than the available account implies.

After February 1961, Bill Mattox took the lead in trying to learn more about these bewildering and conflicting reports. I had become totally frustrated. Bill visited the QPP headquarters in Montréal, where he was given access to the Grenier-Haywood dossier (DM-D-156-60). This provided more disturbing information, as he wrote to me on 11 May 1961. Bill related that he was "almost certain" that André had survived the accident and been able to travel overland "to a location near the Eskimo summer camp." Some letters, scrawled in the sand, had been found near his body, much disturbed by subsequent footprints. Furthermore, the QPP, neither in Montréal or in Québec City, had information concerning the rumor that Brian's remains had been discovered. Bill Mattox also complained that he was not able to obtain information from the McGill Geography Department, and especially from Pat Baird. Indeed, he was not able to obtain a copy of the McGill committee report, written under Pat's chairmanship, that was intended to establish future policy relating to graduate students working in the wilderness. Yet it was Bill's task to encourage his first year's group of graduate students to prepare for fieldwork.

But what of Brian? If he had not been in the canoe he would have had some food, plus the abundant blueberries of autumn, lichen, and possibly fish. Did he try to walk across to the Atlantic side, thinking he could reach Hebron? Of course we will never know, but the perplexed thoughts and sense of frustration remain with me.

How to conclude such a tale? I have always thought that if the McGill University authorities had allowed me to conduct a ground search, we might have rescued André. Had we done so, we then would have been prompted to search for Brian. Difficult questions remain. How could Pat Baird have declared his search complete and recommended presumption of death? How could Ken Hare, or Dr. Cyril James, principal of McGill, have accepted Pat's recommendation and denied me the chance to conduct a ground search?

In essence this is an important part of my life, as well as that of others and especially of the families of Brian and André. I believe that Pat Baird and Ken Hare made errors of judgment. Was it a question of once having denied my request to take part in a search in deference to Pat, Ken could not retract? Who knows? We all make errors of judgment, and I have certainly made some in my lifetime. Would I feel better today if I had disregarded McGill University objections and made an attempt to fly in to the Koroksoak? Would I have got anywhere near Chimo, the essential refueling point, considering the university's and the QPP's apparent determination to prevent me?

After half a century any attempted explanation comes no closer to answering some of the outstanding questions about how Brian and André spent the last days of their lives. The conclusion that the conduct of the search was totally inadequate is unavoidable. Was it reasonable to presume the deaths of both men by drowning? Findings along the Koroksoak after the formal closure of the search clearly indicated this was an error. There remained obligations to do more to determine the manner of death; that would have required a ground party. Contrary to the official McGill University concern that it was not justified to risk additional lives in a futile search, any such effort would not have been particularly hazardous. Furthermore, Rivière André Grenier's remains, or a live but injured André, would almost certainly have been discovered. This, together with transparency in reporting by the McGill authorities, would have short-circuited the damaging rumors, contradictions, and hurtful false news media reports. It would also have avoided the suspicion, widely felt among the graduate students at the time, and by Bill Mattox and myself, that something was being concealed.

I felt a great sense of personal loss over the deaths of Brian and André. I did meet both of their families. I also submitted to the Canadian Permanent Committee on Geographical Names proposals for naming a Rivière Grenier André, a large and unnamed north bank tributary of the Koroksoak, and a Mount Brian Haywood, on the divide between the Atlantic and Ungava Bay that Pauline and I had climbed in 1957 and that provides a fine view to the west far down the Koroksoak. The names Rivière Grenier and Mont Haywood appeared on the 1:250,000 map sheet printed in 1968. Yet even this small detail has been victim of the confusion and uncertainty that plagued the entire episode—the name Mont Haywood on the 1:50,000 scale map is applied to a different summit than the one on the 1:250,000 scale map! I also requested that McGill University grant Brian a posthumous master's degree. This was rejected on the grounds that he had not begun to write his thesis. Much later the small library at the Lab was named in memory of Brian. I wonder whether or not a record of that still remains and why was it not named in memory of both of them.

Transition: 1960–1966

The time period of the previous section overlaps the term of my appointment as field director with that of Bill Mattox (1960–1963). Bill obviously inherited the acutely disturbing episode of the loss of Brian and André on the Koroksoak River. In this he was staunchly supported by Charles McCloughan, who remained for a further year as senior weather observer. My year-end visit, enthusiastically supported by Ken Hare and as a personal houseguest of Bill and Joan Mattox, was very helpful under these circumstances. It enabled me to strengthen the link between the ongoing field research of the Lab and my new responsibilities at the Geographical Branch in Ottawa. There was some hesitation in us pushing ahead with this, as Bill and I waited, in vain, for a copy of McGill's new policy for the Lab's administration of future distant field expeditions. Despite this, one of Bill's first winter's crew, Barry Matthews (University of Leeds), remained keenly interested in taking advantage of the growing network of field studies that had been initiated. In fact, I had recommended the appointment of Barry to the Lab staff following extensive correspondence about the prospects of extending the glacial geomorphology study to the far northwest. Thus Barry used the winter to prepare himself for a summer on the south coast of Hudson Strait, working out from the two small Inuit settlements of Wakeham Bay (Maricourt) and Sugluk Inlet (Saglouc). The proposed research fell well within my Geographical Branch remit so that some logistical support could be anticipated. This plan materialized the following summer.[59]

In the following years, collaboration between the Lab and the Geographical Branch bore substantial fruit. Of the 1961–1962 Lab winter staff, both Martin Barnett (University of London) and David Harrison (Leeds University) began a second phase of the fieldwork on the glacial lake shorelines. Martin, after a summer of very arduous cross-country precise survey, was able to clarify the relationship between the Naskaupi and McLean glacial lakes and to calculate the precise direction and amount of isostatic tilt of the N-2 shoreline. David extended the shoreline work to the vicinity of the newly developing iron-mining towns of Labrador City and Wabush, south of Schefferville. With the additional work of Olav Løken on the tilt of glaciomarine features in the Torngat Mountains (Løken 1962a and 1962b), tilt direction from three different points was determined and it suggested that the area of greatest late-glaciation uplift lay in the vicinity, although to the west of the Kivivik Lake Ice Divide.

The subsequent years, extending into Peter Adams's period in charge of the Lab (1963–1966), saw a further expansion of this process. Jim Peterson (Tasmania University, Lab 1962–1963) worked in the vicinity of Whitegull Lake, well to the south of Indian House Lake, and greatly extended the identification of the N-2 shoreline; Dick Cowan (Carleton University, Lab 1962–1963) studied the ribbed moraine (rippled till) south of Astray Lake. Jim Gray (University of Aberdeen, Lab 1964–1965) initiated what became a career-long involvement in a study of the Ungava Peninsula and Ungava Bay following his first summer in the Mealy Mountains, south of North West River. Jim's leadership led to a major institutional commitment on the part of the Université de Montréal that remains active to this day. Finally, Bob Rogerson (University of Liverpool, Lab 1965–1966) extended the Torngat Mountain work south of Nachvak Fiord, after completing fieldwork along the north coast of Ungava for his McGill doctorate. This was further extended through his appointment to the faculty of Memorial University, St. John's, Newfoundland.

It was during the directorship of Bill Mattox that the permafrost project became a major undertaking. Lennart Annersten, from Uppsala University, Sweden, was offered the NRC permafrost research fellowship and was able to devote himself full-time to extend the ground temperature installations and lay the foundations for a sophisticated study. Although he stayed only a year, the vital observations were carried on by Bill Mattox and his successor, Peter Adams, and various members of the winter graduate student staffs. This resulted in a long series of research publications (Bird 1964; Annersten 1964).

Chapter Five

The Quest for Northern Knowledge

A Permanent Expedition in the Subarctic

The establishment of the McGill Sub-Arctic Research Laboratory in 1954 should be assessed in light of the limited knowledge of, and interest in, Canada's vast arctic and subarctic territories in the immediate years following World War II. As indicated in the prologue and chapter 1, with the exception of scattered small localities, the North remained an enormous empty space to the vast majority of Canadians. Before the war, arctic and subarctic scientific exploration and field research were severely limited by the need to travel by ship and to overwinter for at least one year, if not longer. In this sense, the expeditions of the late 1930s to Melville Peninsula, Foxe Basin, and western Baffin Island (Rowley 2007), and even the summer ship–supported Cambridge University expedition to northeastern Baffin Island,[60] represent the final flowering of the "heroic age" of Canadian arctic research and exploration. Extensive overland travel by members of the Royal Canadian Mounted Police and the Hudson's Bay Company was a complementary part of this. Shipment of prairie wheat from Churchill across Hudson Bay, commercial traffic between Edmonton, AB, and the western arctic coast using the Mackenzie River system, and activities along the Labrador coast by Moravian and Grenfell missionaries were also related.

Technological advances during the war and the beginning of resource development (oil at Norman Wells in the Northwest Territories) initiated rapid change. Exercise Muskox, organized by the Canadian military (1946), and the growing threat of the Cold War prompted Canada's increasing realization of the enormous economic and strategic importance of its northern lands. The RCAF 408 Squadron of Lancasters was vital to the establishment and resupply of the weather stations in the High Arctic. The Lancasters were also vital for the acquisition of trimetrogon air photographic coverage that resulted in the discovery of the Prince Charles and Air Force islands in Foxe Basin, the last large islands to be discovered (1948). In 1949 Tom Manning led a Canadian government expedition sponsored by the newly established Geographical Branch into the ice-choked southeastern Foxe Basin. He navigated the CG MV *Nauja* and made the first landfalls on the islands.

Although the links between McGill University and federal agencies in Ottawa (Defence Research Board, Joint Intelligence Bureau, National Research Council) led to increasing knowledge of the North (see chapter 1) in the immediate postwar years, Canada was almost bereft of young scholars with arctic or subarctic experience and had no short-term prospect of training any. Thus the activities on the McGill campus, with Ken Hare taking a leading role, represented the first Canadian university thrust into northern exploration and research. Due to the shortage of Canadian-born arctic scholars, most of these pioneers were drawn from England and Scotland. They, in turn, attracted to Canada many of the next generation from the Old World, at first mainly British but increasingly from other European countries and New England in the United States. This was mirrored in the appointment of McGill-Carnegie-Arctic research scholars and recruitment of staff for the Lab.

There were important exceptions and Canadian-born enthusiasts were by no means lacking. J. Ross Mackay is perhaps the outstanding example who has achieved unmatchable preeminence, continuing winter research in the Mackenzie Delta until well into his eighties.[61] In the air this was mirrored by the exploits of Keith Greenaway (RCAF), who led the way by developing groundbreaking navigational methods to facilitate aircraft operations across the area of the north magnetic pole and in highest northern latitudes. In this process he navigated the first Canadian flight to the North Pole, discovered Ice Island T-3, and determined that Borden Island (lat 74° N) was not one but two islands (Bergquist 2008). J. Keith Fraser, Denis St-Onge, and Vic Sim, who worked with the Geographical Branch, undertook extensive field surveys in the eastern and central Arctic. The Geological Survey of Canada, founded in 1842, was a major source of Canadian nationals to work in the North, including individuals such as Jim Harrison, Yves Fortier, Ray Thorsteinsson, Bob Blackadar, Bob Christie, Bert Lee, and John Fyles. However, the great majority obtained their graduate training in the United States. Canadian universities were only beginning to awaken to the importance of northern research, and more than half of those presently existing were not founded until after about 1960.

The postwar developments attracted me, as a graduate student, to Canada and McGill in 1954. During those heady days it was possible for a McGill graduate student to be flown north by 408 Squadron, free of charge, to Eureka on Ellesmere Island, Resolute on Cornwallis Island, Igloolik, or Tuktoyaktuk. This ease of access to remote high arctic locations almost seduced me away from central Labrador-Ungava and the Torngat Mountains. In practical terms, Eureka at 79°59' N and Resolute at 74°40' N were more accessible to McGill graduate students than the Torngat Mountains. The glamour of the High Arctic undoubtedly acted as a powerful magnet. It was the reality of a permanent base at Knob Lake, however, that kept me on track. The Lab, in contrast to sporadic locations much farther north, became a "permanent expedition" and one that was most flexible in its proffered opportunity for long-term research program development and individual initiative. Together with the McGill-Carnegie-Arctic scholarship program, the Lab nurtured much of the Canadian university experience that established a platform for the later training of Canadian-born students.

Staffing

The recruitment of the Lab's first winter's staff must have been a struggle for Ken Hare. I have always assumed that Norman Drummond had only three assistants because Ken had not been able to find a fourth. His offer, which reached me in southeastern Iceland a few months before the Lab was due to begin operations, reinforces this view. Thereafter, for the entire life of the Lab (as distinct from its transformation into the McGill Sub-Arctic Research Station from 1971 onward), the composition of the winter staff was overwhelmingly British, with a few exceptions: three from Université de Montréal and Université Laval, one from Norway, one from Tasmania, and three from Dartmouth College. Except for the first winter and the French Canadians, no Canadian-born graduates overwintered until Bruce Findlay (1962–1963) and Jim Gardner (1963–1964). It was 1964–1965 before more than a single Canadian formed the winter's crew (Dick Cowan, Carleton University, and Bruce Findlay, University of Toronto).[62] New immigrants continued to predominate for as long as the DOT weather-observing contract remained in force.

The social problems that developed during the Lab's first winter (1954–1955—see chapters 1 and 2) have perhaps received too much emphasis. In large part they were a reflection of the breaking-in period, although the negative attitude toward women was a real part of it. Only one woman was recruited as winter staff (Rona Bassett, University of Cambridge, 1965–1966) during this nearly twenty-year period, and she did not complete her winter stay. Yet many of the early members of the Lab winter staff were ably assisted with their fieldwork by their wives (Viereck, Ives, Tomlinson, Løken), and the wives of all the successive field directors and senior weather observers made exemplary contributions, including the production of offspring.

While unrelated to the Lab, Beryl Bird accompanied Brian on extensive and rigorous research expeditions in central Keewatin and on Southampton Island, and Ellie Johnson supported Peter for two seasons on the Labrador coast. Eleanor Wheeler, with husband Pep, adopted the traditional Inuit style of living and experienced secure winters on the northern Labrador coast, dependent almost entirely on the available natural resources.[63]

The negative attitude toward women in the wilderness was not limited to Canada. It could be argued that Canada's lack of women stemmed from the colonial and dominion heritage of the mother country. Nevertheless, there were curious exceptions. In addition to the wives mentioned above, "Jackie" Manning overwintered on Baffin Island after going north on the Hudson's Bay Company vessel *Nascopie* to marriage with Tom at Cape Dorset, Baffin Island. Her book, *Igloo for the Night*, became a best seller (Manning 1943). The Norwegians Helge Ingstad and his wife, Ann Stine-Moe, an archaeologist, formed a close field partnership, leading to the first discovery of a Viking settlement in North America at the northern tip of Newfoundland. Moira Dunbar and Margaret Larnder (née Montgomery), as Defence Research Board staff, flew with Keith Greenaway, Tuzo Wilson and Ken Hare across Hudson Bay in 408 Squadron Lancasters. Margaret was also a member of the AINA–McGill 1950 expedition to Baffin Island.[64]

Women nurses worked in the North, and during the long period of HBC operations, post factors took their wives with them, as did Anglican, Moravian, and Grenfell missionaries, many of whom lived in extreme isolation for several years at a time. Similarly, many young Canadian and European women and Roman Catholic nuns were enlisted as teachers in Church boarding schools in the Northwest Territories (Bryant and Bryant 2007). The territories included present-day Nunavut in the 1940s and 1950s.

There is no doubt that the Canadian federal government frowned on the possibility of university women (as well as female federal research staff) working in the Arctic or Subarctic, at least until the 1970s; the exception seems to have been the Defence Research Board. So perhaps it is not surprising that there was a scarcity of women applicants for positions at the Lab. Nevertheless, in the 1960s, when I began to organize a series of expeditions to Baffin Island from Ottawa, there was no shortage of women student applicants once I had broken through the bureaucratic resistance. Today it is hard to get young people to believe that there was such prejudice against women. However, neither the Lab nor the McGill Axel Heiberg expeditions could be regarded as achieving normalcy so long as women—in their own right, rather than as wives—were virtually barred from the wilderness. There is little need for further discussion of this phenomenon other than to recognize here that it was a significant factor. That women "were not strong enough" or that they "were in danger of being assaulted by males isolated through long service on weather stations or DEW-Line sites" has essentially been ridiculed.

Research Results: 1954–1964

To consider the contribution of early Lab research in its broadest sense, it would be necessary to examine the careers of those individuals who undertook the research and the impacts they brought to bear on a significant number of institutions. Some of those broader aspects will be discussed below, although there was a great deal of cross-fertilization between the Lab and those individuals and institutions. This chapter, however, will concentrate, though not exclusively, on the program of distant field research that I had set up during the Lab's earliest years.

Comparison between contributions from early Lab field research (1954–1964) and the present state of knowledge must also take into account the vastly different circumstances that have prevailed for several decades. The early Lab fieldwork depended on foot-slogging, backpacking, and canoe, with transport to and from field areas dependent on charity. Actual research grants were minute ($1,000 to $2,500) or nonexistent. In addition, the availability of topographic base maps and air photographs was minimal compared with even twenty-five years later. Field research over the last two decades or more has been supported by fixed-wing aircraft, helicopter, and marine research vessels. Technological advances, especially in dating techniques and sedimentary stratigraphy, have been extensive. The 1954–1964 period predated the so-called quantitative revolution in the field sciences.

A significant change in field operations has been the result. Many of the more recent field parties have seen researchers flown into chosen field sites, supported for a few days, then flown out again. Transport within chosen field areas has had the benefit of helicopter support. All of this is very much to the good. However, I cannot help wondering that, despite these great advantages, something is missing today. I refer to those long-ago weeks and months of total isolation and something approaching living off the land when the field research, free of radio or cell phone contact, allowed the privileged researcher to obtain a feel for the wilderness that was a significant aid to scholarly intuition, and profoundly unquantifiable.

For a writer who has not conducted field research in remote mountain or arctic regions for the last ten years, my attempt to project the psychology of wilderness research requires some caution. Nevertheless, effort is needed to illustrate the mental environment of entry into a remote Labrador-Ungava of the 1950s.

As far back as the mid-1970s, the George River and Indian House Lake were plastered with an array of commercial fishing and caribou hunting camps, a pattern propagated throughout the great peninsula. In 1975 I made a rendez-vous with an American businessman and adventurer on the lower George River. John Ski (of Polish origin) owned a well-equipped Cessna and had built a small cabin about 30 mi (48 km) upstream from the site of the former Hudson's Bay Company post on the George River estuary, the point where Mina Hubbard completed her historic mission in 1905. I joined John for a few days on my way out from a revisit to the Saglek Moraines in the Torngat Mountains. He had brought with him from New York fresh beefsteaks, cut glass, and fine French wine, together with a lace tablecloth. When I requested a loan of his fishing rod so that we could add fresh arctic char to our exotic menu, he casually informed me that I would not be successful, because the entire river was virtually fished out. Though he was exaggerating somewhat, he did comment that there was no way that I would experience the catches to which fieldwork in 1958 had accustomed me. This was correct, but there are always the rare exceptions.[65] During the same period of the 1970s, the Québec government sold one thousand licenses annually to would-be caribou hunters.

In contrast, the 1950s and early 1960s preserved the utter remoteness of this vast region. So what was the attraction? Certainly there were unlimited research opportunities in much more comfortable and easily accessible localities from the south coast of British Columbia, through the Canadian Rockies, to the St. Lawrence River and Gulf of St. Lawrence.

The attraction, undoubtedly, was the chance to experience a sense of high adventure. Much of this sense of adventure sprang from the British tradition of polar exploration and alpinism that had nurtured numerous student expeditions before and after World War II. It was by no means the only trigger, and Britain certainly had no monopoly.[66] However, it was the predominant one that affected the establishment and expansion of the McGill Sub-Arctic Research Lab.

From a purely personal point of view, I cannot recall an experience that was more intellectually and aesthetically satisfying than backpacking with Pauline through the Torngat Mountains from the Atlantic to the Ungava Bay side in 1956 or tracing the extent of the "parallel roads" along Indian House Lake in 1958. There is no question, in my mind, that much of the same spirit pervaded the entire group of Lab staff facing a subarctic winter at Knob Lake, at least during my directorship. I am equally certain that this sense of adventure was extended to the summer field surveys far distant from the Lab for those who undertook them. This was carried over into north-central and northeastern Baffin Island in the 1960s, although by then we were being spoiled by field radio connections, fixed-wing and helicopter support, icebreakers in the fiords. Despite this, much of the feeling of inaccessibility and adventure remained, and we provided a vehicle for many Canadian-born men and women students to participate. It is also worth recording that many of the immigrant Lab staff found positions in university and government research institutions and became Canadian citizens, or else moved to similar positions in the United States. At least four of the Dartmouth College students who were attracted to graduate work at McGill University in Montréal and/or the Lab became Canadian citizens.

The following attempt to illustrate some of the lasting results of the actual Lab field research should be viewed against the 1950s geography of Labrador-Ungava and the adventure spirit of the times. To this must be added the very small numbers involved and the puny level of financial support available. Most of the relevant results of these early efforts can be itemized briefly under eight separate headings. Several are clearly interrelated.

1. The "Flintian paradigm" of glaciation and deglaciation, widely accepted from the 1940s to the 1970s, was overturned and replaced by the concept of instantaneous glacierization across wide areas of the Labrador-Ungava plateau (Ives 1957, 1960b). This has since become the standard view (Fulton 1989), although many details are still under investigation. The most recent fieldwork now indicates that the Québec highlands north of the St. Lawrence were probably one of the areas to experience earliest accumulation of permanent ice and snow (Dyke 2005; Viellette et al. 1999). This extends rather than contradicts the concept of instantaneous glacierization. There has been no support for Flint's hypothesis since the 1960s and the significance of the "instantaneous" concept has been recently reemphasized.

   Spencer Weart, in his book *The Discovery of Global Warming* (Weart 2003), credited the introduction of the concept to my 1957 paper. Weart writes: "…by *instantaneous* he meant an advance of ice sheets over the course of a few thousand years, which was roughly ten times faster than most scientists had imagined" (italics mine). This statement is appropriately qualified by the meteorological investigations of Barry (1966).

2. As a corollary to (1), it was determined that the Labrador coast and the coastal mountains and plateau edge became ice-free early, and a series of large ice-dammed lakes (Naskaupi and McLean glacial lakes, plus many others subsequently recognized—Jansson 2002) developed between the Atlantic height-of-land and the westward-wasting ice sheet. Ungava Bay was occupied by a northern extension of the Labrador-Ungava ice mass until very late in the process of deglaciation; its eventual collapse led to the northerly drainage of the glacial lakes. The most prominent of the

This schematic map provides a broad outline of the reconnaissance glacial geomorphology that was completed through field research during the early years of Lab operations.

Naskaupi Lake shorelines sloped up toward the southwest at about 2 ft per mi, indicating the direction of location of the thickest ice during at least the later phases of the last glaciation.

3. One of the final wastage areas of the Laurentide Ice Sheet was centered about 25 mi (40 km) north of Schefferville (Kivivik Ice Divide). The pattern of glacial meltwater erosion indicated that the remnant ice sheet was climatically dead and therefore dynamically inactive as the highest summits in the vicinity emerged through the ice. The final pieces of melting ice were located on the valley floors. This final ice sheet disappearance occurred well after the period universally referred to as the end of the Last Ice Age (ten thousand years ago), actually well into the Holocene, or

postglacial thermal maximum. Jansson (2002) and Jansson and Klemen (2004) have carried the interpretation of the glacial lake shorelines (having discovered many more) much further. They conclude that an ice dome over Ungava Bay, necessary to hold up the glacial lakes in question, was the final phase of Labrador-Ungava deglacierization. This challenges my original interpretation of the glacial drainage channels in the center of the peninsula (Kivivic Ice Divide). In turn, Jansson and Klemen's interpretation is opposed by that of Dyke (2005), Veillette et al. (1999), and others. Thus the debate continues undiminished.

A detailed chronology of the events described in points (1) to (3) above has been elaborated subsequent to 1975. Significant modifications have been proposed, especially following the fieldwork of Rogerson and Evans (1986), Clark et al. (1999), Jansson (2002), Veillette et al. (1999), Dyke (2009), and Carlson et al. (2007). The overall pattern of deglaciation determined from the early Lab field research, however, has generated and contributed to two generations of extensive fieldwork and debate.

4. Recognition of the significance of the Saglek Moraines in the southern Torngat Mountains has been retained and reinforced, although recent age determinations appear to relegate them to a substage of the last ice age (Clark et al. 2003; Marquette et al. 2004). Nevertheless, it is significant that the Saglek Moraines and their extensions (Andrews 1963c; Løken 1962b; Rogerson and Evans 1986) are the only prominent landforms that delineate extensive last-ice-age ice sheet margins in northeastern Labrador-Ungava. I suspect that future attempts to refine the "absolute" chronology will witness additional modification.

5. The enigma of the mountaintop detritus (boulder fields or felsenmeer) and summit tors has not yet been fully resolved. The boulder fields are definitely not the product of postglacial weathering, as proposed by Odell (1933) and Tanner (1944). Current claims for the efficacy of the recently developed cosmogenic dating methods, in my opinion, have not yet produced an unequivocal solution. Nevertheless, sometime in the past the highest summits of the Torngat Mountains were probably overtopped by continental ice, possibly rather thin and frozen to the bedrock. The increasingly large number of cosmogenic dates from erratics and rock surfaces in the summit zone in recent years consistently indicate that last glaciation ice has overtopped the highest mountaintops (Gosse and Phillips 2001; Briner et al. 2003; Arthur Dyke, pers. comm., 1 June 2009).

The work of Gray (Lab, 1964–1965) and his research team at the Université de Montréal has resulted in a great increase in understanding of the deglaciation of the Ungava Peninsula and western Ungava Bay.

This work has also been extended to the Torngat Mountains (Marquette et al. 2004), although to date it has been restricted to summits below about 4,000 ft asl (1,219 m). This leaves the highest summits (up to 5,400 ft/1,646 m) theoretically and literally "in the clouds" (but see Briner et al. 2003). Regardless, the conclusions of the 1950s, that thick eroding ice did not submerge the highest summits, has not been challenged. The problem of coordinating the Torngat Mountain depictions with those relating to the interpretation of the glacial lakes Naskaupi and McLean remain. The estuaries of the George and Koroksoak rivers, southeast Ungava Bay, still remain a critical blank in our knowledge; this may have been clarified had Brian Haywood and André Grenier survived in 1960 to complete their work.

6.   Permafrost research, supported by the IOCC and subsequently by establishment of a resident research fellowship at the Lab by the NRC, has made extensive progress (Annersten 1964; Bird 1964; Ives 1960c, 1979; Nicholson 1979). Existence of permafrost more than 200 ft (61 m) thick under the high ridges west of the Lab has been confirmed.

Relationships between ground temperatures and surface characteristics, especially snow depth and vegetation cover, have been elaborated. This had led to southward extension of the supposed southern limit of permafrost, as predicted in the 1950s, by several hundred miles (Ives 1960c). The proposal that patches of sporadic permafrost occur beneath windswept summits along the Laurentian Escarpment and beneath the Shickshock Mountains of Gaspesie south of the St. Lawrence estuary has since been confirmed (Brown 1979). This does not consider the implications of recent climate warming.

7.   The microclimates and their relationships with evapotranspiration from the different cover types of the mosaic of ecosystems between the boreal forest and the arctic tundra, centered on the Lab, have been analyzed (Nebiker 1957; Nebiker and Orvig 1957; Jackson 1958; Orvig 1961).

8.   The snow hydrology and lake ice dynamics of the central Labrador-Ungava peninsula became the objectives of long-term study initiated at the Lab by Peter Adams (Field Director, 1964–1967) and subsequently greatly extended from his base at Trent University (Adams 2007).

From the foregoing outline it will be apparent that a thorough analysis of the research conducted throughout Labrador-Ungava after about 1964 and continuing today will demonstrate the significant impact of the early pioneer efforts described in this book. In this sense alone, Ken Hare's vision of the potential of a McGill research presence at Knob Lake (Schefferville) has been more than fulfilled.

Following the termination of the DOT weather-observing contract in 1971, the Lab, as mentioned earlier, was renamed the McGill Sub-Arctic Research Station. It is no longer a year-round "residential expedition" but supports a great deal of inter- and multidisciplinary research based on shorter visits by McGill and other scientists and students. Its director, Professor Wayne Pollard, is resident on the McGill campus in Montréal. Such developments are far beyond the objectives of this book.

Wider Impacts

During the 1950s, with a few notable exceptions, Canadian arctic and sub-arctic research depended heavily on the efforts of immigrants. As mentioned above, the first major infusion of immigrants who concentrated their careers on northern research occurred immediately before World War II. This set the stage for the postwar developments in that influential figures, such as Graham Rowley, Tom Manning, and Pat Baird, encouraged the tasks that Ken Hare, Brian Bird, and others, who immigrated immediately on demobilization, set themselves. Thus, informal alliances were established that led to the founding of AINA with its original links to McGill.[67]

Other postwar immigrants entered federal government service directly, one of the most notable being Geoffrey Hattersley-Smith. Geoff, as a scientist with DRB, undertook extensive glaciological research in northern Ellesmere Island that led to Operation Hazen (Hattersley-Smith 1960; Hattersley-Smith et al. 1955; Jackson 2006), part of Canada's contribution to the International Geophysical Year (1957–1958). Once again, McGill played a prominent role; for instance, three of the four overwintering members of Operation Hazen, C. Ian Jackson, D. Ingle Smith, and John Powell, were immigrant McGill graduate students. They, in turn, maintained strong personal links with McGill-Carnegie-Arctic scholars and staff of the Lab, while Jim Lotz (Lab 1955 and 1956 summer staff) worked as assistant to Hattersley-Smith on Gilman Glacier and the shelf ice in northern Ellesmere (Lotz 2006).

From this point on it is difficult to separate some of the activities and personnel among Operation Hazen, the McGill-Carnegie-Arctic scholarship program, and the Lab, which later embraced the McGill Axel Heiberg Expedition, led by Fritz Müller, himself coming to Canada in 1954 on a McGill-Carnegie-Arctic scholarship.

It was the Geological Survey of Canada, the Canadian Wildlife Service, and the Arctic Biological Station at Ste. Anne de Belleview, PQ, however, that had attracted the main corps of Canadian-born arctic enthusiasts, such as Jim

Harrison, Yves Fortier, Ray Thorsteinsson, Fred Roots, Bob Blackadar, Bob Christie, John Fyles, John Tener, and others, although even here British immigrants were conspicuous: Digby McLaren, Tim Tozer, Max Dunbar, Arthur Mansfield, and David Sergeant. The AINA–McGill Baffin Island expeditions (1950–1953) also saw a significant presence of Swiss mountaineers, though they were by no means solely professional climbers: Hans Röthlisberger, Jürg Marmet, and Hans Weber had prominent careers in glaciology and geophysics. Röthlisberger and Marmet returned to Switzerland, while Weber became a Canadian citizen and, with wife Meg, produced a son, Richard, who made the first unsupported trek to the North Pole. Hans himself has an outstanding record of geophysical research, including some of the first gravity soundings in the Arctic Ocean as far north as the North Pole itself. He also collaborated with the Geographical Branch (see below) on the Barnes Ice Cap research in the 1960s. The Swiss link was maintained and expanded by Fritz Müller. As a McGill-Carnegie-Arctic scholar he completed his doctorate for the University of Zurich on the formation of pingoes in the Mackenzie Delta and Northeast Greenland. Following his 1956 ascent to the South Col in support of summiteers (led by Jürg Marmet) on the Swiss Everest/Lhotse expedition, he operated jointly from McGill and Zurich in his long career as leader of the Axel Heiberg and North Water expeditions. This had a profound effect on Canada's contribution to glaciology and arctic climatology.

Following this complex of interrelationships further, the McGill Axel Heiberg expeditions provided the Lab with a fundamental boost. Peter Adams, who served as Fritz's assistant on the first venture to Axel Heiberg Island in 1959, again as a McGill graduate student recruited from Sheffield, England, became field director of the Lab from 1963 to 1966.

It is apparent, therefore, that the early Lab staff were closely interconnected with the McGill-Carnegie-Arctic scholarship program, the Axel Heiberg expeditions, the establishment of a northern research program at Trent University, and the development of glaciology and geomorphology in the Geographical Branch of the federal government. It is instructive to trace some of these associations.

Geographical Branch: Ottawa and Baffin Island

My position as McGill Sub-Arctic Research Lab field director led to my appointment as assistant director, and later director, of the Geographical Branch (Federal Department of Mines and Technical Surveys) in Ottawa in 1960. As related earlier, the appointment included responsibility for planning and fielding a series of expeditions to north-central and northeastern Baffin Island (1961–1967) as well as expanding the Lab work in Labrador-Ungava through provision of advice and modest support for Lab graduate students.

In total, six of the Lab staff became associated with the Geographical Branch Baffin Island expeditions,[68] five of whom joined the permanent staff, while Roger Barry came to us for a sabbatical year from his position at the University of Southampton, UK, later joining me as a faculty member of the Institute of Arctic and Alpine Research, University of Colorado, USA. In effect, the Baffin Island development was a direct enlargement of the original fieldwork undertaken through the Lab, with an important additional component—glaciology.

A reconnaissance to north-central Baffin Island was undertaken in 1961; it involved two small parties. I was based to the north of the Barnes Ice Cap and was assisted by Peter Hill (regular Branch staff) and John Andrews (Lab 1959–1960) as graduate student assistant.[69] Vic Sim, assisted by Claude Lamothe, operated across the waist of Baffin Island south of the Barnes Ice Cap. In 1963 Olav Løken (Lab 1958–1959) joined me as chief of the branch's Division of Physical Geography and became co-leader and field party chief of the Baffin Island venture. We attracted Brian Sagar from the Lake Hazen research group, while my participation in Professor Gunnar Hoppe's Abisko Symposium in 1960 (Stockholm IGC) led to the recruitment of Gunnar Østrem. These appointments, the beginning of glaciological studies on Baffin Island, and the start of the International Hydrological Decade resulted in the establishment of the Glaciology Section in the Geographical Branch.[70]

The combined investigation of the glacial geomorphology of Labrador-Ungava and Baffin Island/Foxe Basin produced significant advances in understanding the history of the Laurentide Ice Sheet, the world's largest Pleistocene ice sheet. Perhaps the most immediately important result was the recognition of the collapse of the ice sheet over Hudson Bay and the precipitous entry of Atlantic waters through Hudson Strait all the way south to James Bay about eight thousand years ago (Falconer et al. 1965). This rapid, even catastrophic, event was only understood at the reconnaissance level in the 1960s. The discharge of huge volumes of freshwater, dammed up by the wasting Laurentide Ice Sheet, and its impact on North Atlantic climate was not appreciated at the time. This has been confirmed recently and identified as a major Northern Hemisphere event underpinning much of its postglacial climatic and oceanographic history (Clarke et al. 2004).

The early observations, including study of the status of the Barnes Ice Cap on Baffin Island, have become important components of twenty-first-century research associated with study of the impacts of global warming in the Canadian North. The developments achieved through the work of the Geographical Branch also produced an attempt to create Canada's systematic glacier inventory (Falconer 1962; Østrem 1966).

Trent University and Peter Adams

Trent University, largely through the dedication of Peter Adams, had a fundamental impact on Canadian university teaching and research in the Arctic and Subarctic. It is reassuring that, following Peter's directorship of the Lab (1963–1966), his three years in France and England did not preclude his return to Canada in 1968 as head of Trent University's newly formed Department of Geography (initially a one-person department). Peter articulated "how remarkably my experience at 'The Lab' could be translated into an excellent foundation for a geography department in the Peterborough and Kawartha Lakes region—how snow and ice studies and winter field work could form a special thread for the academic life of a new department" (Adams 2007: 78).

Peter went on to develop a strong department emphasizing northern and ice and snow teaching and research. This knit together both his Lab and Axel Heiberg experience, resulting in many field training ventures using the Lab, and later its transformation into the McGill Sub-Arctic Station, as a base for Trent students. The first group of more than fifty undergraduates was organized in the late winter of 1970 and early spring of 1971. The exercise concentrated on lake ice and snow hydrology survey. It expanded in subsequent years through collaboration with groups from McGill, Sherbrooke, Université de Montréal, Laval, and other universities. Later the program was extended to include field visits to Axel Heiberg Island and the original McGill base founded by Fritz Müller. The emergence of Geography and Northern Studies at Trent, with Peter's remarkable stamp on it, was also influential in the 1976 foundation of the Association of Canadian Universities for Northern Studies (ACUNS) with a permanent secretariat. It is noteworthy that Trent and McGill were founding members of ACUNS, and its first executive director was Trevor Lloyd, who had succeeded Ken Hare as chair of geography at McGill.[71] Later, and for many years, Ken Hare was chancellor of Trent University.

Peter Adams's career thus linked the Lab, the Axel Heiberg expeditions, Trent and McGill, and a web of activities that continued into his second career as a federal member of Parliament. The details of this are provided in full in his recent book, *Trent, McGill, and the North* (Adams 2007).

Université de Montréal and Jim Gray

Jim Gray's 1964–1965 experience as a member of the Lab's winter crew culminated in fieldwork in the Mealy Mountains, south of North West River, that led to his master's and doctoral degrees. He became a faculty member of the Université de Montréal and set about developing a research program to study the glaciation and deglaciation of the Ungava Peninsula and its natural science in general. Given the large number of students and faculty colleagues who became involved, the work constitutes one of the most impressive of any cohesive undertaking in the peninsula. It is highly relevant to the earliest studies emanating from the Lab, particularly in glacial geomorphology and glacial history, as it both confirms and extends some of the initial Lab findings and effectively challenges others (see pp. 133–134). It has also guaranteed a strong Québécois presence in what is, after all, a major part of the territory of the Province de Québec. At the same time, the contribution to the training of Québécois researchers and extensive publication in French is equally important in maintaining a full Canadian perspective.

Epilogue

Short Biographies

Many of the early graduate students went on to illustrious careers. With the passage of half a century, I have lost contact with many of the overwintering staff, while others, regrettably, are deceased. Not all the minibiographies are based on direct contributions; I have composed some of them from various sources. The intent is to illustrate how fortunate McGill University was in being able to attract so many outstanding young graduates who were willing (enthusiastic) to isolate themselves in the wilderness at the very beginning of their careers. Their life achievements would have been highly significant whether or not they had been attracted to the Lab. Nevertheless, I have no doubt that their experiences with the "permanent expedition" to the Labrador-Ungava Subarctic and Arctic and the personal comradeships that developed had a profound influence. The careers of Peter Adams and Jim Gray have already been outlined in preceding sections. The following short biographies are highly selective. (Note: several of the former lab staff expressed a desire to use their own words in these biographies.)

John T. Andrews (Lab 1959–1960)

John was born on 8 November 1937, in Millom, Cumberland, England. He completed his bachelor's degree in geography at the University of Nottingham in 1960. Following graduation he emigrated to Canada, spending his first winter at the Lab. Here he prepared for his master's degree field-work on the Labrador coast north of Nain, while at the same time beginning a study of lake ice growth rates in central Labrador-Ungava. He completed his MA in geography at McGill in 1961, after which he served as graduate assistant in north-central Baffin Island for the federal Geographical Branch. He became a permanent member of the Geographical Branch staff in 1962 and concentrated his efforts on the glacial geomorphological research and the study of sea level response to glacial unloading, 1962–1967. During this period he held a year's sabbatical leave that enabled him to complete his doctoral degree at the University of Nottingham.

In 1968 John was appointed associate professor of geological sciences and assistant director of the Institute of Arctic and Alpine Research, University of Colorado, Boulder. He devoted the remainder of his long career to arctic research from his Boulder base. In 1974 he received the Kirk Bryan Award of the American Geological Association for his monograph *A Geomorphological Study of Post-Glacial Uplift with Particular Reference to Arctic Canada*, and in 1978 he was awarded a D.Sc. degree by the University of Nottingham. The University of Colorado recognized him as Distinguished Research Professor.

John has advised and supported numerous graduate students and published several hundred papers in a wide range of scientific journals. His mature research is best described as the study of terrestrial and marine glacial systems. This recognizes the progressive expansion of his fieldwork from the eastern Canadian arctic islands to the fiords and continental shelves of Greenland, Baffin Island, Labrador, and Iceland. Throughout the entire period from 1970 to present he has been the dominant figure in the highly effective annual series of Arctic Workshops, originating at INSTAAR in Boulder and subsequently extending to alternate-year locales in Canada, the eastern United States, Norway, and Iceland. He has developed long-standing research collaboration with the Atlantic GeoScience Centre (Canada), the universities of Tromso and Iceland, and GeoMar, Germany. In 2002 the American Geological Society recognized John's extensive contribution by devoting a special session to his honor during its annual meeting in Denver. He is probably the single-most prolific scientist in his field.

William Barr (Lab 1963–1964)

William "Bill" Barr was born in Coventry, England, on 1 October 1940. During his high school and undergraduate education (University of Aberdeen) his facility for language led to training in French and German. This had a profound effect on the development of his later career.

After completing his University of Aberdeen MA, he emigrated to Canada during the summer of 1963 and spent the 1963–1964 winter at the Lab. His McGill M.Sc. was based on a field study of the fluvioglacial features near Schefferville. Subsequently he undertook research on the raised marine shore features of Devon Island during the 1965–1967 field seasons. He joined the faculty of the Geography Department, University of Saskatchewan, in 1968, rising to the rank of full professor. Bill held the position of departmental head for twelve of the thirty-one years until he took early retirement in 1999. He then moved to Calgary to become a resident research associate of the Arctic Institute of North America.

While he taught extensively on topics such as introductory physical geography and geomorphology, especially glacial geomorphology, his research was focused almost entirely on the history of arctic exploration. Here his facility with language, now including Russian, came into play. Over a period of ten years, for instance, he translated into English almost the entire contents of the Russian journal *Polar Geography and Geology*. He has published seventeen books, with two more in press, and over one hundred journal articles. With the exception of two books on the history of antarctic exploration, most of his writings have dealt with the Arctic. Bill Barr has become the doyen of arctic historians and has made an outstanding contribution to our understanding of this fascinating field of high-latitude research.

For the past seven years he has served as series editor for the *Northern Lights Series*, copublished with the University of Calgary Press. In recognition of his contribution to the historiography of northern Canada, in 2006, the Canadian Historical Association presented him with the Clio Lifetime Achievement Award. Since 1994 he has penetrated almost all corners of the Arctic and Antarctic as lecturer and member of the "expedition team" on various polar cruise ships. To conclude with a personal quote: "All of which, I suppose, led indirectly from my year at Schefferville."

Roger G. Barry (Lab 1957–1958)

Roger was born in Sheffield, England, in 1935, where he attended High Storrs Grammar School. In 1952 he joined the British Meteorological Office as scientific assistant doing weather observations and plotting charts. In 1954 after failing the National Service health examination due to bad eyesight, he decided to take a degree in geography at Liverpool University. He graduated in 1957 specializing in climatology. After his 1957–1958 year at the Lab he completed his master's degree at McGill under Professor Ken Hare in 1959. It involved the analysis of airflow patterns over Labrador-Ungava, using the conditions in two contrasting winters (1956–1957 and 1957–1958) as proxies for those favoring glacierization, and not, in the region.

In 1960 Roger was appointed assistant lecturer in geography at the University of Southampton, where he obtained his PhD in 1965 on moisture transport over Labrador-Ungava, with Ken Hare as external examiner. He was lecturer there until 1968. During this period he spent a sabbatical year (1966–1967) with the Geographical Branch, Canadian Department of Energy, Mines and

Resources, working on the climate of Baffin Island with Olav Løken and Jack Ives. In October 1968, he joined Jack Ives and John Andrews at the Institute of Arctic and Alpine Research (INSTAAR), University of Colorado, Boulder. Roger's work in Boulder followed two main lines: arctic climatology and alpine climatology, with emphasis on paleoclimatology, climate change, and synoptic climatology. In 1976 he became director of the World Data Center (WDC)–A for Glaciology, transferred to the University of Colorado from USGS Tacoma. This began a long-standing collaboration with the Institute of Geography, Russian Academy of Sciences in Moscow, on Russian glaciology and snow and ice data, and later with the Arctic and Antarctic Research Institute in St. Petersburg on sea ice data.

In 1981 Roger transferred from INSTAAR to the Cooperative Institute for Research in Environmental Sciences (CIRES) and in 1982 the WDC was expanded to include the National Snow and Ice Data Center (NSIDC) from NOAA. In 1993 it became a Distributed Active Archive Center (DAAC) for NASA's Earth Observing System program and began managing satellite data streams. Through this and the appointment of scientists to the center, it began to steadily expand, exceeding ninety employees by the early 2000s. NSIDC became internationally known, and its tracking of arctic sea ice decrease and trends in hemispheric snow cover received wide attention. Roger's research turned more toward the cryosphere—all components—but focusing on snow cover, arctic sea ice, and later, permafrost. He served on the Polar Research Board of the National Academy and, 2000–2006, was co–vice chair of the Climate and Cryosphere project of the World Climate Research Programme.

Roger's scientific papers and chapters exceed two hundred. He has also coauthored (with Richard Chorley) nine editions of *Atmosphere, Weather and Climate* (latest ed. 2009) and translated into Spanish and Korean; has written three editions of *Mountain Weather and Climate* (latest ed. 2008) and translated into Russian and Taiwanese; coauthored *Synoptic and Dynamic Climatology* (with Allen Perry), *Synoptic and Dynamic Climatology* (with Andrew Carleton, 2001), and *The Arctic Climate System* (with Mark Serreze, 2005); and coedited *Arctic and Alpine Environments* (with Jack Ives, 1974).

Roger has held many visiting appointments, including a Guggenheim Fellowship in 1982–1983 and a Fulbright Teaching Fellowship at Moscow State University in 2001. In 1999 he was appointed fellow of the American Geophysical Union, and in 2004 the University of Colorado appointed him as Distinguished Professor of Geography. He was awarded the Goldthwaite Polar Medal of the Byrd Polar Center in 2006, and the Founder's Medal of the Royal Geographical Society in 2007. He currently holds a Humboldt Research

Award at the Commission for Glaciology of the Bavarian Academy of Sciences in Munich, Germany.

Edward Derbyshire (Lab 1956–1957)

Ed was born in Liverpool, England, on 18 August 1932. He married Maryon Derbyshire (née Lloyd) in 1956 and they had three sons and eight grandchildren (the eldest researching in metamorphic geology).

Ed obtained his BA with honors at Keele University, England, in 1954; MS at McGill University in 1960; and his doctorate at Monash University (Australia) in 1968. His PhD thesis title was "Glacial Geomorphology and Climate of Western Tasmania."

Ed was demonstrator in geography, Keele University, England, from 1958 to 1960; lecturer in geography, University of New South Wales, Australia, 1960–1962; lecturer and senior lecturer, Monash University, Australia, 1962–1966; lecturer, senior lecturer, reader, and professor of geomorphology, University of Keele, England, 1967–1985; professor and head of department, University of Leicester, England, 1985–1991; and Belle Van Zuylen Professor, University of Utrecht, The Netherlands, 1992.

Currently he holds several positions: research professor in physical geography and Quaternary science, Royal Holloway, University of London, England; emeritus professor in physical geography, University of Leicester, England; and honorary research professor, geological hazards research, Institute of Gansu Academy of Sciences, Lanzhou, China.

Academic distinctions: Antarctic Service Medal of the U.S. (1974); Back Award of the Royal Geographical Society of London, for contributions to glacial geomorphology and research in China (1982); Exemplary Foreign Expert, Government of Gansu, China (1992); Honorary Life Member, International Union for Quaternary Research (1999); Honorary Life Member, Quaternary Research Association (2000); the Varnes Medal of the International Consortium on Landslides, UNESCO and IUGS (2008). Other honors include Honorary Colonel of the Commonwealth of Kentucky in the United States (2006) and Goodwill Ambassador, UN International Year of Planet Earth (2008).

Ed has research experience in Antarctica, Argentina, Australia, Canada, China, France, Iceland, India, Ireland, Italy, Nepal, New Zealand, Pakistan, Scandinavia, Spain, Tibet, Tunisia, the United Kingdom, and the United States. Hi major research interests are (1) sedimentology, stratigraphy, and bulk properties of loess, especially in China; (2) geomorphology, sedimentology, and deformation in Quaternary diamictons: China, India, and Pakistan; (3) landslides in thick loess; (4) geohazards, especially in China and the Himalaya; and (5) medical geology, with reference to mineral particulates.

Other scientific experience: Consultant on major civil engineering works, including the largest reservoir in Europe, stability of oil and gas platforms in the North Sea, collapsible soils and foundation problems in the oil and gas fields of Azerbaijan, and loess cliff stability in the Channel Islands.

Other public service: Royal Army Educational Corps, NATO HQ, Fontainebleau, France, 1954–1956.

External offices held: Honorary Secretary, British Geomorphological Research Group (1971–1975); Chairman, British Geomorphological Research Group (1982–1983); Member, Geological Sciences Research Awards Committee of the UK Natural Environment Research Council (1983–1985); Executive Committee Member, Mt. Everest Foundation (1985–1988); President, Section E (Geography), British Association for the Advancement of Science (1990); Secretary-General, International Union for Quaternary Research (INQUA) (1991–1995); member of the UNESCO Director-General's International Scientific Advisory Board (1997–1999); Chairman, Scientific Board of the International Geological Correlation Programme (IGCP: UNESCO) (1996–2001); United Kingdom Correspondent, IGCP 425 (1998–2002); Member, Earth Resources Committee of the Royal Society (1994–2003); Chairman of the Committee for Research Directions of IUGS (2001–2004); IUGS delegate to IGBP (2001–2004); Member, External Relations Committee (ERC) of the Geological Society of London (1999–2006); Member, United Kingdom Commission to UNESCO, Natural Sciences Committee (2004–present); Secretary for Foreign and External Affairs of the Geological Society of London (GSL) (incorporating the Chairmanship of the External Relations Committee of GSL, the UK National Committee for the IGCP and the UK National Committee for the International Year of Planet Earth [2007–2009]), 2007–present; Member of the Council of the Geological Society of London, 2007–present.

Scientific publications: 268.

James S. Gardner (Lab 1963–1964)

Jim completed his bachelor's degree at the University of Alberta in 1963, proceeding from there to his winter's appointment at the Lab. Research for his McGill master's degree focused on periglacial geomorphology and its mapping in the Schefferville region. This was not his first field experience because he had worked previously as a research assistant on glaciological and geomorphological projects in the Canadian Rockies. He explained, however, that his work at the Lab was a truly formative experience in shaping his academic and research career.

On completing his M.S. degree in 1965, supported by a National Research Council of Canada scholarship, he began studies, also at McGill, leading toward his PhD, which he received in 1968. His thesis research examined slope morphology and processes in the Lake Louise District of the Canadian Rockies. This interest in contemporary slope process was extended with a Killam Postdoctoral Fellowship at the University of Calgary and two academic appointments at the University of Iowa (1969–1973) and the University of Waterloo (1973–1991). Much of this research was supported by grants from the Natural Science and Engineering Research Council of Canada and produced a considerable number of scientific journal publications and conference presentations.

While at the University of Iowa, Jim developed an interest and gained experience in undergraduate teaching and graduate supervision leading to the development of new courses and teaching materials, including an introductory textbook, *Physical Geography*, published in 1974. This commitment to teaching and graduate student supervision extended over thirty-five years to the present at the universities of Iowa, Waterloo, Manitoba, and Victoria. His current activity in this regard is carried out in his capacity as professor emeritus at the Natural Resources Institute, University of Manitoba, and adjunct professor in the Department of Geography, University of Victoria. At Victoria he teaches disaster management and planning, and field studies in coastal geomorphology. He regularly assists with the annual field courses in mountain geomorphology and glaciology. In addition to the many rewards of working with hundreds of undergraduates and scores of graduate students, Jim's teaching has been recognized with awards from the University of Waterloo and the National Council on Geographic Education (U.S.).

Although teaching and research have been the mainstay of Jim's academic career, he developed strong interests in the administration of higher education and management. This resulted in appointments as associate dean of the faculty of environmental studies, and dean of graduate studies (1987–1991), University of Waterloo, and provost and vice president (academic), University of Manitoba (1991–2002), and executive director, International Relations, University of Manitoba (2002–2006). Despite these heavy administrative responsibilities, with support from various institutions, staff, colleagues, friends, and family, Jim was able to continue with some teaching and research.

Jim explained that the primary lesson gained from the McGill Lab experience pertained to the importance of systematic and long-term field-based research. Having grown up in the shadow of the Rockies, where skiing, mountaineering, and trekking were part of everyday life, the new experience of academic research at the Lab showed the way to a convenient marriage of vocation and avocation. This involved participation in projects in many parts of the mountain world: studies of high-altitude rock slope failure, glacier headwall weathering; avalanche and other mountain slope hazards, glacier fluctuation and mass balance, glacier sediment transport, and community-based hazard and resource management. These projects have entailed research in the Canadian Rocky and Columbian mountains, the Karakoram and Western Himalaya in northern Pakistan, the Kullu and Garhwal Himalaya and the Darjeeling Hills in India, and the mountains of southwest China. In addition, Jim's administrative and research interests have led to participation in various health, social development, and hazards and resource management projects in South India, Sri Lanka, and Sichuan, as well as elsewhere in China, Kenya, South Africa, and Botswana.

Jim has published nine books and more than 120 papers in scientific journals. His committee work and general service activities are prodigious. Awards and national and international recognition include: the Wiley Lecture, Canadian Association of Geographers (2003); Distinguished Career Award, Mountain Speciality Group, Association of American Geographers (2003); Queen Elizabeth II Golden Jubilee Medal (2002); fellow of the Royal Canadian Geographical Society (1992); Thomas Roy Award, Engineering Geology Division, Geotechnical Society of Canada (1990); National Council for Geographic Education (U.S.), Distinguished Teaching Achievement Award (1988); and Distinguished Teacher Award, University of Waterloo (1979). (Bio compiled from Jim's direct contribution, with minor modifications.)

Roger Kirby (Lab 1958–1959)

I was born on 10 February 1934, in Plymouth, England; completed two years of National Service in the Royal Air Force; and entered University College, London, as an undergraduate. I led a student expedition to Swedish Lapland (the North Sweden Research Group) and completed an honors degree in geography before taking up the meteorological assistantship at the McGill Sub-Arctic Research Laboratory, Knob Lake. This proved to be an entirely different experience—both for its scientific novelty and, I would guess, for major character building. Even after this interval of fifty years, the year spent at the Lab remains extremely vivid and fresh in my memory. It was a very barren country, but the pioneering population were always helpful; it was a time when free lifts by airplane or helicopter were readily available. I suppose it will all have changed today, but a reasonably accurate record of the geography of central Labrador for that time is contained in the Hammond Innes novel *The Land God Gave to Cain*, first edition 1958.

In the Lab's function as a meteorological station, we were responsible for hourly weather observations, working shifts around the clock. The trick became how to wait until the last moment possible before beginning the repetitive task of dashing out into the cold, making accurate observations at the Stevenson screen, and producing a teletype tape in time to transmit in correct sequence with other weather stations. In the winter, the six-hourly balloon observation was not a favorite job, but observing the aurora borealis as part of the International Geophysical Year was a delight.

In the Lab's other function as a field station of McGill University, we were all postgraduate students with plenty of winter hours for studying and a surprisingly good reference library. The downside was that we couldn't get away from our academic director (Jack Ives), who lived next door and kept us at our course work! The interaction within our small group was basically trouble-free, and of course we also had an RCAF station and a modern company mining town in the background with some facilities to help keep us sane.

The cold winter of meteorological work was in total contrast to the hot summer devoted to our own fieldwork, in my case glacial geomorphology using till fabric analysis of deposits in the surrounding district. The fieldwork went well, in spite of the mosquitoes and black flies, and led directly to an MS thesis and five published papers (Kirby, 1959–1964) and to subsequent work in the United Kingdom. A highlight of the summer season was an extended trip to Grand Falls (later renamed Churchill Falls) with Jack Ives and Brian Hayward. Using a brand-new Land Rover that was Jack's pride and joy, we started at Mile 106 on the Quebec North Shore and Labrador Railway and drove to the falls on an exploration track. Grand Falls had not at this time been developed, and the area was little known. An expedition on foot without compass was not a success. Brian, a fellow student from University College, London, died on fieldwork in the Arctic the following season.

On a lighter note, another personal highlight was a summer fishing trip with Ervil Bentley, a radio engineer and accomplished backwoodsman who rented accommodation at the Lab. He helped me catch my largest fish ever, a 13-lb (6 kg) landlocked salmon. I also remember the royal visit to Knob Lake of Her Majesty Queen Elizabeth II and the Duke of Edinburgh on a very hot and dusty summer day; it was to be another forty-eight years before I was to speak to them personally!

While still at McGill, I responded to an advertisement in *The Times* (London) for an academic position at Edinburgh University and was appointed there. My research eventually led me from geomorphology to cartography, GIS, photogrammetry, and remote sensing. At Edinburgh I established remote-sensing laboratories and was part of the team teaching the M.S. in GIS, the first such course in the United Kingdom. I led the UK delegation to the International Society of Photogrammetry and Remote Sensing in the Netherlands 1996 and was president of the Photogrammetric Society, 1998–2000. Apart from a visiting professorship at the University of Winnipeg (1975–1976) and consultancies in the Netherlands, the United Arab Emirates, and China, I remained at Edinburgh University until retirement.

Olav Løken (Lab 1958–1959)

Olav was born in Ålesund, Norway, on 23 February 1931. He completed his cand. real. degree (comparable to an M.S.) at Oslo University in 1956. The following year he overwintered in the Antarctic at Wilkes Station as a member of the U.S. IGY expedition. He emigrated to Canada in 1958 and went immediately to Knob Lake. This led to his first summer in the Torngat Mountains, after which he studied in Montréal on a McGill-Carnegie-Arctic Research scholarship and spent his second summer in northernmost Labrador with his wife, Inger Marie. These two summers provided material for his doctoral degree, awarded by McGill University in 1962. He accepted a position in the Geography Department of Queen's University in September 1961, returning to northern Labrador the following summer, using the Hudson Bay Company's post at Port Burwell as his base. His research on the glaciation of northern Labrador and the glaciomarine relationships produced the first definition of late-glacial isobases for the eastern Canadian Arctic. This was supported by the first Labrador radiocarbon dates on marine molluscs.

Olav joined the Geographical Branch in 1964 as chief of its Division of Physical Geography and took the major leadership role in the Branch's long-term Baffin Island expeditions, 1964–1967. This included pioneering work with government ice-breaker support to map the continental shelf and fiord bottom topography.

In 1967–1976 Olav was chief of the Glaciology Division, Natural Resources, Environment Canada. He directed field studies in all the glacierized regions of Canada and developed an ice physics laboratory and the glacier inventory in Ottawa. There was a strong emphasis on glacier mass balance measurements as related to water resource problems.

Between 1976 and 1984 Olav directed the Northern Environmental Protection Branch, responsible for planning, directing, and coordinating environmental assessment of oil and gas projects and for recommending terms and conditions for regulatory authorization. This included the Norman Wells Oil Field Expansion and Pipeline Project, the Beaufort Sea Hydrocarbon Production Proposal, and the Lancaster Sound, and South Davis Straits drilling proposals.

Olav's main area of work after retirement in 1990 involved the Far South. He served as secretary of the Canadian Committee for Antarctic Research that promoted participation of Canadian scientists in antarctic research and led to Canada's associate membership of the Scientific Committee for Antarctic Research (SCAR). During this period he contributed to the passage of Canada's Antarctic Environmental Protection Act.

He has published numerous scientific papers and technical reports that have significantly advanced our understanding of the polar regions.

William G. Mattox (Lab Field Director, 1960–1963)

Bill was born on 3 October 1930, in Philadelphia in the United States. He attended Dartmouth College, NH, where he studied local peregrines with Professor Charles Proctor and College Naturalist Doug Wade. As a colleague junior he sailed to Greenland on the McFadden-Turner Arctic Expedition. He completed a bachelor's degree in geography (specializing in northern areas) in 1952. There followed an academic year at Uppsala University on a Swedish government grant and a year at the University of Iceland. During this time he worked on fishing trawlers, studied the Icelandic language, and gathered material for his McGill master's degree.

In 1956 he was drafted into the U.S. Army and served as a language specialist stationed at Stuttgart, Germany, where he met and married his wife, Joan, the following year. They spent a further two years at McGill, where Bill presented his master's and doctoral theses, studies of the fishing industries of Iceland and West Greenland. In the fall of 1960 they moved to Schefferville, where Bill took on the position of field director of the Lab.

In 1964 Bill was appointed fellow of the Institute of Current World Affairs, under whose support he moved to Denmark, where he studied northern economic development, publishing in the Danish arctic journal *Meddelelser on Grønland.* For most of his career he worked for the State of Ohio, Department of Natural Resources, until his retirement in 1992. During this period he supervised water programs such as coastal management, flood plains, and wetlands. In 1972 he became cofounder and director of a study of nesting peregrine falcons in West Greenland, which evolved into the Greenland Peregrine Falcon Survey and was transferred to The Peregrine Fund in 1998. Bill led twenty-five annual field trips to coordinate this study, which involved more than ninety field researchers and developed one of the longest uninterrupted data sets for this species.

Bill and Joan founded the environmental consulting company Greenfalk and, between 1990 and 1996, undertook a long-term study of the effects of military activities on birds of prey in Idaho. In 1994, to broaden their activities to embrace other environmental issues, Bill and Joan formed the nonprofit Conservation Research Foundation. In 1998 they moved permanently from Ohio to Boise, where Bill continued his avian research specializing on wintering raptors in southwest Idaho.

Bill assisted Kent Carnie in publishing the first volume of *The Archives of Falconry* (TAF) *Heritage* publication series. He spent 2008–2009 editing John Swift's long-anticipated *Bibliotheca Accipitraria II.*

Robert James Rogerson (Lab 1965–1966)

Bob was born on 4 July 1943, in Lancaster, England. He emigrated to Canada in 1965 after completing a BA in geography at the University of Liverpool. He was awarded a master's degree by McGill University in 1967 based on fieldwork from the Lab on the northern coast of Ungava. He worked as a scientific officer in the Glaciology Division, Department of Energy, Mines and Resources, Ottawa, until 1969, when he accepted a position as lecturer in the Geography Department of Memorial University, NL. This was later changed to a cross-appointment with geology/earth sciences.

From his position in St. John's he advanced to the rank of full professor and served as head of department (1986–1988), assistant director of the Labrador Institute for Northern Studies (1985–1988), and executive director of the Oceans 2000 Secretariat (1988). During his twenty-year period in Canada's far east, he made many research trips to Labrador, especially the Torngat Mountains, and introduced a generation of students to mountain fieldwork.

In 1988 Bob was appointed professor of geography (1988–2006) and dean of arts and sciences (1988–1990) at the University of Lethbridge, AB, from where he extended his research to the Canadian Rockies, especially the Yoho Valley. He also found time to serve as chair of the Geography Department at Lethbridge (1994–1997; 2003–2006) and took a two-year secondment as executive director of the Canadian Centre for GIS in Education (1990–1992) in Ottawa. He "retired" in 2006 to become vice president (academic) of University Canada West, in Victoria, BC.

Bob handled many other offices with distinction. A sample includes: National Research Council, Sub-Committee on Glaciers (1975–1985); Organizing Committee, Canadian Institute of Mining and Mineralogy conference on Mineral Prospecting in Glaciated Terrain, St. John's (1982–1983); President, Geological Association of Canada, Newfoundland Section (1985–1986); Chair, Western Deans of Arts and Sciences (1990); President, Western Division, Canadian Association of Geographers (2007–2009); Member, British

Columbia Ministry of Advanced Education–Degree Quality Assessment Board (2008–2010). He also taught extensively throughout his career in geomorphology, glaciology, hydrology, glacial and Quaternary geomorphology, and the Arctic region.

Bob's awards include the Canadian Association of Geographers 2001 Award for Excellence in the Teaching of Geography and the J. Louis Robinson Award (2005) for Service to the Discipline of Geography. He has written twenty-six scientific papers and chapters in books and has co-authored the book *Forever Better: Continuous Improvement in Higher Education*. He has published a considerable amount of "creative" writing and poetry, much of it under the pseudonym Anyon Wright.

Bob and Maria Luzvisminda Calulo were married in 1968; their daughters, Neriza and Luiza, were born in 1970 and 1982. Bob also asked that mention be made of important items not in his formal curriculum vitae (from which the foregoing was extracted). He became a proud grandfather on 18 January 2009, with the birth of Luiza's son, Dylan James Grillo Rogerson. The garden of his new house on Moss Street in Victoria is full of rhododendrons and contains a beautifully polished roche moutonnee.

Geoffrey Sherlock (Lab 1957–1958)

Geoff was born in Epsom, Surrey, England, on 8 April 1936. He graduated in geography from Leeds University in 1957 under the guidance of Professor Ronald F. Peel and set out for Montréal in early July. He recollects that the Heathrow departure lounge was then a marquee, and the flight took some thirteen hours in a BOAC Stratocruiser. He joined the rest of the 1957–1958 Lab crew to attend the McGill Summer School at Stanstead, where he also met the group who were destined to spend the following year at Lake Hazen, northern Ellesmere Island. The Lab group then endured a three-week meteorological training session at Dorval (Pierre Elliot Trudeau) Airport. He notes that this was a dismal experience with an instructor who knew less about his subject than Don Macnab.

Geoff frankly admits that his year at the Lab convinced him that academia was not to be his life's course, although he came to realize that the experience provided him with a remarkable foundation for his eventual career choice. The Lab stay included not only the strictures of met observations, but the worthwhile learning experience of living in a very limited social atmosphere. He was a leader in developing the local Boy Scouts and undertook an adventurous canoe trip on the Howells River with Roger Barry and Erv Bentley. He returned to England in July 1958 to spend a year back at Leeds University, taking a postgraduate Certificate of Education including outdoor activities. This led him into teaching deprived inner-city children, where he took groups on their first outings to the Peak District and the Pennines. He describes a subsequent three and a half years teaching at a boys' grammar school in Rotherham, where his Knob Lake sojourn gave him a decided edge as a teacher with an adventure experience.

Geoff and Shirley, another Leeds University geographer, were married in April 1960. By 1963 Shirley, sensing her husband's growing restlessness toward teaching, spotted an advertisement in the *Guardian* for a BBC radio producer to create school programs in geography. He was offered the position, and they moved to London. From this point Geoff's real career took off—planning new BBC radio series and contributing to the early development of Radiovision. He claims that the informal photography instruction at the Lab, provided by Roger Tomlinson, gave him an advantage, as he became a "one-man band" traveling widely, conducting interviews, taking photographs, editing, and writing scripts and often presenting them on the air. Eventually this led to program formulation based on worldwide travel and included programs about Knob Lake, the James Bay hydroelectric power project, and similar topics in such far-flung locales as Australia and China.

Geoff's contributions to geographical education led to his election as fellow of the Royal Geographical Society in 1975 and he received the RGS Cuthbert Peek Award in 1985. He became an active member of the Council of the British Geographical Association, chairing one of its committees, and a member of the Education Committee of the RGS. In conclusion, it is relevant to quote directly from Geoff's notes: "I hope this makes clear how much I valued my time in Knob Lake and that it made a huge difference to my career. I did not contribute much to the academic community but...I may well have enthused a lot of young geographers."

Geoff's far-reaching influence has probably exceeded that of many of his Lab colleagues.

Roger F. Tomlinson (Lab 1957–1958)

Roger was born in Cambridge, England, in 1933. After completing his national service as a pilot with the RAF, he studied for his bachelor's degree in geography at the University of Nottingham. He emigrated to Canada in 1957 and proceeded immediately to the Lab. After completing his master's degree at McGill in 1959 he served briefly as assistant professor at Acadia University. He next worked as manager of the computer mapping division of Spartan Air Services in Ottawa. This was followed by private consulting for the federal government and then a position as the director of regional planning systems with the Canadian Department of Forestry and Rural Development.

While with the federal government he initiated, planned, and directed the development of the Canada Geographical Information System, the world's first computerized GIS.

University College, London, awarded him a doctoral degree for his dissertation entitled "The Application of Electronic Computing Methods and Techniques to the Storage, Compilation, and Assessment of Mapped Data." In 1977 he founded the consulting firm Tomlinson Associates Ltd. and has led the organization, with branches in Australia, Canada, and the United States, up to the present.

Roger served as chair of the International Geographical Union Commission on GIS for twelve years, during which time he pioneered the concepts of world-wide geographical data availability. He is widely recognized as the father of Geographical Information Systems and has received extensive recognition, including the Order of Canada in 2001 for "changing the face of geography as a discipline." In 2003 he was awarded the Gold Medal of the Royal Canadian Geographical Society. He is a past president of the Canadian Association of Geographers. The Association of American Geographers awarded him the James R. Anderson Medal for Applied Geography in 1995 and the Robert T. Aangeenbrug Distinguished Career Award in 2005. He is an honorary fellow of the Royal Geographical Society and the 1988 recipient of its Murchison Medal. In 1996 he was awarded the GIS World Lifetime Achievement Award. He is a fellow of University College, London, and has been awarded honorary degrees by the University of Nottingham, Acadia University, the University of Lethbridge, and McGill University.

Charles Rowland Twidale (Lab 1955–1956)

R owl" was born on 5 April 1930, in Lincolnshire, England. He obtained a first-class honors BS in geography at Bristol University in 1951, followed by an MS two years later. After working with CSIRO in Australia, he arrived in Montréal in September 1955 and proceeded to Knob Lake shortly thereafter. He undertook fieldwork in periglacial geomorphology and carried out his share of the weather observations and associated duties. He obtained his doctorate at McGill in 1957. His recollections of life at the Lab include the conviviality of his colleagues and good relations with the local Bell Telephone Company and RCAF personnel, although he also has memories of the weather room: noise—the continual chatter of the teletype printer and the frequent slamming of doors.

Rowl and his wife, Kate, were married in Montréal in May 1956. Ken Hare gave away the bride, and Helen Hare took care of most of the arrangements.

They had decided that, if possible, they would return to an academic post in Australia, preferably at the University of Adelaide. The timing was not entirely perfect, so they took the opportunity to spend time with family and friends in England and were duly invited to Adelaide in 1958.

The University of Adelaide provided Rowl with his lifelong base, first in the Department of Geography and later (1988) in the Department of Geology and Geophysics, where, in "retirement," and as honorary visiting research fellow, he still maintains an office. His lecture courses in geomorphology were widely acclaimed, and his research and publication record is prodigious. His special interests were with granite landforms and landscapes. The structural impacts of neotectonic events, fold mountain belts, desert forms, pediments, duricrusts, anthropogenically induced changes, and the identification and dating of old landscapes also feature in his publications. He found that Adelaide was an excellent center for field research and states that "teaching was a joy."

His international experiences were extensive: at various times, visiting professor at Rensselaer Polytechnic Institute; University of California, Berkeley; University of the Western Cape, Cape Town; University of Austin, Texas; Texas A&M University; Universidad de Salamanca; and Universidad de Coruña, among others.

Rowl's research publications have received universal recognition. They include authorship of fifteen books, coeditorship of ten others, and more than 350 essays and papers in refereed monographs, books, and journals, together with about a hundred short, unrefereed booklets, articles, and reviews.

His accomplishments resulted in numerous awards and honors, including a D.Sc. from Bristol (1977); Doctor Honoris Causa, Universidad Complutense de Madrid (1991); National Science Foundation Senior Foreign Scientist Fellowship (1965–1966); Verco Medal, Royal Society of South Australia (1976); Serton Memorial Lecture, Stellenbosch University (1978); and the Mueller Medal, ANZAAS (1993). In 1998 he was appointed honorary professor at Coruña in perpetuity. He toured the United States as Australian government lecturer in 1999. He served on several editorial boards, was consultant to the Commonwealth Railways and Northern Territories Geological Survey, and undertook geotechnical work on the then-proposed Alice Springs-Darwin railway (1980–1983), in addition to working on (and continuing to be engaged in) other projects.

Rowl and Kate have two sons and a daughter, eight grandchildren, and, as of April 2009, one great-granddaughter.

A concluding quotation provides an especially attractive insight: "I have been fortunate in my collaborators, both in Australia and overseas, and I have benefited enormously from various travel and research grants . . . from various visiting posts in universities in U.S., Spain, and Africa. In spite of being a loner and nonjoiner, I feel fortunate to have been and still to be a member of that wonderful global club called Academe."

Leslie A. Viereck (1930–2008; Lab 1954–1955)

Les, born in South Dartmouth, Massachusetts, graduated from Dartmouth College in 1952. During his U.S. military service in Alaska, with three colleagues he pioneered the South Buttress route on Mount Denali (Mount McKinley) and completed the first summit traverse. He arrived at the Lab in time for its opening in September 1954. During the 1955 summer he undertook extensive botanical research that led to his MS degree at the University of Colorado, Boulder. Thereafter, he transferred his research attention back to Alaska and completed his doctorate under Professor John Marr, also at the University of Colorado. He married Eleanor "Teri" Norton in 1955. Together they traveled to Fairbanks, where Les took a position with the University of Alaska. He worked with Project Chariot; from today's viewpoint, this seemingly reckless project aimed to excavate a harbor on Alaska's northwest coast by detonating a nuclear device. It provoked a crisis in Les's career, during which his lifelong high principles cost him his position. In his letter of resignation, he wrote, "A scientist's allegiance is first to truth and personal integrity and only secondarily to an organized group such as a university, a company, or a government." In 1993 the university granted him an honorary degree, emphasizing his courageous stand in those early years of his career.

Les worked with the Alaska Department of Fish and Game and, from 1963 until his retirement in 1999, he was principal plant ecologist with the Institute of Northern Forestry, U.S. Forest Service. He coauthored the immensely popular field guide *Alaska Trees and Shrubs*. He was elected fellow of the Arctic Institute of North America and served on its board of directors. He also served as associate editor of *Arctic* and *Arctic, Antarctic, and Alpine Research*. His scientific production included numerous papers on many aspects of Alaskan ecology, including plant succession after fire, flooding, and glacier retreat. He became recognized informally as the dean of Alaska botany. Les and Teri had two sons and a daughter, all of whom were introduced to life in the Alaska wilderness from their earliest years.

[This account relies heavily on an obituary written by David F. Murray and published in 2008 in *Arctic* 61(4):451–452.]

John Welsted (1935–2009; Lab 1958–1959)

John was born in Norwich, England, on 6 December 1935. He obtained his BSc (geography with geology) from the University of Bristol in 1958 and proceeded to Montréal and Knob Lake that summer. John wrote the following letter, and it is reproduced verbatim, because it provides an especially interesting personal reflection.

When writing about my year at Knob Lake (1958–1959) it is impossible to separate academic from personal matters. Although I had just obtained a good B.Sc. from the University of Bristol, I was still recovering from the death of my mother a few months earlier. I had travelled little outside Britain. When I arrived at Knob Lake I was not sure whether I had "bitten off more than I could chew."

This feeling was emphasized by the fact that two of my compatriots at the McGill Sub-Arctic Research Lab (Roger Kirby and Olav Løken) seemed so much more adept than me. I was intimidated/in awe of them. At times I considered abandoning my quest for a master's degree, but fortunately I did not.

My choice of a thesis topic was largely by a process of elimination. I did not feel confident of travelling in interior Labrador-Ungava, nor along the mountainous northeast coast. This led me to the St. Lawrence Estuary and eventually to the large "delta" at the mouth of the Natashquan River. This was reasonably accessible by train from Knob Lake to Sept-Îles and then by boat along the North Shore. I had arranged with Ray Holt (the fourth student in my year at Knob Lake) to accompany me and help me with my fieldwork. Unfortunately for me—good for Ray—he got a job at Knob Lake a couple of weeks before we were due to leave. So I was on my own at Natashquan for about 12 weeks although I got some help from a member of a First Nation based at Old Post Village at the mouth of the Natashquan River. The language barrier was quite a strain. However, I was lucky that Brian Haywood got permission from the Lab to come to help me for two weeks. These were spent almost constantly surveying the landforms of the "delta." To my great sorrow, Brian disappeared the next year while doing his own fieldwork in Labrador/Ungava. The choice of the Natashquan Delta as a thesis topic was sound in that it was a tightly defined topic, not too large for an M.Sc.

Two events stand out during my time at Knob Lake: first, the fire at the Iron Ore Company of Canada warehouse on New Year's Eve, 1959, resulting in a major set back for the IOCC; second, a visit by the Queen and Prince Philip during the summer of 1959. On a day-to-day basis I remember—not particularly fondly— doing weather balloon observations at 2.00 a.m. with a −30 degree Celsius temperature and determining ice thickness on Knob Lake with an auger that did not function very well.

During my time at Knob Lake the group consisted of: Don Mcnab, in charge of weather observations: four students (Ray Holt, Roger Kirby, Olav Løken, and John Welsted), and Erv Bentley. We also had close contact with Stan Saines, one of the radio operators. I have lost contact with all of them except Roger Kirby, who I visited at his home in Haddington, Scotland in 1990. We have maintained contact since and I hope Roger will be able to visit us in Victoria.

I have mixed emotions about my year at Knob Lake. Academically it was a struggle but I persisted and eventually obtained an MSc. This gave me the confidence to tackle a PhD some years later, which led to a career in academia (mainly at Brandon University) that I enjoyed immensely. Aside from academic things, during the winter Olav taught me to ski. Although I never became very proficient at downhill skiing, over the years I did become reasonably good at cross-country skiing. It was my main physical recreation during the winters I lived in Brandon (1965–2002).

After receiving his MS degree from McGill in 1960, John taught geography at Maidenhead Grammar School, England, for a year, returning to Canada to teach at Oromocto High School, New Brunswick (1962–1964). A fourth crossing of the Atlantic saw John as demonstrator in geography at the University of Bristol that led to the award of a doctorate in 1971. Finally, he moved to Brandon University, MB, in 1965, rising to full professor in 1978. He was awarded emeritus status on his retirement in 1997. His main fields of interest have been air photo interpretation and remote sensing, geomorphology, and water resources. He served as acting head and head of the department of geography at Brandon, as well as a member of the university senate and senate representative on the university's board of governors.

John's research papers include studies of the land emergence and morphology of the Bay of Fundy coastline and of the landforms, geomorphology, and water resources of Manitoba. He has published over forty papers in scientific journals and chapters in books. In 1996 he coedited the book *The Geography of Manitoba: Its Land and Its People*, and in 2008 he authored the online monograph "Manitoba from the Air: A Geographical Interpretation" (http:// mbair.brandonu.ca).

For his air photo interpretation of the Bay of Fundy coastline, John received the Autometric Award of the American Society of Photogrammetry in 1979 and the John H. Warkentin Award of the Prairie Division of the Canadian Association of Geographers in 1996. In 2001 he received the Award for Service to Geography in the Western Interior presented by the Prairie Division of the Canadian Association of Geographers, which was renamed in his honor as the John Welsted Award.

John has lived in retirement in Victoria, BC, since 2002. It was with great sadness that I learned of John's unexpected death shortly after compiling his biography.

H. Anthony Williamson (1935–2004; Lab 1957–1958)

Tony was born in 1935 in Quaker Hill, Pawling, NY. He completed his undergraduate studies at Dartmouth College in 1957 and arrived at the Lab shortly afterward. He received his master's degree from McGill in geography in 1964, although had become heavily involved with the Department of Anthropology and was already drawn into Labrador coast affairs. From 1965 until 1967 he was a research fellow with the Institute of Social and Economic Research, Memorial University, Newfoundland, becoming the university's extension service representative, Labrador Coast, for the following three years. During this time he was resident at Cartwright. These years were the beginnings of his lifelong commitment to the Innu and Inuit of Labrador and related matters of resource use and appropriate environmental management.

During the 1970s and 1980s Tony carried out an assessment of the inshore fisheries for the Canadian Royal Commission on Labrador, an evaluation of the Newfoundland-Canada Native Peoples Agreement, and assessment of communication needs along the Labrador coast. Memorial University pioneered in the use of telecommunications for distance education, and the interactive loop along the Labrador coast was used not only for delivery of university programs but by local and regional organizations for such purposes as board meetings and community consultations. Tony was a major factor in the success of all these many-sided activities. As the founding director of Memorial's Labrador Institute of Northern Studies, located in Goose Bay-Happy Valley, he raised $4 million between 1979 and 1985. This supported participatory research in Métis land use and occupancy studies, the value of country foods for aboriginal communities, and the establishment of pilot programs in the training of aboriginal people in renewable resource technology and management.

The last ten years before his retirement in 1996 were devoted to promoting international partnerships and building institutional capacities with partner universities to meet the development needs of their respective countries. These efforts were primarily funded by the Canadian International Development Agency (CIDA) and the International Development Research Centre (IDRC). After his retirement he remained extremely active as president of H. A. Williamson and Associates, Community Services, with involvements ranging all the way from assessment of the economic and environmental effects of military flight training, to analysis of the importance of seals and sealing to the Labrador Inuit, to study of the potential impacts of nickel exploitation at Voisey's Bay. He pursued these many activities with vigor until his final illness.

Appendices

Appendix 1: Glacial Drainage Channels

Dr. Carl Mannerfelt, a Swedish geographer, was a pioneer in the study of these remarkable steep-sided, water-eroded channels that appear in closely spaced groups sloping obliquely down hillsides and mountain slopes in Norway and Sweden. Frequently there are sets of up to twenty or thirty on a single mountain slope, with a vertical spacing of 10 ft (3 m) to 30 ft (9 m). Mannerfelt determined that the most uniform of them had been formed by meltwater streams that flowed between a wasting glacier or ice sheet margin and the adjacent hillside. As the ice progressively thinned, each successive year witnessed the formation of a new channel. The approximation of the slope and rate of melting of the wasting ice sheet or glacier could be obtained by careful survey. A plot of the directions of channel slope over a wide area would give a good indication of the location of the last remaining sections of a former ice sheet.

As glacial drainage channels were found high on hillsides and mountain ridges, it could be assumed that the snowline (equilibrium line) of the time was close to, or above, the highest land as it emerged through the wasting ice mass. This led to the conclusion that the ice mass was climatically dead and stagnant, or moving only very slowly.

More detailed work, of which the studies around Helluva Lake represent a small part, led to the conclusion that many of these channels had not been formed strictly lateral to the ice margin but had cut their way beneath the ice (sublateral channels). The extreme form, the so-called subglacial chutes, indicated that meltwater had flowed under gravity down the steepest slope beneath the ice. Careful study of such forms has greatly assisted our understanding of glacier and climate conditions during the closing phases of the last ice age. It has also been instructive to study the process of their formation along the margins of present-day glaciers.

Appendix 2: Tors

The tors of Dartmoor in southwestern England were some of the earliest of these occasionally spectacular features to attract the attention of geomorphologists. Well-developed tors appear as prominent irregular upstanding rock masses, sometimes with balancing blocks littered over them, and attracted much local superstition in past centuries. They are the hard cores of bedrock that have resisted erosion, in contrast to their "softer" surrounding rock. In the late nineteenth century, when the great controversy concerning the thickness and extent of the former ice sheets of the ice ages arose in Scandinavia and the United Kingdom, tors were frequently cited as proof that they were located above and/or beyond the limits of the former ice sheets. This contention has always been in dispute, ignored by antagonists or assumed to have been formed after the ice ages by rapid frost-splitting in the cold climate of mountain tops or arctic and subarctic lowlands.

Protagonists insisted that they had not been formed postglacially and that they could not have been overridden by the ice or they would have been eroded away. Therefore, they became important indicators of former ice sheet thickness and extent. The latter opinion was widely held in the 1950s and 1960s. Thus, discovery of glacial erratics (see appendix 3) lying on top of tors in the Torngat Mountains and the mountains of Baffin Island proved highly enigmatic. More recent interpretation, based on newer methods, such as cosmogenic dating, assumes that the tors were covered by ice sheets at their maximum extent but were protected because the ice was so thin that it was frozen to the bedrock and so was not able to erode. Some movement of the ice was necessary, however, to carry the erratics to their unlikely perches.

Appendix 3: Erratics

The term refers to anomalous rocks or boulders that are foreign to the underlying bedrock on which they are found. This implies that they have been transported there by some natural process, at least when found on remote mountaintops where human interference can be discounted. A glacial erratic, therefore, is assumed to be a foreign rock that has been detached from a contrasting type of bedrock distant from the place where it was found and transported there by a glacier or ice sheet. Blocks perched on mountaintops have also been the cause of controversy. Some may be the result of weathering out of inclusions from the underlying bedrock—blocks incorporated into the original magma deep within the earth's crust and not completely assimilated.

In such regions as the Canadian and Fenno-Scandinavian shield country, where the bedrock is a complicated mix of granites, gneisses, and other metamorphic rocks, clear differentiation of glacial erratics is often impossible. At the other extreme, if a block of limestone, for instance, were discovered on a Torngat summit, underlain by Canadian Shield rocks, there would be no uncertainty. However, depending on the position of an unusual block, other mechanisms, such as landslides, rockfalls, soil creep, or even sea ice or floating lake ice, could be responsible. Delicately perched blocks on mountain tops, and especially if they are lying on tors, would be accepted as glacial erratics. In geomorphology, multiple discovery of the same type of evidence strengthens any conclusion. Despite this, tors and glacial erratics, or presumed erratics, have been subject to controversy for more than a century.

Appendix 4: Isobase

An isobase is a theoretical line that connects points of equal postglacial uplift, or emergence, along sea coasts, fiords, and inlets, or around former ice-dammed lakes. During the ice ages, the great weight of the ice sheets depressed the earth's crust, in extreme cases by more than 1,000 ft (305 m). The greatest amount of depression of the crust roughly coincided with areas where the ice sheets were thickest. On their disappearance at the close of the last ice age, the depressed crust rebounded, but with a significant time lapse—some areas, such as southeastern Hudson Bay, James Bay, and the Gulf of Bothnia between Sweden and Finland, are still slowly recovering (on the order of inches, or centimeters, a century). In coastal areas the land has emerged from the sea, leaving raised marine shore features up to several hundred feet (100 m or more) above present sea level. Marine mollusc shells associated with the raised shore features provide the necessary carbonaceous material for radiocarbon dating. The strandlines, or raised beaches, have been tilted because of the differential degree of the original depression determined by distance from the centers of the former ice sheets. Similar sets of features are associated with regions that were formerly flooded by ice-dammed freshwater lakes, such as the Naskaupi Glacial Lakes of the Indian House Lake area.

A combination of precise leveling of the raised marine and lake shore features and their dating by radiocarbon isotope methods can provide information about the relationship between glacier retreat and falling sea levels (conversely, rising land), and also about deep-earth geophysics. Application of these methods has been extremely rewarding for studies in glacial geomorphology throughout northern Canada and in many other formerly glacierized regions.

Endnotes

1. When Dr. Svenn Orvig, director of the Montréal Office of the Arctic Institute of North America, delivered my first monthly scholarship paycheck, the amount was surprisingly large. Orvig was amused and thought I was in luck. It turned out to be a payment at the level of a university lecturer. Hare had forgotten to readjust his precautionary act. It took so long to sort things out that we were worried that we wouldn't be able to pay the month's rent.

2. The photograph of the 1954 jökulhlaup is included to illustrate the great significance of summers in southeast Iceland in terms of my research efforts in Labrador-Ungava and Baffin Island. I did not realize until I started to tackle fieldwork in Labrador-Ungava how rewarding the Icelandic experience had been. It was a great advantage to have become familiar with glacier processes, especially the gigantic glacier floods, in trying to understand the significance of landforms influenced by similar processes but several thousand years earlier and, by the 1950s, totally inactive.

3. After the expedition Malcolm went to the Antarctic with the Australians and produced a monograph on what, for many years, stood as the standard reference on the physics of blowing snow. Jim spent two years with the British Antarctic Survey obtaining the Polar Medal. Cuchlaine was appointed to a personal chair of geography at Nottingham University and succeeded Professor Edwards on his retirement. She also joined me on Baffin Island in the 1960s.

4. This arduous piece of fieldwork was to provide "ground truth" (to cross-check actual investigations on the ground with the air photograph images) across a range of vegetation cover types, as part of an ambitious scheme of air photograph interpretation covering the entire Labrador-Ungava peninsula—another component of Hare's master plan for a better understanding of the geography of this forbidding and little-known part of eastern Canada.

5. The original mining exploration camp was called Burnt Creek. Knob Lake was incorporated in May 1958 as Schefferville. The name *Knob Lake* will be used throughout the text.

6. Alan Rayburn in *A Dictionary of Canadian Place Names* (Oxford University Press, 1997: 198) explains: "its name may be traced to the Portuguese *lavrador* (meaning small land-holder) João Fernandes. Fernandes explored the coasts of North America at the end of the 1400s and the beginning of the 1500s. In 1500 he identified Kalaalit Nunaat (Greenland) as *Tiera del Lavrador*, and the present Labrador was called *Tiera del Corte Real*, given for another *lavrador*, Gaspar Corte-Real. About 1560, after the name Greenland was found to be in general use, mapmakers shifted Labrador to the mainland."

7. For a full discussion of the provincial boundary dispute from the Québec point of view, see Courville (2008: 4–15).

8. Various spellings have been used over the last 150 years. The Hudson's Bay Company established the short-lived "Fort Nascopi" in the mid-nineteenth century. A. P. Low used "Nascaupee River" and Mrs. Leonidas Hubbard followed Low's usage and also referred to the "Nascaupee" people. Lawrence Coady (2008) uses "Naskapi." "Naskaupi River" is used on Canadian government maps. Today the Naskaupi and Montagnais First Nations are known collectively as Innu.

9. John ("Jock") Tuzo Wilson was a preeminent promoter of the theory of plate tectonics, bringing the earlier and, for the time, discredited work of Alfred Wegener (1880–1930) out of obscurity for serious scientific examination and validation. Tuzo Wilson is credited with being one of the major contributors to the concept of sea-floor spreading that revitalized the earth and natural sciences.

10. The Canadian Government's production of trimetrogon air photography (RCAF) of its entire area in a very short time was a remarkable achievement and provided an outstanding tool for examination of enormous tracts of land that otherwise would have remained virtually unknown for years to come.

11. This statement represents a viewpoint based on British or European academic tradition, an approach that, for northern Canada, Hare was attempting to overthrow or at least modify.

12. Pep Wheeler recounted to me his basis for choosing Labrador as the region to which he devoted his life. He had applied to Vilhjalmur Stefansson to accompany him to the High Arctic. All he received was a postcard that read briefly: "Other rivers flow into the Arctic. Yours Stefansson."

13. Tanner used the term *Labrador Peninsula* as synonymous with Hare's *Labrador-Ungava*; hence Tanner's *eastern part of the Labrador Peninsula* refers to the area that today is the mainland section of the Province of Newfoundland and Labrador.

14. There are two summits on the same massif, on or close to the height-of-land in the Torngat Mountains south of Nachvak Fiord. This has provided further fuel to the seemingly permanent dispute between Québec and Newfoundland. The former seized the initiative and secured its preferred name for the 5,420-foot summit. Subsequently, and somewhat ironically, it was discovered that a separate high point clearly within Newfoundland territory was slightly higher. The Newfoundland authorities named it Mount Caubvik.

15. Although he was not a field man, Hare's enthusiastic support aided many students and colleagues in their field research. His autobiography has been archived recently by the Royal Geographical Society (pers. comm., R. G. Barry, 10 April 2008).

16. However, given that access in those days was restricted to travel over land, this was not surprising in itself. Nevertheless, the vast gap in geographical knowledge needed to be filled.

17. This was already being transformed based on the provision of the trimetrogon air photography (author's qualification).

18. The initial suspicion that Hudson Bay froze over by early January was based on a McGill University master's study by Margaret R. Larnder (née Montgomery), who recorded the sudden cut-off of heavy snowfall and unusually high air temperatures along the east coast of the bay, thereby indicating that the nearby source of warm open water had been eliminated. She, together with colleague Moira Dunbar of the DBR staff, accompanied the airborne missions. However, the coordinator of the flights was Keith Greenaway, who explained that the account given above is somewhat oversimplified. He and several other observers accompanied the Lancaster

flights. The regular route was northward from Ottawa up the east coast of Hudson Bay to Hudson Strait, across to Coral Harbour, then down the west coast to Churchill. There was a rest-stay in Churchill then a return in the reverse direction. The issue was really one of definition. In Keith's recollection (pers. comm. 15 March 2009), the bay was never frozen solid, but choked with floating ice. Local people on the east coast, facing a prevailing westerly wind, would observe total ice cover after the beginning of January. Local people on the west coast, with a predominantly off-shore wind, would often be able to observe open water from the edge of the land-fast ice to the horizon. This is a significant reinterpretation of Hare's view although it does not detract from his concern over the need to fill in the vast tracts of virtual geographical unknown.

19. George Jacobsen's fascination with the Canadian Arctic subsequently placed him at the forefront of establishing in 1960 the internationally acclaimed Axel Heiberg expeditions, led by Fritz Müller, one of the McGill-Carnegie-Arctic Scholarship Program beneficiaries (1954–1956). George was subsequently conferred a McGill honorary degree, became an officer of the Order of Canada, and served as the highly successful president of the Canadian Equestrian Olympic Committee.

20. When I eventually had a chance to conduct detailed field studies in 1958, it became apparent that this initial interpretation was oversimplified (see pp. 92–94).

21. Teri was a student of animal ecology and eventually received her PhD under Professor Robert Pennack at the University of Colorado, Boulder, where Les was awarded his PhD in plant ecology guided by Professor John Marr. In retrospect this was a remarkable coincidence, as I was destined to succeed Marr as director of the Institute of Arctic and Alpine Research at the University of Colorado, although that would be twelve years later.

22. After completing their doctorates at the University of Colorado, Les and Teri became professionally committed to Alaska.

23. It was obvious that part of the personality problem was related to the widespread male chauvinist notion of the times that wilderness and arctic was a man's world and that the "weaker" sex was decidedly weaker. This viewpoint pervaded the Canadian Federal Government. The Geological Survey of Canada, for instance, had a rigid policy of not allowing women to work in the northern wilderness. It set up a confrontation for me that I had to struggle against several times, both in the context of the Lab and fieldwork in Labrador-Ungava, and later in Baffin Island in the 1960s.

24. This surprised us as we were well aware of the origin of the word *pemmican.*

25. By Canadian, read "non-American."

26. There was a single possibility. AINA was in the process of negotiating with the Canadian federal government for a contract that would involve preparations for publication of a new *Arctic Pilot* (1959). It would require several research staff, and Svenn Orvig, as director of the AINA Montréal office, had suggested that I leave a CV and an expression of interest.

27. Here we learned that the camp had been anticipating the arrival of the lieutenant governor of Newfoundland. Fortunately for us, his arrival at Makkovik had been delayed by ice conditions. This released the Beaver and so permitted our flight north to the Torngats. An additional, if minor, benefit was that we were given the sandwiches that had been prepared for the VIP.

28. Professor Hare, however, made three stipulations: first, since the location of the Lab was just within the border of Québec Province, I must become fluent

in French; second, I must learn to swim, as I would be dependent upon canoe traverses; and three, I must break with my English formality and address him as Ken. He only had the satisfaction of the third requirement being fulfilled; the second did not follow until after my sixtieth birthday; and the first . . . !

29. The SS *John Biscoe* was the name of the supply ship under charter to the British Falkland Islands Dependencies Survey (FIDS). It later became the British Antarctic Survey.

30. My recent observation of current Ottawa TV weather forecasts indicates that our innovative graduate student observer of all those years ago should be taken on as adviser.

31. The Naskaupi were Protestant. Their Montagnais confreres on the opposite side of the town were Roman Catholic, strictly the "property" of the priest, and ne'er the twain did meet.

32. "Sammy," of course, was his anglicized name. He became a frequent visitor to the Lab and a great friend. Through him I obtained my first mountain snowshoes (circular and difficult to adjust to, although he took me out a couple times to teach me). It was with great sadness that I met him when I returned to the Lab some twenty years later for a visit and found him suffering from the effects of alcohol addiction. Nevertheless, I was delighted that he had remembered me and had come to the Lab to say hello.

33. This was usually so effective that it prompted the keeping of a jug of water in the refrigerator because drinking water from the taps was always warm.

34. The visit to Montréal and McGill proved routine, a convivial reunion with the faculty. Martha Mount, Ken Hare's indomitable departmental secretary, claimed that my sunburned face gave me away. Martha insisted I could hardly deny that I had sneaked away for at least a week in Florida, the last thing I would have contemplated.

35. The problem of persuading senior government officials to allow women students to visit arctic facilities arose again a few years later in connection with a series of expeditions that I organized to Baffin Island. The field program depended on access to the DEW Line (Distant Early Warning Line). The gracious reception we experienced at Indian House Lake, although on a much larger scale with respect to Baffin Island, was repeated. And, in balance, the difficulty of breaking through the "opposition" was so much greater.

36. This stream is named Ruisseau Natikamaukau on the 1:250,000 map of Lac Brisson, published in 1983.

37. For the purpose of our 1958 survey, we had taken the 980-foot (298.7 m) mean of a series of radar spot heights (Ives 1960a).

38. *Isobase* is a term used for a line that joins points of equal isostatic land uplift across the surface. In this case, the regional pattern of isobases would give an indication of the location of the greatest thickness of a former ice sheet.

39. Much of this proposed work was completed over the next decade (Matthew 1961; Harrison 1963; Barnett 1964, 1967; Barnett and Peterson 1964; Peterson 1965; Matthews 1967).

40. I don't know the origin of this curious, if disrespectful, name. With the rapid opening of the iron ore mines and the production of special topographical maps, scale 1:50,000, a large number of new place names were urgently needed to allow adequate identification of lakes, campsites, ore bodies, and other topographical features. IOCC staff indulged in a flourish of naming everything after wives, children, girlfriends, and senior IOCC personnel. Thus we have indelibly glued

to official topo maps such names as Mary-Jo Lake, Carol Lake, John Lake, Geren Mountain, etc. ad infinitum. All such names break most of the stringent rules set by the Canadian Permanent Committee on Geographical Names. Regardless of a certain lack of aesthetics, the sheer demand for several hundred place names won out—a salutation to all those early wilderness pioneers who did so much for Canada's developing economy in the early postwar years.

41. Ed had served as the member of the Lab's 1956–1957 winter crew and had spent the 1957 summer for his McGill master's thesis researching the deglaciation of the Howells–Goodwood Valley, concentrating on the glacial drainage channels. His findings supported my Kivivic Lake Divide hypothesis. However, with my absence at Indian House Lake I had not heard of his successful application to the Banting Fund (AINA) for a return visit. He had arrived at Knob Lake after our departure for Helluva Lake and reached the head of the IOCC trail by the Lab jeep, walking in from there. My next chance meeting with Ed proved to be more than two decades later in west-central China!

42. To the best of my knowledge, all the winter staff of the first ten years of Lab operations either enthusiastically endorsed this viewpoint or else willingly accepted it. However, it should be kept in mind that the majority were geography honors graduates from the United Kingdom who had themselves taken courses in climatology during their undergraduate training, and several of them had had previous practical experience.

43. His application to AINA was funded and that allowed him to invite a Norwegian colleague, Arve Fiskerstrand, to cross the Atlantic and serve as his field assistant in the Torngat Mountains during the 1959 summer. Olav emerged as one of the most outstanding Lab members, and our close collaboration continued for many years, leading to an excellent expedition partnership in Baffin Island.

44. He died tragically on the Koroksoak River in 1960 (see pp. 112–123).

45. During the 1956 and 1957 summers, the IOCC had employed Ben Bonnlander, a McGill graduate who had been with the AINA/McGill 1953 expedition to Baffin Island. Ben had installed strings of thermocouples in mining test holes to depths of more than 200 ft (60 m). He had determined that much of the Ferriman ore body, as well as surrounding areas at higher altitudes, was underlain by permafrost, in places more than 200 ft (60 m) thick. The IOCC had terminated the project, satisfied that they had obtained all the data necessary.

46. I had been aware that during the previous late summer the IOCC had been obliged to reject such a late-season order because of uncertainties about frozen ground.

47. The primary reason for the royal visit to Canada was that Queen Elizabeth was to join President Eisenhower for the ceremonial opening of the St. Lawrence Seaway.

48. Eventual comparison of the mean air temperature of the ridge crest with the ten-year official DOT mean showed a close coincidence despite the difference in altitude. Detailed examination of the data showed that winter temperatures at the Lab were consistently lower than those from the higher station, because the Lab was influenced by strong temperature inversions. During the summer the reverse was the case, and ridgetop temperatures were also somewhat depressed in comparison with the Lab by the greater frequency of cloud and fog cover. This indicated the unreliability of drawing microclimatological generalizations based on differences in altitude alone.

49. Professor Hamelin visited the Lab the following spring and we successfully conducted Camille's formal thesis examination. This was the first occasion when award of a graduate degree was confirmed at the Lab.

50. Both Brian's and John's work led to papers being accepted for publication in scientific journals.

51. The Duplessis years in power became known as *Le Grand Noirceur*, or "The Great Darkness."

52. I have wondered to this day why the official date of his death is recorded as 7 September. While the Duplessis regime was partly based on an alliance with the Church, to assume that the "powers that be" want it on record that he had died on a Sunday seems to be a stretch of the imagination.

53. The so-called Abisko Symposium proved a highly significant turning point. This was how I met Dr. Gunnar Østrem, who later joined me in Baffin Island, and many other international experts, several of whom have remained colleagues for life.

54. Roger G. Barry (Lab 1957–1958) also presented his first professional paper at the same conference (Barry 1961).

55. The same Max Budgell whom I had met in Nain in 1957.

56. Anne-Marie had been one of the ski cottage group at McGill during the winters of 1954–1955 and 1955–1956 and a close friend. Her work on Great Bear Lake was intended for her master's thesis at McGill.

57. The discovery of the life jackets, in particular, had raised much controversy. In practice, however, to upset a canoe on such a cold lake would more likely result in death through hypothermia rather than drowning.

58. Considering that the body discovered was initially identified as that of Brian, this raises a serious question: how to explain the tent and André's diary that was located upstream of the accident site? Nor does it explain the fact that it was André's personal possessions that were recovered downstream of the wrecked canoe, not Brian's.

59. I met Barry at Frobisher (Iqaluit) in the following June (1961) as I was on my way to north-central Baffin Island. Barry had reached Frobisher, en route to the Hudson Strait south coast. It was a very fortuitous meeting, as a vital part of his field equipment had been misplaced in transit and I was able to replace most of it from my own supplies.

60. The expeditions cited above originated in England, although they provided Canada with a corps of arctic specialists who were major players in the postwar surge of interest: Graham Rowley, Tom Manning, and Pat Baird.

61. Actually, Ross Mackay was born to missionary parents in China (Taiwan). After a brief time at McGill with Ken Hare, he moved to the University of British Columbia, where he became a fixture of far-reaching influence.

62. It is curious that, with the exception of Norman Drummond, not a single McGill graduate took part in the early winter staffing of the Lab.

63. The marriage of Pep and Eleanor Wheeler occurred many years into Pep's Labrador wilderness research. Eleanor described the urgency of fitting into her new husband's efficiently set ways. Pep had adapted a canoe for rowing on the open sea. With a rifle across his knees, he had trained himself to shoot at any suddenly appearing seal in a single movement. But with his new wife in the stern, a place previously empty, his instinctive move almost cost Eleanor somewhat more than her hat.

64. Margaret related to me that her initials procured the acceptance of her application, as they were mistaken for Mr. rather than M.R. Montgomery. But she may have been joking; Professor and Mrs. Pierre Dansereau were also members.
65. In fact, I amazed everyone, including myself, by taking a large arctic char with my first and only cast; I demurred from making a second cast despite jocular provocation—stop while you are ahead!
66. Dartmouth and Bowdoin colleges, New England, also had a well-established arctic expeditionary tradition.
67. AINA was transferred from McGill University to the University of Calgary in 1975.
68. John T. Andrews, D. Martin Barnett, Roger G. Barry, David A. Harrison, Olav H. Løken, and myself.
69. The following year John obtained permanent Geographical Branch status and went on to make a major contribution to the field research. As with Roger G. Barry, he joined the faculty of the Institute of Arctic and Alpine Research at the University of Colorado in 1968, where he also completed a most influential career.
70. This was the first formal institutionalization for glaciology in Canada. It has evolved, enlarged, and experienced several administrative relocations under the leadership of such dynamic individuals as Olav Løken, Simon Ommaney, and the late Roy "Fritz" Koerner. Today it is an internationally recognized unit for glaciological research, being given a further boost at the onset of the current International Polar Year. It is worth recording that the establishment of glacier mass balance studies in the Canadian Rockies for the Geographical Branch by Gunnar Østrem (in particular on the Peyto Glacier) has produced a permanent record of observation, 1964 to present, the longest in Canada.
71. Trevor Lloyd was also the founding director of the Geographical Branch (1947) and, subsequently, chair of Geography at Dartmouth College, New Hampshire.

References

Adams, P. *Trent, McGill, and the North: A Story of Canada's Growth as a Sovereign Polar Nation*. Peterborough, ON, Canada: Cover to Cover, 2007.

Andrews, J. T. "Variability of Lake Ice Growth and Quality in the Schefferville Region, Central Labrador-Ungava." *J. Glaciol.* 4, no. 33 (1962):337–347.

———. "The Analysis of Frost-Heave Data Collected by B. H. J. Haywood from Schefferville, Labrador-Ungava." *Canadian Geogr.* 7, no. 4 (1963a):163–174.

———. "The Cross-Valley Moraines of the Rimrock and Isortoq River Valleys, Baffin Island, NWT: A Descriptive Analysis." *Geogr. Bull.* 19 (1963b):49–77.

———. "End Moraines and Late-Glacial Chronology in the Northern Nain-Okak Section of the Labrador Coast." *Geogr. Ann.* 45 (1963c):158–171.

Andrews, J. T., and C. H. McCloughan. "Pattern of Lake Ice Growth on Knob Lake, 1954–1960." *McGill Sub-Arctic Research Papers* 11 (1961):64–89.

Annersten, L. J. "Investigations of Permafrost in the Vicinity of Knob Lake, 1961–62." *McGill Sub-Arctic Research Papers* 16 (1964):51–143.

Barnett, D. M. "Some Aspects of the Deglaciation of the Indian House Lake Area, with Particular Reference to the Former Glacial Lakes." MSc thesis, McGill University, Montréal, 1964a.

———. "Temperatures in the Northwest Room at the McGill Sub-Arctic Research Lab." *McGill Sub-Arctic Research Papers* 18 (1964b):60–64.

———. "Glacial Lake McClean and Its Relationship with Glacial Lake Naskaupi." *Geogr. Bull.* 9 (1967):96–101.

Barnett, D. M., and J. A. Peterson. "The Significance of Glacial Lake Naskaupi 2 in the Deglaciation of Labrador-Ungava." *Can. Geogr.* 8 (1964):173–181.

Barry, R. G. "A Note of the Synoptic Climatology of Labrador-Ungava." *Quat. J. Roy. Met. Soc.* 86 (1960):557–565.

———. "The Application of Synoptic Studies in Palaeoclimatology: A Case-Study for Labrador-Ungava." *Geogr. Ann.* 42 (1961):36–44.

———. "Meteorological Aspects of the Glacial History of Labrador-Ungava with Special Reference to Vapour Transport." *Geogr. Bull.* 8, no. 4 (1966):319–340.

———. "Variations in the Content and Transport of Water Vapour over Northeastern North America during Two Seasons." *Quart. J. Roy. Met. Soc.* 93 (1967):535–543.

———. "Vapor Flux Divergence and Moisture Budget Calculations for Labrador-Ungava." *Cahiers de Geographie de Québec* 12, no. 25 (1968):91–102.

Bell, R. "Observations on Geology, Mineralogy, Zoology and Botany of the Labrador Coast, Hudson's Strait and Bay." *Geological Survey of Canada, Report of Progress*, 1882–1884, vol. 1, Pt. D (1884):5–62.

Bergerud, A. T., S. N. Luttich, and L. Camps. *The Return of the Caribou to Ungava*. Montréal: McGill-Queens University Press, 2007.

Bergquist, K. *Great Circles: The Keith Greenaway Story*. Ottawa, ON, Canada: Kathy Berquist, 2008.

Bird, J. B., ed. *Permafrost Studies in Central Labrador-Ungava*. Montréal: McGill University, 1964.

Bonnlander, B., and G. M. Major-Marothy. "Permafrost and Ground Temperature Observations, 1957." *McGill Sub-Arctic Research Papers* 16 (1964):33–50.

Briner, J. P., G. H. Miller, P. T. Davis, P. R. Bierman, and M. Caffee. "Last glacial Maximum Ice Sheet Dynamics in Arctic Canada Inferred from Young Erratics Perched on Ancient Tors." *Quat. Sci. Reviews* 22 (2003):437–444.

Brown, R. J. E. "Permafrost Distribution in the Southern Part of the Discontinuous Zone in Nouveau-Québec and Labrador." *Géogr. Phys. Quat.* 33 (1979):3–4.

Bryant, M., and J. Bryant. *Then…Friends Sharing Memories*. Ottawa: Mary and Joe Bryant, 2007.

Carlson, A. E., P. U. Clark, G. M. Raisbeck, and E. J. Brook. "Rapid Holocene Deglaciation of the Labrador Sector of the Laurentide." *J. Climate* 20 (2007):5126–5133.

Clark, P. U., R. B. Alley, and D. Pollard. "Northern Hemisphere Ice-Sheet Influences on Global Climate Change." *Science* 286 (1999):280–283.

Clark, P. U., E. J. Brook, G. M. Raisbeck, F. Yiou, and J. Clark. "Cosmogenic [10]Be Ages of the Saglek Moraines, Torngat Mountains, Labrador." *Geology* 31 (2003):617–629.

Clarke, G. K. C., D. W. Leverington, J. T. Teller, and A. S. Dyke. "Paleohydraulics of the Last Outburst Flood from Glacial Lake Agassiz and the 8200 BP Cold Event." *Quat. Sci. Rev.* 23(2004):389–407.

Coady, L. *The Lost Canoe: A Labrador Adventure*. Halifax, NS, Canada: Nimbus, 2008.

Coleman, A. P. "Northeastern Part of Labrador and New Quebec." *Canadian Geol. Surv.* (1921): Memoir 124.

Courville, S. *Quebec: A Historical Geography*. Vancouver: University of British Columbia Press, 2008.

Daly, R. A. "The Geology of the Northeast Coast of Labrador." *Harvard Univ. Mus. Comp. Zool. Bull.* 38 (1902):2056–2270.

Derbyshire, E. "Glaciation and Subsequent Climatic Changes in Central Quebec-Labrador: A Critical Review." *Geogr. Ann.* 42, no. 1 (1960):49–61.

———. "Fluvioglacial Erosion Near Knob Lake, Central Labrador-Ungava, Canada." *Bull. Geol. Soc. Am.* 73 (1962):1111–1126.

Dyke, A. S. "Late Quaternary Vegetation History of Northern North America Based on Pollen, Macrofossil, and Faunal Remains." *Géogr. Phys. Quat.* 59 (2005):211–262.

———. "Laurentide Ice Sheet." In *Encyclopedia of Paleoclimatology and Ancient Environments*, ed. V. Gornitz. Dordrecht, The Netherlands: Springer, 2009, 517–520.

Falconer, G. "Glaciers of Northern Baffin and Bylot Islands." *N.W.T. Geogr.* (1962): Paper 33.

Falconer, G., J. D. Ives, O. H. Løken, and J. T. Andrews. "Major End Moraines in Eastern and Central Arctic Canada." *Geogr. Bull.* 7 (1965):137–153.

Flint, R. F. "Growth of the North American Ice Sheet during the Wisconsin Age." *Bull. Geol. Soc. Am.* 54 (1943):325–362.

———. *Glacial Geology and the Pleistocene Epoch.* New York: John Wiley, 1947.

———. *Glacial and Pleistocene Geology.* New York: John Wiley, 1957.

———. *Glacial and Quaternary Geology.* New York: John Wiley, 1971.

Forbes, A. *Northernmost Labrador Mapped from the Air.* New York: American Geographical Society, 1938.

Fulton, R. J., ed. *Quaternary Geology of Canada and Greenland.* Geological Society of America, vol. K-1, 1989.

Gosse, J. C., and F. M. Phillips. "Terrestrial in situ Cosmogenic Nuclides: Theory and Application." *Quat. Sci. Rev.* 20 (2001):1475–1560.

Hare, F. K. "The Climate of the Eastern Canadian Arctic and Sub-Arctic and Its Influence on Accessibility." PhD diss., Université de Montréal, Canada, 1950.

———. A *Photo-Reconnaissance Survey of Labrador-Ungava.* Memoir 6, Geographical Branch, Ottawa, 1959.

Harrison, D. A. "The Tilt of the Abandoned Lake Shorelines in the Wabush-Shabogamo Lake Area, Labrador." In *Geographical Studies in Labrador. Annual Rept. 1961–62, McGill Sub-Arctic Research Papers* 15 (1963):14–22.

Hattersley-Smith, G. "Some Remarks on Glaciers and Climate in Northern Ellesmere Island." *Geogr. Ann.* 42 (1960):45–48.

Hattersley-Smith, G., A. P. Crary, and R. L. Christie. "Northern Ellesmere Island, N.W.T." *Arctic* 8 (1955):3–36.

Henderson, E. P. "A Glacial Study of Central Quebec-Labrador." *Geological Survey of Canada, Bull.* 50 (1959).

Hubbard Jr., Mrs. Leonidas. *A Woman's Way Through Unknown Labrador.* London: John Murray, 1908.

Ives, J. D. "Glaciation of the Torngat Mountains, Northern Labrador." *Arctic* 10, no. 2 (1957):66–87.

———. "Proposal for the Adoption of a Standard Nomenclature." In *Field Research in Labrador-Ungava, McGill Sub-Arctic Research Papers* 6 (1959a):77–82.

———. "Glacial Drainage Channels as Indicators of Late-Glacial Conditions in Labrador-Ungava." *Cahiers de Géographie de Québec* 3 (1959b):57–72.

———. "Former Ice-Dammed Lakes and the Deglaciation of the Middle Reaches of the George River, Labrador-Ungava." *Geogr. Bull.* 14 (1960a):44–70.

———. "The Deglaciation of Labrador-Ungava: An Outline." *Cahiers de Géographie de Québec* 4, no. 8 (1960b):323–343.

———. "Permafrost in Central Labrador-Ungava." *J. Glaciol.* 3 no. 28 (1960c): 789–790.

———. "Indications of Recent Extensive Glacierization in North-Central Baffin Island, NWT." *J. Glaciol.*, 4 (1962):197–205.

———. "A Proposed History of Permafrost Development in Labrador-Ungava." *Géogr. Phys. Quat.* 33, nos. 3–4 (1979):233–244.

———. *Skaftafell in Iceland: A Thousand Years of Change.* Reykjavik: Ormstunga, 2007.

Ives, J. D., and J. T. Andrews. "Studies in the Physical Geography of North-Central Baffin Island." *Geogr. Bull.* 19 (1963):5–48.

Ives, J. D., and R. G. Barry, eds. *Arctic and Alpine Environments.* London: Methuen, 1974.

Jackson, C. I. "Insolation and Albedo in Quebec-Labrador." *McGill Sub-Arctic Research Papers* 5 (1958).

———. *Does Anyone Read Lake Hazen?* Edmonton, AB, Canada: Canadian Circumpolar Institute, 2002.

Jansson, K. N. "Glacial Geomorphology of North-Central Labrador-Ungava, Canada." PhD diss., Stockholm University, 2002.

Jansson, K. N., and J. Kleman. "Early Holocene Glacial Lake Meltwater Injections into the Labrador Sea and Ungava Bay." *Paleoceanography* 19 (2004): PA 1001, doi:10.1029/2003.

Løken, O. H. "On the Vertical Extent of Glaciation in Northeastern Labrador-Ungava." *Can. Geogr.* 6 (1962a):106–119.

———. "The Late-Glacial and Post-Glacial Emergence and the Deglaciation of Northernmost Labrador." *Geogr. Bull.* 17 (1962b):23–56.

Lotz, J. *The Best Journey in the World: Adventures in Canada's High Arctic.* Lawrencetown Beach, NS, Canada: Pottersfield Press, 2006.

Manning, E. W. *Igloo for the Night.* London: Hodder and Stoughton, 1943.

Marquette, G. C., J. T. Gray, J. C. Gosse, F. Courchesne, L. Stockli, G. Macpherson, and R. Finkel. "Felsenmeer Persistence under Non-erosive Ice in the Torngat and Kaumajet Mountains, Quebec and Labrador, as Determined by Soil Weathering and Cosmogenic Nuclide Exposure Dating." *Can. J. Earth Sci.* 41 (2004):19–38.

Matthew, M. E. "Deglaciation of the George River Basin, Labrador-Ungava." Paper 29, Geographical Branch, Ottawa, 1961.

Matthews, B. "Late Quaternary Land Emergence in Northern Ungava, Quebec." *Arctic* 20, no. 3 (1967):176–202.

Nebiker, W. A. "Evapotranspiration Studies at Knob Lake, June–September 1956." *McGill Sub-Arctic Research Papers* 3 (1957).

Nebiker, W. A., and S. Orvig. "Evaporation and Transpiration from an Open Lichen Woodland Surface." *Proc. IUGG, Toronto* 3 (1957):379–384.

Nicholson, F. "Permafrost Spatial and Temporal Variations near Schefferville, Nouveau-Québec." *Géogr. Phys. Quat.* 33, nos. 3–4 (1979):265–277.

Odell, N. E. "The Mountains of Northern Labrador." *Geogr. J.* 82 (1933):193–210; 315–325.

Orvig, S. "Net Radiation Flux over Sub-Arctic Surfaces." *J. Met.* 18, no. 2 (1961):199–203.

Østrem, G. "Mass Balance Studies on Glaciers in Western Canada, 1965." *Geogr. Bull.* 8, no. 1 (1966):81–107.

Peterson, J. A. "Deglaciation of the Whitegull Lake Area, Labrador-Ungava." *Cahiers de Géographie de Québec* 9, no. 18 (1965):187–196.

Prichard, H. H. *Through Trackless Labrador.* New York: Sturgis and Walton, 1911.

Rayburn, A. *Dictionary of Canadian Place Names.* Oxford: Oxford University Press, 1997.

Rogerson, R. J., and D. J. A. Evans. "Glacial Geomorphology and Chronology in the Selamuit Range/Nachvak Fiord Area, Torngat Mountains, Labrador." *Can. J. Earth Sci.* 23 (1986).

Rowley, G. W. *Cold Comfort: My Love Affair with the Arctic.* Montréal: McGill-Queen's University Press, 2007.

Tanner, V. "Outlines of the Geography, Life and Customs of Newfoundland-Labrador." *Acta Geographica Fenniae* 8, no. 1 (1944).

Viellette, J. J., A. S. Dyke, and M. Roy. "Ice-flow Evolution of the Labrador Sector of the Laurentide Ice Sheet: A Review, with New Evidence from Northern Quebec." *Quat. Sci. Rev.* 18 (1999):993–1019.

Wallace, D. *The Lure of the Labrador Wild.* New York: Fleming H. Revell, 1905.

Weart, S. R. *The Discovery of Global Warming.* Cambridge, MA: Harvard University Press, 2003.

Wenner, C. G. "Pollen Diagrams from Labrador: A Contribution to the Quaternary Geology of Newfoundland-Labrador." *Geografiska Annaler* 29, nos. 3–4 (1947):137–373.

Wheeler, E. P., II. "The Nain-Okak Section of Labrador." *Geogr. Rev.* 25, no. 2 (1935):240–253.

———. "Topographical Notes on a Journey Across Labrador." *Geogr. Rev.* 28, no. 3 (1938):475.

———. "Pleistocene Glaciation in Northern Labrador." *Geol. Soc. Am. Bull.* 69, no. 3 (1958):343–344.

Index

Note: *Italicized* page numbers indicate photographs.

A

Abisko Symposium, 137, 170n53
Abloviak Fiord, 29, 43, 46, 61
  photo, *46*
Adams, Peter, 124, 134, 136, 138
Air Force Island, 126
Alaska Trees and Shrubs (Viereck and Little), 157
Allington, Kathleen, 63
Amor, Hugh, 70
Amor, Jean, 70, 102
Ananek, Stanley, 116
Andrews, John T., 100, 107, 109, 113–14, 119, 137, 171n69
  biography, 141–42
  photo, *112*
Annersten, Lennart, 124
Arctic Biological Station, 135
Arctic Institute of North America (AINA), 167n26
  establishment of, 10–11
  Ives work for, 53–56
  U.S.-Canadian schisms in, 11–12, 34
Arctic Pilot, 10, 167n26
Association of Canadian Universities for Northern Studies (ACUNS), 138
Astray Lake
  canoe trip to, 16–24
  geographic position, 18, 19
  photo, *19*
aurora borealis, 26, 67, 149

B

Baffin Island, 1, 60, 110, 125
  Barnes Ice Cap on, 54, 137
  expeditions, 11, 26, 66, 110, 114, 125, 128, 130, 136–37
  glacierization and deglaciation, 74

Baird, Patrick D., 10–11, 135, 170n60
  and Grenier-Haywood tragedy, 114, 115, 116–18, 121, 122
  as McGill Lab director of field studies, 66, 111
Barnett, Martin, 123
Barr, William, 142–43
Barry, Roger G., 63, 66–67, 69–70, 95, 137
  biography, 143–45
  photo, *74*
  research areas, 72, 74, 144
bears, 85–86
Beavan, Paul, 35, 36, 56, 74, 113
  and glacial research project, 32–33, 38
Bell, R., 6, 7, 31
Bentley, Ervil, 16, 27, 63, 67, 149
  photo, *74*
Bird, Beryl, 9, 113, 128
Bird, J. Brian, 9, 113, 135
Bishop, Barry, 114
Blackadar, Bob, 126, 135–36
Boesch, Hans, 66
Bonnlander, Ben, 63, 99, 169n45
Borden Island, 126
Bowdoin Canyon, 5
Bowdoin College, 5, 6
BRINCO (British Newfoundland Corporation), 8
BRINEX (British Newfoundland Exploration)
  founding of, 8
  support to McGill Lab, 32, 40, 56, 65, 74, 93, 113–14
  in Torngat Mountains, 30, 33, 36, 38, 42–43
Brown, Roger, 99
Budgell, Max, 39, 116

179

G

Galloway, Jock, 14, 16
Gardner, James S., 127
  biography, 146–48
Gathorne-Hardy, G. M., 86
Geografiska Annaler, 56
Geographical Branch, 113, 126, 171n70
  Ives position with, 110, 112, 114,
    136–37
  support to McGill Lab, 79, 93, 113,
    118, 123–24
Geological Survey of Canada, 15, 126,
  135, 167n23
George River, 5, 83, 130, 134
  naming of, 4
Geren, Dick, 93, 96, 99, 100
Glacial Lakes McLean, 84–85, 134
Glacial Lakes Naskaupi, 83–84, 134
  photos, *82, 84, 85*
Glacial Map of Canada, 79, 88
glacierization and deglaciation, 8, 131–35
  directional movement of, 50–51, 52,
    61–62
  and erratic rocks, 59, 60, 133, 162–63
  Flint hypothesis on, 8, 30–31, 50, 51,
    52, 131
  glacial drainage channels, 14–15, 55,
    90, 91, 98–99, 133, 161
  Henderson thesis on, 55
  increased understanding of, 137
  instantaneous, 52, 72, 131
  isobases, 88, 150, 163, 168n38
  Ives hypotheses on, 52, 88, 91
  Odell theory on, 7, 31, 51, 133
  permafrost research and, 98–99, 103,
    134
  schematic map, *132*
  and semipermanent snow patches, 98
  shorelines, 88, 123
  and Torngat Mountains, 7, 31, 51–52,
    59, 61–62, 88, 124, 133–34
  tors, 60, 162
  See also Laurentide Ice Sheet
global warming, 137
Gold, Lorne, 99
Goodfellow, Joan, 118
Grand Falls. *See* Churchill Falls
Gray, Jim, 124, 133, 138–39
Greenaway, Keith, 126, 128, 166–67n18
Grenfell, Wilfred, 4, 30
Grenfell missionaries, 4, 125, 128

Grenier, André, 97, 101, 105, 109, 112
  about, 113
  fatal journey, 113–23, 170n58

H

Hamelin, Louis-Edmond, 97, 119–21,
  170n49
Hare, F. Kenneth, 18, 33, 123, 128,
  135–36
  air photo research by, 3, 88
  and Baird, 111, 118
  biographical information, 9
  as chancellor of Trent University, 138
  and Dartmouth College, 26
  and establishment of McGill Lab, 2,
    8–9, 10, 11
  and Grenier-Haywood tragedy, 114,
    115, 117–18
  Ives and, 55, 65, 75, 79, 97, 110, 114,
    115, 167–68n28
  as new immigrant, 135
  on schisms within research agencies,
    12
  on success of McGill Lab, 12
  unpublished autobiography, 9, 166n15
  and vegetation research, 26
  on winter observation, 12, 93, 127
Harrison, David, 123
Harrison, James, 118–19, 126, 135–36
Hattersley-Smith, Geoffrey, 55, 135
Haywood, Brian, 100, 105, 107, 109, 112
  about, 112–13
  fatal journey, 113–23
  photos, *108, 112*
Hebron, 4, 41, 48
  evacuation of Inuit from, 39–40, 42
Helluva Lake, 90–92, 168n40
  photo, *93*
Henderson, Eric, 55–56
Hesketh-Prichard, Hesketh V., 5, 80, 86
  Through Trackless Labrador, 71
Hettasch, Katie and Seigfried, 40, 41, 42
Hill, Peter, 137
Holt, Ray, *97,* 105, 158
Hopedale, 4, 105, 113–14
Hoppe, Gunnar, 15, 56, 109, 114
Hubbard, Leonidas, 5, 17, 24, 35
Hubbard, Mina, 35, 80, 86, 130
  *A Woman's Way Through Unknown
    Labrador,* 5–6
Hudson, Henry, 1

Hudson Bay, 1
  during Ice Age, 31
  ice cover during winter, 10, 11,
    166–67n18
Hudson's Bay Company, 1, 4, 5, 125
Hustich, Ilmari, 7
hydroelectric power, 2, 8, 18

I

Ice Age. *See* glacierization and
  deglaciation
Igloo for the Night (Manning), 128
Indian House Lake (Lac de la Hutte
  Sauvage), 79–89
  commercial development of, 130
  photos, *81, 87*
Ingstad, Helge and Ann Stine-Moe, 128
Innes, Hammond, 148
International Geographical Congress
  (IGC), 109, 112
International Geophysical Year (1957–
  1958), 67–68
Inuit, 30, 123
  evacuation from Hebron, 39–40, 42
  and missionaries, 4
Iron Ore Company of Canada (IOCC),
  78, 102, 104, 108, 134
  McGill Lab relations with, 70, 93, 95,
    96, 99
isobases, 88, 150, 163, 168n38
Ives, Anthony "Tony" Ragnar, 98
Ives, Jack D.
  children of, 98, 100, 102
  fundraising by, 96, 113
  and Grenier-Haywood tragedy, 114,
    117–18, 119–20
  and Hare, 55, 65, 75, 79, 97, 110, 114,
    115, 167–68n28
  at Helluva Lake, 90–92
  at Indian House Lake, 79–89
  on Knob Lake in 1955, 13–28
  as McGill Lab field director, 55, 63,
    65–79, 92–111
  photos, *19, 22, 45, 49, 74, 97, 112*
  position with Geographical Branch,
    110, 112, 114, 136–37
  at Torngat Mountains, 33–62, 130
Ives, Nadine, 98, 100, 102
Ives, Pauline, 27, 28, 65, 67, 75–76, 78,
  113, 114, 119
  on Astray Lake canoe trip, 16–24
  on Helluva Lake field trip, 91–92

on Indian House Lake field trip,
    80–88
  job with CIL, 20, 29
  as "librarian," 70–71
  map compiler and computer job, 53,
    56
  outdoor skills, 7, 21
  photos, *19, 22, 25, 74, 85*
  pregnancies and childbirths, 99–100
  with Queen Elizabeth, 102
  on Torngat Mountains field trip,
    33–50, 57–61, 122, 130

J

Jackson, C. Ian, 63, 135
Jacobsen, George, 11, 167n19
James, Cyril, 11
Jansson, K. N., 133
Johnson, Peter and Ellie, 33, 35, 36,
  62–63, 112, 128

K

Kangalaksiorvik Lake, 43–49
  photo, *43*
Kaumajet massif, 41
Kimble, George, 9
Kirby, Roger, 105, 112
  biography, 148–50
  photo, *97*
Kleman, J., 133
Kmoch, George, 4
Knob Lake
  airstrip, 13
  geographic position, 24–26
  glacial geology of, 15
  incorporation as town of Schefferville,
    99
  Ives at, 13–28
  photos, *25, 63*
Koerner, Roy "Fritz," 171n70
Kohlmeister, Gottlieb, 4
Komaktorvik Lakes, 29, 43, 46
  photos, *47, 49, 50*
Komaktorvik River, *47*
Koniak, George, 116
Koroksoak River, 6, 8, 57, 61, 134
  Grenier-Haywood fatal trip down,
    105, 113, 114, 118
  photo, *62*
Kranck, Hakan, 7
Krüger, Anne-Marie, 118, 170n56

L

Labrador Lake Plateau, 18, *23*
Labrador Trough, 8
Labrador-Ungava, 1–12
  air photography of, 3, 10, 18, 79, 129,
    166n10
  creating maps of, 3, 5, 6, 10, 129
  economic development, 2, 8, 130
  first settlements, 4–5
  geography, 2–3
  iron ore in, 2
  lack of knowledge about prior to 20th
    century, 3–4, 10
  Mid-Canada Line sector in, 13
  modernization of fieldwork in, 129
  mountaineering in, 8
  navigation of waterways in, 2–3
  origin of name, 1
  Québec-Newfoundland dispute on,
    1–2
  scientific expeditions in, 5–8
  vegetation, 26, 31, 134
  winter temperatures, 3, 68, 71, 103,
    169n48
Lamothe, Claude, 137
Land God Gave to Cain, The (Innes), 148
Langlois, Jean-Claude, 13, 26
Larnder, Margaret R., 53, 128, 166n18,
  171n64
Laurentide Ice Sheet
  advances in understanding of, 137
  disintegration of, 91
  Flint's hypothesis on, 30–31
  and glacial channel formation, 15
  Ives hypothesis on, 52, 91, 132–33
  Odell's conclusion on, 8
  outlet glaciers from, 59
  photos, *46, 85*
  See also glacierization and
    deglaciation
Lee, Bert, 126
lemmings, 44
Lewis, Cyril "Cy," 14, 16
Lewis, Vaughan, 114
Linton, David, 10, 114
Lloyd, Trevor, 11, 138, 171n71
Løken, Inger Marie, 109, 112
Løken, Olav, 105, 109, 112, 124, 137,
  169n43, 171n70
  biography, 150–51

  joins McGill Lab, 95
  photos, *97, 109*
loons, 20
Lotz, Jim, 14, 16, 17, 63
Low, A. P., 8, 166n8
  at Astray Lake, 16, 18, 19
  detects iron ore, 2
  maps Labrador-Ungava, 5

M

Mackay, J. Ross, 126, 170n61
Macnab, Don, 71, 75, 92, 96, 97, 100
  in Antarctic, 65, 66, 71
  joins McGill Lab, 63, 66
  leaves McGill Lab, 106
  marriage, 75–76
  photos, *74, 77*
  and weather monitoring, 90, 95
Macnab, Jean, 75–77, 92, 97, 100, 106
  photos, *77*
Makkovik, 4, 38
Manley, Gordon, 65–66, 98
Mannerfelt, Carl, 15, 56
Manning, "Jackie," 128
Manning, Tom
  expedition of 1949 by, 126, 135,
    170n66
  as head of AINA, 34, 53
Mansfield, Arthur, 136
Marble Lake, 18, 22
Marchant, Peter, 32
Marmet, Jürg, 136
Marr, John, 167n21
Matthew, Mike, 100, 107, 113–14, 117,
  119
  photo, *112*
  research area, 108, 112, 123
Matthews, Barry, 123, 170n59
Mattox, Joan, 123
Mattox, William G. "Bill," 102, 123, 124
  biography, 151–52
  and Grenier-Haywood tragedy, 119,
    121, 122
McCloughan, Charles, 107, 111, 114, 123
  photo, *112*
McConnell, J. W., 11
McGill Axel Heiberg expeditions, 128,
  135, 136
McGill-Carnegie-Arctic scholarship pro-
  gram, 11, 32, 95, 126, 127, 135, 136

McGill Sub-Arctic Research Laboratory
   accomplishments of, 12, 125, 127
   becomes McGill Sub-Arctic Research
      Station, 127, 135
   and bureaucratic schisms, 11–12,
      28, 34
   complaint to DOT about, 101
   contributions of to IOCC, 93, 95
   creation of, 2, 9–12
   demonstrated importance of field
      research, 147
   establishment of Knob Lake base,
      13–14, 127
   funding, 11, 32, 96, 99, 113, 129
   Ives as field director, 55, 63, 65–79,
      92–111
   Ives resignation from, 111
   living accommodations for staff, 28, 67
   meteorological responsibilities of,
      68–69, 71, 92–93, 95, 149, 169n48
   in 1958–1959, 97–108
   in 1959–1960, 107–11
   in 1960–66, 123–24
   predominance of immigrants in, 126,
      127, 135
   support from Geographical Branch,
      79, 93, 113, 118, 123–24
   and Trent University, 138
   winter staff in, 12, 93, 127
McGill University
   in arctic and subarctic research, 8–9,
      11, 12, 126, 135
   and Grenier-Haywood tragedy, 118,
      120, 121, 122, 123
   offers professorship to Ives, 110
McLaren, Digby, 136
McLean, John, 5
Mellor, Malcolm, 75
Melville Peninsula, 125
Mercer, John, 53–54
Merry Adventures of Robin Hood, The
   (Pyle), 70
Michie, George, 13, 79, 90
   research of, 26
Michie, Margaret, 79, 90
Mid-Canada Line, 13, 93, 107
Montagnais indigenous people, 3, 18,
   166n8
Mont D'Iberville/Mt. Caubvik, 8,
   166n14

Mont Haywood, 122–23
   photo, 62
Moravian missionaries, 3, 4, 125, 128
   photo, 41
Morgan, Millet, 16, 26, 67
Morris, Art, 13
Mortensen, Erik, 83, 91
   photo, 94
Mount, Martha, 96, 168n34
Mount Tetragona, 29, 49
Mowat, Farley, 61
Müller, Fritz, 66, 135, 138, 167n19
   about, 136

N

Nachvak Fiord, 4
Nain, 38–41, 48
   photos, 39, 41
   transfer of Inuit to, 39–40
Nakvak Lake, 56, 57, 60
Naskaupi indigenous people, 3, 68, 72,
   102, 166n8
   and Christian missionaries, 69,
      168n31
National Research Council (NRC), 12,
   98, 107
Neal, Carol and "Buzz," 70
Nebiker, Walt, 63
Never Cry Wolf (Mowat), 61
Newfoundland, 8
   and control of Labrador-Ungava, 1–2
Nicholson, Norman, 55, 79, 110, 114
Northwest Passage, 1, 2
North West River, 4–5, 35
Nunatak Hypothesis, 31

O

Odell, Noel, 6–7, 8, 10, 29
   on glacierization, 7, 8, 31, 51, 133
   Ives and, 34, 59
Okak, 4
Ommaney, Simon, 171n70
Operation Hazen, 135
Orvig, Svenn, 26, 93
   Ives and, 33, 52–53, 165n1, 167n26
Østrem, Gunnar, 114, 137, 170n53,
   171n70
Outlines of the Geography, Life and
   Customs of Newfoundland-Labrador
   (Tanner), 7
Owen, Liz, 80

P

Parallel Roads of Glenroy, The, 78
Peacock, Reverend and Mrs., 39
Peel, Ronnie, 114
permafrost, 98–99, 103, 134
  photo, *104*
Perry, Budd, 71
Peterson, Jim, 124
Philip, Prince, 71, 102
*Photo-reconnaissance Survey of
  Labrador-Ungava* (Hare), 3
Pilgrim, Mr. and Mrs., 41–42
Piloski, Edna, 48
Piloski, Murray, 36, 38, 48, 56, 59
Pilot of Arctic Canada, 53
Pollard, Wayne, 135
Pollen Diagrams from Labrador
  (Wenner), 7
Porsild, Erling, 7–8, 54, 55
Powell, John, 135
Precipice Mountain, *47*
Prince Charles Island, 126
Prosser, Tony, 98
Pyramid Hills, 88, 108, 114, 115–16,
  117
  photo, *89*

Q

Québec Province, 61, 72, 108, 130
  and control of Labrador-Ungava, 1–2
  importance of researchers from, 139

R

Ramah, 4
Rivière Grenier, 122
Rogerson, Robert James "Bob," 124, 133
  biography, 152–53
Romaniuk, Al and Marge, 70
Roots, Fred, 135–36
Ross, Doug, 75
Röthlisberger, Hans, 136
Rousseau, Jacques, 55, 56, 83, 85, 86, 113
  contributions to arctic and subarctic
    research, 7–8
Rowley, Diana, 11, 55
Rowley, Graham, 11, 55, 135, 170n60
Roy, Camille, 97, 100, 105, 120, 170n49
  photo, *112*
  research by, 103, 107
Royal Canadian Air Force, 13, 93, 98,
  125–26

Royal Canadian Mounted Police (RCMP),
  4, 115

S

Sagar, Brian, 137
Saglek Moraines, *58,* 60, 62, 133
Salmon, G., 101
Sammy, 72, *73,* 168n32
Saunders, Paul, 38, 40, 42, 48, 56, 57, 62
Schytt, Valter, 114
Selleck, Barbara, 80
Selleck, David and Barbara, 70, 80, 98
Sergeant, David, 136
Sherlock, Geoffrey, 66, 71, 76, 80
  biography, 153–54
  photo, *74*
Shoreline Lake (Lac Tasiguluk), 61
Sim, Vic, 126, 137
Ski, John, 130
Slanting Brook, 87
Smith, D. Ingle, 135
Snowden, Don, 116
Southern, Richard M., 53
Stamp, Dudley, 10
Stanstead Summer School on Arctic
  Geography, 10, 11
Starkel, Leszek, 114
Stefansson, Ragnar, 98
Stefansson, Vilhjalmur, 10, 166n12
St. Laurent, Louis, 9–10
St-Onge, Denis, 126
Strowger, Alan, 112, 113–14
Swithinbank, Charles, 55

T

Tanner, Väinö, 7, 31, 166n13
Tener, John, 135–36
Thompson, Andrew, 12
Thornthwaite, Warren, 26
Thorsteinsson, Ray, 126, 135–36
Through Trackless Labrador (Hesketh-
  Prichard), 78
Tomlinson, Jocelyn, 74, 97, 112
Tomlinson, Roger F., 63, 66, 74, 75, 97,
  102, 112
  biography, 154–55
  photo, *74*
Torngat Mountains, 1, 4
  elevation, 30, 166n14
  glacierization and deglaciation in, 7, 31,
    51–52, 59, 61–62, 88, 124, 133–34